MW01485627

The Heroes of Hosingen
Their Untold Story

By Alice M. Flynn

with a foreword by Allyn R. Vannoy

23.99

SEP   2016

www.heroesofhosingen.com

On the cover: Hosingen water tower, *(background)* newspaper articles
written about the 110th Infantry Regiment, 28th Infantry Division
during January 1945
Designed by Catherine Lewis

Copyright © 2015 by Alice M. Flynn
The Heroes of Hosingen: Their Untold Story
All rights reserved. Sky Blue Publishing, LLC

ISBN-10: 1517268338
ISBN-13: 9781517268336

In "Heroes of Hosingen," Alice Flynn–whose father was 1st Lt Thomas Flynn, executive officer of K Company during the defense of Hosingen–has combined archival research with personal anecdotes and other research to assemble a detailed and compelling portrait of the valiant but doomed American defense of this small Ardennes village. She introduces us to many of the principal characters of the main drama by recounting their horror stories from the Hürtgen Forest, then brings us forward with them to December of 1944 and the epic, awesome, and awful ordeal they endured at Hosingen, trying with all their might and courage to block the road to Bastogne. Flynn has also managed to accumulate an impressive selection of photographs of the battle area, so that the reader can see Hosingen as the men who fought to defend it did. She manages to wrap a wealth of information that would delight an historian in a narrative worthy of a novelist, and the result is a true story, well told, that is hard to put down.

So many of the heroic stories of the Battle of the Bulge tend to get lost in the glare of epics like the defense of Bastogne or the fight to trap Kampfgrupper Peiper. The defense of Hosingen–conducted in part, as historian Bob Phillips has called it, "To Save Bastogne"— is one of those tales that is now finally told as it should be.

Jay Karamales, Co-Author of *Against the Panzers, United States Infantry versus German Tanks, 1944-1945*, 2006

HELEN M. PLUM MEMORIAL LIBRARY
LOMBARD, ILLINOIS

3 1502 00823 2843

Dedication

I dedicate this book to the brave men of the 28th Infantry Division, 110th Infantry Regiment, who tenaciously fought off Hitler's massive assault at the beginning of the Battle of the Bulge from December 16-18, 1944. Ordered to "Hold at all cost" by Maj. Gen. Troy Middleton, outnumbered more than ten to one and surrounded, they sacrificed themselves to help delay the advance of Hitler's army long enough to allow the 101st Airborne Division to arrive at Bastogne on December 18, 1944.

www.koorosh1970.blogfa.com

Acknowledgments

Since the publishing of my first book, *Unforgettable: The Biography of Capt. Thomas J. Flynn,* in 2011, I have been very fortunate to have been in contact with a number of individuals; both veterans and children of veterans who fought with my father in the Hürtgen Forest and the Battle of the Bulge in Hosingen, Luxembourg. Their kind words have touched my heart and the additional stories and historical information they have shared with me has inspired me to write a second book that tells the story of what happened in the small Luxembourg town as told by the men who were there; either written by them, stories told to their children, or documented in a personal interviews they gave.

Unlike most books that end with the Americans' surrender to the Germans on December 18, 1944, I felt it was important for those reading this story to understand the sacrifice that General Middleton's "Hold at all cost" battle command had on these men as prisoners of war–following eight men from their capture to liberation. For many of them, being a prisoners had a more lasting and profound impact on the rest of their lives than the rest of their time as soldiers.

Thanks to a generous gift by my Luxembourg friend, Martin Gleis–a young teenage boy during the German occupation–I was able to travel to Luxembourg to continue my research in 2014 and I would like to express a heartfelt thank you to him. In addition, fellow countrymen–Yves Rasqui, Marcel Scheidweiler, Tom Scholtes and Pierre Eicher–all generously contributed their time during my visit to help me better understand the story of what happened in Hosingen, Luxembourg in December 1944. I was happy to discover that my earlier book had also provided them details which they were not aware of. Hopefully this one will do the same.

In addition, Jacques Heinen, Mayor of Hosingen, and Yves Rasqui very generously gave their consent for me to use the WWII era photos that have been included in this story. WWII expert and author, Jay Karamales, created the detailed map that shows where each photo was taken, thanks to information provided by Mr. Rasqui. They are an invaluable contribution that will help you envision this story as it unfolds.

The individuals that have shared their father's personal stories with me are Mark Erickson, Anne Gracie, Scott Guenther, Jim Gustafson, Hank Miller, Robert Morse, Jim Putz and Edward Seidel. Though most of us have not met in person yet, we all felt an immediate bond that will last our lifetime and we are proud to share our fathers' stories with you. We are affectionately calling ourselves the '110 Kids Club". New members are welcome.

I am honored to have been able to get to know some of the veterans of the 28th Infantry Division, 110th Infantry Regiment that served with my father. I thank them not only for their dedicated service to our country during WWII but for their willingness to help tell their story for others to learn from: Pvt. Robert Phillips (medic for the 110th), historian, and author of *To Save Bastogne*; Pfc. Sam S. Oliveto, Sgt. Albert W. Burghardt, Sgt. James S. Arbella, Pfc Edwin H. J. Cornell and Pvt. Joe R. Reed.

Finally, I have been very excited to get to know some of the authors over the last few years, whose books were key to helping me learn about the 110th Infantry Regiment and in particular, K Company's story in Hosingen. The very first book I read my father's name in was *Against the Panzers* by Allyn Vannoy and Jay Karamales, which changed my life forever as it gave me answers to so many questions about my father who had passed away in 1993. Thank you both for writing that book and for lending your knowledge, wisdom and talents to helping continue to tell this amazing story of heroism and courage. Allyn, you're attention to detail and editing my book has been greatly appreciated. I feel very blessed to call you my friend.

Table of Contents

ADDITIONAL MATERIALS

By Larry Newman:
...A Saga of Gallant Men; How Heroic 28th Halted Nazis And Saved Our Armies

By Morley Cassidy:
...28th Division Battle a Tale of Incredible Heroism

...Every Man on the 28th Gave All he Had–and more- in
   Week of a Thousand Battles
...28th Wipes out Nazi Force After Feigning Retreat
...28th Holds off 9 German Divisions, Upsets Offensive;
   Keystoners Share Glory of Great Feat of U.S. Military History

By Ivan H. (Cy) Peterman:
...Full Weight of Foe Hit Jinxed 28th Division, (Second of a Series)
...110th Followed Orders, But Cost Was Terrible, (Second of a Series)
...28th Stood Up Against Big Odds (Fourth of a Series)

Typical Unit Structure in the World War II US Army[1]

These are approximations, as strength levels, attached units, and command structure often varied.

Army Group: Between 250,000 and 600,000 soldiers; commanded by a four-star general

Army: Between 60,000 and 120,000 soldiers; commanded by a lieutenant (three-star) general

Corps: Between 30,000 and 60,000 soldiers; commanded by a senior-level major general

Division: 14,000 soldiers, commanded by a major (two-star) general; two or more divisions per corps

Regiment: 3,500 soldiers, commanded by a colonel; three regiments per division

Battalion: 900 soldiers, commanded by a major or a lieutenant colonel, three battalions per regiment

Company: 190 soldiers, commanded by a 1st lieutenant or a captain; four companies per battalion

Platoon: Forty soldiers, commanded by a 2nd lieutenant; four platoons per company

Squad: Twelve soldiers, commanded by a buck sergeant; three squads per platoon

---

1   John C. McManus, *Alamo in the Ardennes: The Untold Story of the American Soldiers Who Made the Defense of Bastogne Possible* (New York: NAL Caliber, 2008), p xx.

Foreword

The action of K Company at Hosingen and those of other units of the 110th Infantry Regiment might be one of the most overlooked stories of the many actions that chronicled the US Army's greatest battle–the Battle of the Bulge. Were the efforts of the GIs that fought there dismissed because their losses were so few in comparison to the other units that suffered so much during the first few days of the German counter-offensive? Was it because of issues related to the 110th Infantry's commanding officer, Colonel Hurley E. Fuller, who previously had been relieved of commander of the 23th Infantry during operations in Normandy? Or was the 110th eclipsed by the beleaguered 101st Airborne Division at Bastogne?

In 2008, Brigadier General Jerry G. Beck, Jr., CO of the 28th Infantry Division, directed the creation of a study group to re-examine the historical information pertaining to the actions of the 110th Regimental Combat Team, 28th Division, during the Ardennes Offensive, and to determine if a request for the awarding of the Presidential Unit Citation was warranted. The study group included several volunteers–retired Army officers, Army War College professors, United States Army Command and General Staff College instructors, writers, and historians who have studied the Ardennes Offensive for decades.

They reviewed US Army Center of Military History documents and publications, 28th Infantry Division historical records, division and regimental operations and intelligence journals, messages, after action reports, and German Army records. Local historians in Luxembourg were interviewed along with 110th Regimental Combat Team veterans of the battle. The Luxembourg historical organization Circle of Studies on the Battle of the Bulge provided independent analysis. The Pennsylvania National Guard Military Museum, the Pennsylvania Military Museum, the National Archives, the 28th Infantry Division's Command Historian, and the Pennsylvania National Guard's Command Historian provided information from their files.

The conclusion of the study group was that information existed that satisfied the criteria for the awarding of the Presidential Unit Citation to the 110th Regimental Combat Team for their actions in Luxembourg. The group concluded that the denial of the original citation application in 1946 set the tone for subsequent denials and was based on incomplete and immature information. That information had come to light that provided a clearer understanding of the events of 16-19 December, 1944. They felt that had this information been available at the time of the original request in June 1945, the Presidential Unit Citation would have been awarded.

And yet, their request was denied.

On three separate occasions, the 110th RCT was recommended for a Presidential Unit Citation for its stand in the Ardennes. The unit accomplishing its mission under hazardous circumstances, and resisted enemy action until they no longer had the means to do so further. Yet, all applications were rejected.

The first application was made on 22 June, 1945, by Brigadier General Basil H. Perry. It was accompanied by letters of endorsements from Colonel Hurley E. Fuller and Colonel Theodore E. Seely, both former commanders of the 110th Infantry Regiment. But the request did not include an endorsement from Major General Norman Cota, who was on leave at the time, nor did it include an endorsement from the VIII Corps commander, General Troy Middleton. Middleton was in the United States at the time the proposal was developed.

This was highly regrettable since Middleton had told Fuller, by letter, of his desire to strongly endorse such an application and was highly complementary of the 110th in post-war correspondence to Colonel S. L.A. Marshall.

The War Department Decorations Board did not consider this first request until 5 March, 1946, at which time they recommended disapproval. Disapproval may have been due to the comments of Colonel S. L. A. Marshall, Theater Historian, with General George S. Patton concurring. Marshall's comments are somewhat unusual: "It is the belief of the Theater Historian, based upon the examination of all evidence that the Regiment's conduct during 16 and 17 December was exceptional and that it contributed materially to the victory of other troops whose own exploits were more apparent, as at Bastogne. These were not the ordinary hazards of battle. They were exceptional hazards."

Following this rejection there was a flurry of letters to the War Department from General Cota, General Strickler, and General Middleton requesting a reconsideration. Cota even wrote General Eisenhower (9 September, 1947) asking for his assistance in getting the unit its citation, but to no avail. Daniel Strickler, by this time a Brigadier General in the Pennsylvania National Guard, was even more irritated when he was told that the 112th Infantry Regiment had received, a Presidential Unit Citation for its action in the Ardennes, but not the 110th. None of the letters, however, caused the War Department to change its position.

The original application did not have all the supporting information to properly assess what the 110th did nor did not have the correct endorsements. The 110th was a shattered unit. Thus, some of those who could have supported the application were casualties of the Ardennes. Personnel losses and transfers were only part of the problem. Most of the elements of the 110th involved had lost their records though destruction or captured during 16-18 December 1944. Regimental records at Clervaux were burned in the Claravallis Hotel before the headquarters staff left. K Company, and attached units, at Hosingen, destroyed all of their records except for the morning reports before surrendering.

Another application was submitted in 1983. Its origin was unique. Captain Roger Cirillo, then an instructor at the U.S. Army Command and General Staff College, during research of the 110th's stand in the Ardennes, was so impressed by the units' actions that he used the 110th in his instruction. He became convinced the 110th should have received a PUC and submitted an application to the U.S. Army Center of Military History.

This application was referred to the U.S. Army Military Personnel Center, the action agent for such applications, who refused to act on the application because such applications for World War II units were supposed to be submitted no later than May 1951. Since Cirillo's application was not received in the proper time frame, it was rejected. In the letter of rejection, Lt. Col. James L. Hickman, justified this rejection by noting that some 28th Division elements had received the PUC for the Ardennes service, and that this showed a conscious effort on the part of the 28th Division leadership to recognize certain units and not others. And since they had failed to recommend the 110th, their wishes should be respected.

It's doubtful that Lt. Col. Hickman was aware of the post-application efforts of Generals Cota, Strickler, and Middleton.

A factor that may have cast the unit in an unfavorable light, was the number of casualties the regiment suffered. In the original board deliberations, it was noted that approximately 2,240 men from the 110th were missing in action. The board summary stated that "the loss of approximately 2,240 missing in action, including the loss of two regimental commanders was exceedingly large." But no one bothered to determine if this figure was correct or what it meant. Even if these figures were correct, a unit that had to hold at all costs and had followed orders, should have a much higher casualty rate than one which had the latitude to maneuver. Thus, the figure may have been misinterpretation.

In an independent study in 2009, Camille P. Kohn, President of the Circle of Studies on the Battle of the Bulge, Grand Duchy of Luxembourg, concluded: "I do not know another Regiment that has accomplished such a performance in Luxembourg than the 110th Infantry! This outstanding unit deserves really an appropriate mark of distinction if only for those indescribable achievements in Luxembourg during the dark days 1944. In their combat zone they contributed in a very rarely manner, to prevent the Hitler aggressors to conquer Bastogne and last but not least reach the final objective, the harbour of Antwerp."

Maybe some future military authority will reconsider the heroic efforts of the men that fought at Hosingen in December of 1944.

Allyn R. Vannoy, Co-Author of *Against the Panzers,*
United States Infantry versus German Tanks, 1944-1945, 2006

CHAPTER 1

Bloody Buckets fight their way across Europe: July 25–October 31, 1944:

European Theatre of Operation (ETO)

It wasn't until Japan attacked Pearl Harbor on December 7, 1941, where over 3,600 American servicemen and civilians were killed or wounded in less than an hour, that the United States, England, other Western Allies, and China declared war on Japan. In response, Germany, along with other members of the Tripartite Pact, responded by declaring war on the United States.

With the power of the American military behind them, the Western Allies were able to force the Germans to retreat in both Italy and North Africa, while American and British bombers carried out attacks on German industrial targets and cities, disrupting the flow of raw material and finished goods. The Allied naval forces had also dealt with the threat of German submarine attacks, allowing the massive build up in the British Isles of Allied military personnel, weaponry, and supplies that would be needed to mount a major offensive against Germany. France and its neighboring countries had been under German control for four long years, and the Allies were determined to finally drive the Germans from Western Europe and ultimately destroy the Nazi regime.

As part of this plan, the Pennsylvania National Guard unit, the 28th Infantry Division, spent over two years training for combat in the States until finally ships filled with its soldiers set sail on October 7-8, 1943. After ten days on rough, stormy seas, the 28th arrived at Fishgard, Wales, where they would continue to train while they waited for orders.

On June 6, 1944, the Western Allies, commanded by US Army Gen. Dwight D. Eisenhower, landed on the beaches of Normandy in northern France, beginning an assault against Hitler's Germany. Dozens of minesweepers led the way for the enormous warships across the English Channel followed by hundreds of ships and watercraft, while three divisions of paratroopers (two American, one British) were dropped behind the beaches.

They arrived at their strike zones just before daybreak. Guns from the warships bombarded German positions inland and six divisions (three American, two British, and one Canadian) stormed ashore on five main beaches, code named "Utah," "Omaha," "Gold," "Juno," and "Sword." After two months of bloody battles, the Allies' continual assaults forced the Germans to retreat, enabling the Allies to drive deeper into northern France.

The Bloody Buckets

Originally included as part of the D-Day follow-on force, their orders were delayed until the end of July. Landing on Omaha Beach on July 25, 1944, the 28th observed Normandy beaches littered with signs of the fierce battles that had been fought. The small green field on the hill above Omaha Beach, covered with rows and rows of white crosses, turned all vague ideas of what war was like into a cold, harsh reality. As they worked their way to the front lines, they passed many fields scattered with German corpses and dead horses. On July 30, they entered into their first combat near the town of St. Lo. As the 28th fought its way across France it earned a fierce reputation among the German troops. The

Germans mistakenly interpreted the red Keystone emblem on the left shoulder of each soldier's jacket and helmet as a "Bloody Bucket," believing the insignia reflected the toughness of the unit's fighting ability, and the name stuck.

The 28th Infantry Division, composed of the 109th, 110th and 112th Infantry Regiments, had been in the middle of intense combat since shortly after arriving in France. However, parent headquarters, not seeing the results it had counted on, perceived a lack of leadership and notified Major Gen. Norman D. Cota on August 13 that he was to take command of the division. Under General Cota, the 28th began to move briskly through France and the number of German prisoners taken increased significantly. After completing these missions, the 28th was reassigned to Major Gen. Leonard Gerow's V Corps.

The Allies' successful landing in southern France in August had forced the German army to retreat toward its homeland, liberating the city of Paris on August 25, 1944. On August 29, the 28th Division was selected to represent the U.S. Army in a 'Victory Parade' through Paris-passing through the Arc de Triumph down the Champs-Elysées to a cheering Parisian crowd. The parade provided an uninterrupted route through the city. Eight hours later the 28th was back fighting remnants of German units just outside the city limits.

The Division continued to push the Germans across France and swept through Belgium, averaging seventeen miles a day against heavy German resistance. The 109th and 110th Infantry Regiments then continued on to liberate the northern part of Luxembourg. On September 11, the 28th became the first Allied unit to reach the German border, where it destroyed or captured 153 pillboxes and bunkers. Along the West Wall, better known to Allied soldiers as "the Siegfried Line," were approximately 150 miles of anti-tank, steel-reinforced, concrete pyramids standing over four feet tall, referred to as "dragon's teeth." With the Soviet Union pressing Hitler's armies back from the east, Germany was being forced back toward its homeland from all sides.

Photo: "American troops of the 28th Infantry Division march down the Champs Elysees, Paris, in the 'Victory' Parade." 08/29/1944, Poinsett, Photographer, (National Archives Identifier: 531209); Signal Corps Photographs of American Military Activity, 1754–1954; Records of the Office of the Chief Signal Officer, 1860–1982; Record Group 111; U.S. National Archives and Records Administration.

During September and October of 1944, the accomplishments of the 28th were great; however, General Cota had to not only deal with the exhaustion of his troops, some of whom had been fighting for several months, but also the training and incorporation of thousands of replacement troops needed to fill his depleted division during this period.

Finally, on October 1, the unit was sent to the rear for rest and recovery. Many soldiers went on leave to Paris while others stayed behind to train the new soldiers from the Allied Ground Forces Replacement System who were being added to the unit. Most of the replacements arrived as individuals and the majority of the enlisted men had little or no infantry training. The war was taking its toll on the supply of trained military personnel as all front line units were losing men faster than their replacements could be properly trained. The battle-weary veterans were leery of the new men, concerned that their severe lack of combat training might put them at risk during intense fighting—like the fighting they had just experienced. K Company's 4th Platoon, veterans with the 110th, included Sgt. James Arbella, Staff Sgt. Henry Shanabarger, Pfc Harry H. Seidel, and Pfc Sam S. Oliveto, messenger for 1st Lt. Bernie Porter's 2nd Platoon, were hesitant to even speak to these new men and ask their names as they had already learned it was too painful to get to know somebody that would probably be wounded or dead within a week. It was best to not take a personal interest in any of them.

Because of what the 28th and other key divisions had been able to achieve so far, the morale of the American soldiers was very high, having helped the Allies push the German army back across France, Belgium, Luxembourg, to the German border in just a few weeks. It was during the first weeks of September, that the European Allied commanders began to believe that the German army was exhausted, dispirited, and disorganized and that the war might be over by Christmas. It was also widely believed that the next breakthrough would lead to certain victory for the Allies.

By mid-October, the German army had retreated far inland and the 150-mile western border of Germany, nicknamed the Siegfried Line, became the primary objective of the American Army. The Battle of the Hürtgen Forest had begun on September 12, 1944, when the 9th Infantry Division was sent to seize control of the crossroads village of Schmidt and, thus, secure the right flank of VII Corps before a larger offensive was to begin. The Army experienced major communications problems within the chain of command and had entered the Hürtgen Forest before proper intelligence had been gathered on German strength in the area. As a result, the 9th Infantry Division was suffering a much higher casualty rate than expected and the Army began moving thousands more replacement troops into the area for quick deployment, when and where they were needed.

K Company killed in Northern France: July 25-September 2:

- S/Sgt. Harold G. Myers*   7/31/1944
- Pvt. Leon J. Dinino*   8/2/1944
- Pvt. Charles Drenocky*   8/2/1944
- Pvt. Henry F. Hampton*   8/2/1944
- Pvt. Louie Iaquinto*   8/2/1944
- Pfc Robert E. Landau*   8/2/1944
- Sgt. Harry B. Leasure*   8/2/1944
- Pvt. Arley Harris*   8/3/1944
- T/Sgt. Joseph Skurla*   8/3/1944
- Pfc John L. Gagne*   8/4/1944
- Pfc Harry L. Lemley*   8/4/1944
- Pvt. Carlo Tiberio*   8/4/1944
- Pvt. Charles S. Wosilek*   8/4/1944
- Pfc John Kittle*   8/6/1944
- S/Sgt. Edgar R. Sandidge*   8/10/1944
- Pfc Herman B. Evix*   8/12/1944
- Pfc Richard T. Hochreiter*   8/13/1944
- S/Sgt. James E. Monroe*   8/13/1944
- Sgt. Homer J. Stengel   8/13/1944
- 2nd Lt. Carl P. Tuisl*   8/13/1944
- Pfc Thomas J. Peterson*   8/24/1944
- Pfc Sol Fine   9/2/1944

K Company killed in Rhineland: September 3-November 1:

• S/ Sgt. John J. Bell*	9/9/1944
• Pfc John O. Thauren	9/14/1944
• Pvt. Harvey E. Stephens	9/17/1944
• Sgt. Robert L.Bond	9/19/1944
• Pfc Eugene F. Seifert*	9/19/1944
• Pfc James L. Staten	9/19/1944
• Pvt. Eugene M. Dzieszkowicz*	9/22/1944
• Sgt. Edward A. Fisher*	9/30/1944
• Pfc Oral Gandee*	10/1/1944
• Pvt. Alva R. Haun*	10/1/1944
• S/Sgt. Charles Kertesz*	10/1/1944
• S/Sgt. Milford E. Matthew*	10/1/1944
• Pfc John A. Spinelli*	10/1/1944
• Sgt. Carl R. Buchman*	10/5/1944
• Pfc John H. Kieby	10/27/1944
• Pfc Jesse J. Riddell	11/1/1944

* Member of the original K Company, 110th Infantry Regiment, 28th Infantry Division that landed on Omaha Beach July 25, 1944.

CHAPTER 2

The Hürtgen Forest: November 2-14, 1944

The Hürtgen Forest was one of the largest forests in Germany, covering an area of approximately fifty square miles between Aachen, Monschau, and Duren on the Belgian-German border. At its widest points, the forest was twenty miles in length from north to south and ten miles wide from west to east. The forest was part of the northern portion of the Ardennes region of Belgium and Luxembourg and the Eifel region of Germany. The area contains some of the most rugged terrain in Europe, characterized by steep, wooded slopes reaching 1,000 feet in elevation, with numerous, deep valleys and ravines and very few roads or trails.

The Siegfried Line ran right through the middle of the forest whose 75- to 100-foot tall fir trees were so dense they impeded both foot and motor traffic, preventing the sun from reaching the forest floor. Even at high noon, the sunlight barely reached the spongy bed of pine needles and decaying logs at the base of the forest.

The enemy soldiers who awaited the American soldiers in this sector were certainly not Germany's finest; for the most part, they were the very young and the very old. However, they were mixed in with combat veterans, who provided the backbone for the units in the area.

The Germans had turned the forest into a labyrinth of well-camouflaged earth and log bunkers and concrete pillboxes, many still intact from WWI. These structures provided excellent interlocking fields of fire and were augmented with booby-trapped concertina wire and minefields designed to restrict all enemy movement. Throughout the forest, the Germans also had laid dense belts of barbed wire and planted thousands of mines and booby traps; many designed to maim rather than kill. One mine was notorious for amputating legs and the male genitals. The numerous bunkers in the area were the Germans' key centers of resistance. They defended the few roads and trails that bisected the forest with intense machine gun and artillery fire. The rough terrain complicated the situation, as advancing soldiers easily became confused and disoriented in the dense forest and large groups could become separated, lost, and disorganized.

The Germans knew well how to use the terrain to their advantage. They turned even the thick forest of evergreens into weapons as artillery blasts were frequently aimed to explode in the treetops, spraying the American soldiers below with both wood and steel splinters. Soldiers learned quickly that lying prone on the ground while receiving artillery fire was the worst possible thing to do. Instead, soldiers learned to crouch or stand close against a tree, minimizing the bodily surface area exposed to the blast. Still, there was no safe place to hide from the tree bursts.

The Battle

After stubborn fighting by the German army in the Hürtgen Forest throughout September and early October, the Americans reevaluated the situation and decided there was no way the war would be over by Christmas. The 9th Infantry Division had done its best but had little in the way of positive results to show after almost six weeks of heavy fighting and suffering more than 4,500 casualties. The division desperately needed a break to rest and rebuild, and on October 26, the 28th Division moved forward to replace the 9th.

Further attacks were postponed until the 28th Infantry Division was able to move northward to the Hürtgen Forest. Much to the frustration of General Cota, Major General Gerow of V Corps ordered the three regiments of the 28th Division to split up, giving each a different objective. General Cota was concerned that each regiment had to attack a different objective, each moving out in opposite directions across some of the most difficult terrain in western Europe. The mission of the 110th was to clear the woods next to the River Kall, capture Simonskall, and maintain a supply route for the advance on the town of Schmidt—an objective the 9th Infantry Division had failed to achieve.

In hindsight, it seems clear that General Cota failed to demand detailed intelligence on the area before making a decision on the plan of attack. As a result, the main supply route he chose for the 28th was the Kall Trail, which was just that, a trail. In good weather, the dirt trail was barely adequate for vehicle travel. In bad weather, it was practically impassable, even for tracked vehicles, yet this route was chosen to be the main supply route for the entire division of men, vehicles, and equipment. By early November, the rain and snow had turned the Kall Trail into a muddy lane with mud six to ten inches deep in some places.

November 2

The 28th began its attack on November 2, 1944, after an intense hour of bombing by tactical air support. Each regiment moved out from the woods west of Germeter towards its assigned target– Vossenack, Simonskall, and Schmidt. The weather had taken a turn for the worse over the previous week. It started to rain a cold and relentless drizzle, and with the Hürtgen Forest now covered in fog and mist, further air support was suspended until November 5.

*Photo: E Company, 110ᵗʰ Infantry Regiment, 28ᵗʰ Infantry
division enters the Hürtgen Forest on November 2, 1944,
U.S. National Archives and Records Administration.*

The 110ᵗʰ Infantry Regiment's 2ⁿᵈ (E, F, G, and H companies) and 3ʳᵈ battalions (I, K, L, and M companies), moved south out of Germeter—directly into the heart of the Siegfried Line pillboxes— toward the town of Simonskall and a fortified strongpoint called Raffelsbrand. The 1ˢᵗ Battalion (A, B, C, and D companies) remained in the rear as a small division reserve.

Moving into the sector just vacated by 9ᵗʰ Infantry Division was a horrifying experience for the soldiers of the 28ᵗʰ, particularly for the large number of replacement soldiers, like Pvt. William Gracie, with no combat experience. As the black, shattered trees swallowed up the 28ᵗʰ, the soldiers were shocked by what they saw and the morale of the men plummeted from the moment they entered the tangled fir forest. The forest bore the scars of war: the record of the bitter contest waged by the 9ᵗʰ was apparent as abandoned helmets, gas masks, blood-soaked field jackets, and loose mines lay all about. Water-filled shell holes were everywhere. Even worse, the bodies of German and American soldiers, some of which had been booby trapped by the Germans overnight, lay entangled in the sucking troughs of mud, lying unclaimed by Graves Registration units. It was a grotesque and gloomy landscape. Sgt. Al Burghardt, K Company mortar squad leader, noted the forest floor had a thick layer of branches from the broken tree tops above, which made it difficult to walk in a straight line. The somber-faced men of the Graves Registration units quietly moved among the bloated, mutilated corpses that now stank, unceremoniously slinging them on the backs of their trucks. Soldiers who had expected an easy victory were shocked by the hard realization that severe fighting lay ahead.

The enemy was not the only source of casualties with which the 28th would have to contend. Cold and wet November weather, with temperatures hovering around freezing, would take a terrible toll on the soldiers. Many were still wearing the summer clothing they had been issued when they first went into battle. Without proper cold-weather gear—items such as over boots, field jackets, woolen caps, and long underwear—trench foot and respiratory infection cases skyrocketed. K and C rations, the standard combat issue for each soldier, were intended to provide three nutritional and satisfying meals a day, whether served hot or cold. However, given the conditions under which the soldiers were fighting, many men lost their appetites and ceased eating altogether. Battle conditions were much too dangerous to risk bringing hot meals or drinks forward. The soldiers also were unable to build fires to warm up, dry off, or to heat their food in order to make it more palatable, since their proximity to the enemy was sure to draw rifle and mortar fire. All too often, enemy soldiers lay hidden just a stone's throw away. The continual lack of hot rations, constant cold and wet conditions contributed significantly to the declining health and morale of many of the soldiers.

Within the 3rd Battalion, K Company was to move to the right and capture Simonskall. L Company was to move to the left, penetrate enemy defenses, and capture the horseshoe bend in the road east of Simonskall. Only two hours prior to departure, patrols in the area had reported a German defensive line south of

Germeter made from concertina wire–barbed wire laid out in large coils. Two rolls stretched side by side through the trees, with a third placed on top of them, creating a six-foot tall barrier. In front of the wire, German troops had hand dug a shallow ditch that varied in width from four to six feet and strategically positioned several machine-guns to saturate the defensive perimeter in-between the well-concealed bunkers and pillboxes. Unfortunately, this report did not make it down to the men on the line leaving them blind to the obstacles that lay ahead.

L Company came under immediate fire after leaving the woods west of Germeter, but continued to fight until they reached the ditch. K Company made it to the ditch, but heavy German machine-gun fire immediately wounded or killed twelve men, with most injuries occurring from the waist down because of the low position from which the enemy fired. The soldiers were suddenly living out their worst nightmares, learning quickly what tree bursts were. The men prayed even as they searched for ways to protect themselves. Some even tried to cut the fallen trees, arranging them for protection over a dugout.

Third Battalion commander, Lt. Col. William Tait, called the battalion back to the line of departure late in the afternoon, as no progress toward their objective had been made.

November 3

At 0700 on November 3, K and L Companies set out again and tried twice more to capture their objectives. Each time, they suffered so many casualties that they had to fall back and regroup. Unbeknownst to them, the Germans had strengthened their defensive position overnight by over 200 riflemen and K Company experienced much heavier losses than the day before. Once again, at 1600 hours, Lt. Col. Tait ordered those who were able to move back to the line of departure. Some of the men had to remain in position as they were pinned down by enemy fire.

November 4

At 0430 on November 4, the 1st Battalion was added to the attack plan and set off to approach the objective from the north, from Vossenack. The 2nd and 3rd battalions were to hold their positions and exert pressure on the Germans to cover the attack. Using this strategy, the 1st Battalion met little enemy resistance and captured both the bend in the road and Simonskall, but it was now surrounded and in danger. The men dug into position for the night.

The 109th and 112th regiments were experiencing similar results throughout the forest, as the men of the 28th tried their best to do as they had been ordered. But advance after advance was halted as the Americans had been ordered to advance through heavily mined areas. Constant German machine-gun fire and mortars kept engineers from clearing the minefields or evacuating the dead. And all too often, wounded soldiers who lay helpless and stranded on the cold, wet ground would freeze or bleed to death during the night.

After only two days under these conditions, the 110th was no longer an effective fighting unit. Despite its weakened condition, however, it continued to attack when ordered. With each passing hour, the number of casualties grew, yet it made no measureable progress toward taking its assigned objectives.

Due to the heavy casualties taken by the 110th, the 41st Replacement Battalion left France on November 5, en route to the Germeter and Vossenack area to join the 28th Infantry Division in the Hürtgen Forest.

November 5

Around 1030 on November 5, General Gerow arrived at General Cota's command post (CP), where General Cota assured him that despite the failed attack on Schmidt, a plan was being drafted to take the town the following day. Of great concern to General Cota, though, was the fact that for the past four days his division had been the only Allied division attacking into Germany along a 150-mile front. Worse still was the fact that the VII Corps attack had been postponed indefinitely until the weather improved. General Cota perceived that the Germans would now be able to concentrate their forces on the lone enemy division trying to take Schmidt.

To appease his commanding officer, General Cota created Task Force Ripple on November 5, under the leadership of Lt. Col. Richard W. Ripple, commander of the 707th Tank Battalion. Task Force Ripple was to consist of the already weakened 3rd Battalion, 110th Infantry Regiment, (now numbering only 316 men of the original 871 and of which only 200 were infantrymen), eight tanks, and nine tank destroyers. The plan was to move the task force out through Vossenack, pass through the Kall Valley, and join forces with the depleted and exhausted 112th Infantry Regiment that was pinned down on Kommerscheidt Hill, and then combine forces to take Schmidt.

November 6

Task Force Ripple left the line of departure near Germeter at 0245 hours on November 6. As it moved through Vossenack, it once again encountered a barrage of artillery fire. Waiting for the bombardment to end, an artillery shell hit the ground near Pfc Oliveto. While it didn't explode, the force of its impact threw him into the air. Shaken but uninjured, Oliveto once again took cover, but another shell soon knocked him out of action with a concussion and ruptured eardrum. He would not wake up until three months later in a Paris hospital.

Anxious to move forward, the tank destroyer crewmen asked for infantry support to accompany their guns down the Kall Trail. Colonel Ripple refused the request. The four supply jeeps of the task force left on their own, without support, and headed south along the Kall Trail. They were soon ambushed, and half the men in the party were killed or wounded. It now became apparent that the Kall Trail was completely controlled by the Germans, so Colonel Ripple ordered the remaining vehicles to return to Germeter. Because his infantry force was already too depleted, Ripple tried to avoid a fight along the trail by taking a firebreak paralleling the trail 200 yards to the west instead. The change in tactics made no difference, though, and almost from the moment the infantry entered the woods at the firebreak, they came under small arms fire that lasted all the way to the Kall River. It was mid-day before they reached Colonel Peterson's troops on Kommerscheidt Hill. Colonels Tait and Ripple reported they had lost another fifteen men and two officers along the firebreak.

The scene that Task Force Ripple found upon arrival on Kommerscheidt Hill was one of misery and desolation. The American tanks and tank destroyers in Kommerscheidt had prevented German infantry from forming to attack. However, enemy tanks were positioned on the higher ground around Schmidt, and poured round after round into Kommerscheidt and positions held by the 112th. Maneuvering on the lower ground around Kommerscheidt, American tanks and tank destroyers were no match for the German Mark IVs and Vs. It was apparent that even the combined forces would be no match for a continued attack on Schmidt.

Colonel Ripple and Colonel Peterson, commander of the C Company 112th, in Kommerscheidt, postponed the joint attack on Schmidt as they assessed their situation. As the officers discussed their options, the situation quickly worsened. In a matter of minutes, German snipers concealed in the woods wounded or killed the 3rd Battalion commander, Colonel Tait, the executive officer, S-2 officer, and a company commander. Colonels Ripple and Peterson finally decided that without supplies or armor, outnumbered by enemy forces, and with their men shattered by exhaustion, cold, and unrelenting fear, that the mission of Task Force Ripple was out of the question. They judged it would be impossible to mount a successful attack under these conditions. Canceling the proposed attempt to retake Schmidt, Colonel

Peterson told the men of Task Force Ripple to dig in along the woods line north of Kommerscheidt instead, to strengthen their defensive position.

While Task Force Ripple and the 112th waited for reinforcements on Kommerscheidt Hill, the Germans counterattacked. Some of the exhausted men simply fled in panic, as they couldn't take the fighting anymore. The soldiers who stayed on Kommerscheidt Hill as ordered, endured another night of freezing cold and rain.

Also on Monday, November 6, General Cota left his division command post in his jeep and made his only recorded visit to the forward positions of his divisional units during the Vossenack-Kommerscheidt-Schmidt battle. He was finally face to face with the reality of the conditions under which his men operated and the true condition of the Kall Trail he had designated as the 28th's main supply route. General Cota finally admitted to himself that this was an impossible battle to win, and he sought and received approval for his units to fall back behind the Kall River. Unfortunately for the 28th, the retreat was to be temporary, as once his units had regrouped and replacement troops were added, General Cota was ordered to renew the attack. Cota reluctantly committed to being ready in three days if sufficient replacements arrived, General Hodges, commander of First Army, having only approved the withdrawal from beyond the Kall River under those conditions.

November 7

News that Colonel Tait had been injured reached Lt. Col. Theodore Seely at the 110th CP, but it was uncertain whether he had been wounded or killed. Captain George "Howdy" Rumbaugh had just arrived at the regimental CP and was anxious for an assignment along the front line. He was ordered to take several tracked vehicles ('Weasels') and four jeeps with supplies to the men in Kommerscheidt, find out Colonel Tait's condition, and take command of 3rd Battalion, if needed. Through many close calls, with much effort, and despite the loss of most of the supplies, Captain Rumbaugh arrived in Kommerscheidt at 0500 on November 7. Upon discovering that Colonel Tait had been evacuated, he assumed command of the 3rd Battalion.

November 8

On Wednesday, November 8, during a drenching rainstorm, the battle-worn survivors began their withdrawal to the rear, disabling and abandoning any equipment as quietly as possible so the Germans would not know they were retreating. The men carried as many wounded as they could, but the men were physically exhausted and retreating units were forced to leave behind scattered groups of soldiers, some badly wounded, and others who had not received the notice to withdraw. On the way out of the woods, the men met up with Task Force Davis, which had been organized to help guide them out of the woods. When they reached the task force, however, they were told to dig in for the night and that they would resume their march out in the morning. The men escaping from Kommerscheidt were forced to spend yet another miserable night in the nearly freezing temperatures, most of them soaked from the waist down after crossing the Kall River.

K Company's mortar squad leader, Sgt. Burghardt, and his crew were trapped on the reverse slope outside of Kommerscheidt when they were radioed to abandon their position and destroy all the equipment they couldn't carry out. It was late that night before they started to work their way out, crossing the Kall River. Choosing to avoid the Kall Trail, eighteen GIs climbed the steep slopes in the dark. Everyone remained quiet except for the platoon sergeant's helmet that somehow dislodged from his head and rolled all the way down the rocky hillside, crashing at the bottom. Miraculously they received no incoming fire as a result.

The men collapsed to the ground when they reached the top of the slope. Medics made their rounds the next morning to see who might need medical attention. Burghardt suffered from frozen feet so he was tagged and sent to the hospital, where he would remain the rest of the war.

Also arriving at Cota's Division Headquarters that day were a number of American commanders – Major Gen. Leonard Gerow, Lt. Gen. Courtney Hodges, General Omar Bradley and even Supreme Commander, General Dwight D. Eisenhower – anxious for General Cota to explain exactly what had happened to the 28th.

While Task Force Ripple and the 112th were retreating, the 41st Replacement Battalion had begun to arrive at the rear assembly area near Germeter to fill out Colonel Seely's depleted troops. Maj. Harold M. Milton, who was part of the Replacement Forces, had taken command of the 3rd Battalion until Captain Rumbaugh could return to the rear assembly area, and he assigned 1st Lt. Thomas Flynn as commanding officer of K Company, 110th Infantry Regiment. Lt. Flynn had been trying to get to know the non-commissioned officers (NCOs) in the group prior to arriving on the front lines. Flynn began to evaluate the situation, waiting for the veterans to return from the frontline.

Over the next two days, 500 replacements were added to the 110th, 200 of whom went to the 3rd Battalion with one hundred of them assigned to K Company. Flynn handpicked his NCOs while enlisted men were assigned in groups of tens and twenties to platoons and companies. But even the 500 new bodies barely qualified the 110th to be considered ready for combat duty, as the regiment was still far from being considered full strength and most of the new soldiers had only the minimum basic training and no combat experience.

November 9

By 0530 on November 9, it had begun to snow. Captain Rumbaugh was anxious to get his men out of the woods and so he told the 3rd Battalion to fall in behind him. He led the survivors the rest of the way back to Germeter (approximately 200 of the 316 who had set out in Task Force Ripple). Stragglers continued to arrive throughout the day. The men were given quick but thorough medical checks and those suffering from trench foot, battle fatigue, or other injuries or ailments were evacuated to the rear for rest or hospitalization. Out of the original 871 men in the 110th's 3rd Battalion that had entered the forest on November 2, only seventy-five men were still capable of fighting. The battalion had lost its commanding officer, executive officer, S-2 intelligence officer, S-3 operations officers, regimental surgeon, and its medical assistance officer. There was only one officer left with K Company, and since Lt. Flynn had already selected his NCOs, he was reassigned as the transportation officer for the 110th.

Men from other units stationed in the area made temporary shelters with heat, blankets, and straw for bedding for the men that had escaped from Kommerscheidt Hill. They even arranged for the replacing of lost equipment. Officers donated their liquor so that those who returned might each get a small drink. As soldiers arrived, aid men met them to tend their wounds and issue them their small ration of liquor. Vehicles were serviced or replaced and mess kits and new clothing provided. Flynn and the other replacement officers made a point to talk to the survivors about the battlefield conditions they had experienced in preparation for their next mission. The weather was not letting up and the snow continued to fall.

Men who were wounded at Kommerscheidt but couldn't escape were scattered all along the trail back to Germeter and several medical officers, including medic Wayne Erickson and Sgt. George McKnight, with the 103rd Medical Battalion assigned to K Company, located at the aid station in the Kall Gorge negotiated a temporary cease-fire on their own for both sides to evacuate their wounded. Oddly enough, despite the intense fighting, German soldiers helped evacuate some of the wounded American soldiers and gave up their coats to help keep them warm while they awaited evacuation.

The few veteran enlisted men who were able to return to battle were allowed only one day to rest. Lt. Flynn and the other company officers were notified at 2200 hours on November 9 that at 0700 the next day, the 110th was to move out to assault the enemy stronghold at Raffelsbrand, capture it, and continue the attack toward Monschau. This left minimal time for the new officers to conduct satisfactory ground reconnaissance or work out company-level assault plans, so they were not happy with the decision. By now, almost a foot of snow had fallen.

From what they had seen and heard in the two days since arriving in the area, it was clear they were up against what appeared to be insurmountable odds. The sheer number of casualties in the unit in just a week could hardly be dismissed or give the new officers much hope that their efforts would result in any better outcome. Many of the men of the 28th referred to the forest as the "Green Hell" and the "Death Factory" and the soldiers believed the officers in charge were simply unwillingly to admit defeat.

November 10-13

As 0700 approached, Lt. Flynn's K Company and the rest of the 3rd Battalion—armed only with small arms—left the Germeter assembly area still short of automatic weapons, mortars, and appropriate clothing for the winter weather. The men slogged through snowdrifts as the guns rumbled and thundered and as machine guns rattled not far away. The main objective for K Company that day was the line of pillboxes outside the village of Raffelsbrand…again.

En route to Raffelsbrand, Flynn and the new replacements witnessed the carnage, giving them a glimpse of what the veterans of this battle had already experienced. The men moved cautiously through a recent battlefield scattered with wounded and dead. Out of the corner of his eye, Flynn caught the movement of a German medic attending to a wounded German soldier. As the GIs passed by, the medic raised his gun to shoot at Flynn's men and Flynn responded without hesitation; the medic fell dead in the snow.

Based on the information he had been able to gather while still in Germeter, as well as from reports by the veterans in his unit,

Flynn believed that the main roads in the area were filled with anti-tank and anti-personnel mines. He tried to avoid having his men needlessly injured by skirting areas suspected to be heavily mined. At some point along the route, Flynn and his men were stopped by an officer, said to be a West Pointer, in a jeep, who ordered Flynn to take his men down the road, rather than avoiding it. He refused and tried to explain that the road was mined. The officer became angry and threatened to write Flynn up for insubordination. As the officer drove off down the road, he passed over a buried mine. The explosion killed the officer. After that incident, Flynn concluded that being a graduate of West Point didn't necessarily mean that one was smart.

K Company encountered heavy fighting all morning as they worked their way toward Raffelsbrand, Pvt. Joe Reed was one of the many wounded or killed as they attempted to attack the line of pillboxes that defended the town. By 1230, Flynn was ordered to have K Company replace Task Force Lacy, a special composite unit under the command of 1st Lt. Virgil Lacy. Their mission for the next several days would be to move northeast to protect the left flank of the regiment, coordinating their movement with that of the 109th Infantry to their north.

On the night of November 10, after the troops of K Company had dug in for the night, Flynn went to check on his men in the forward positions and came under intense enemy fire. He dove to the ground to avoid the gunfire, and unable to see the unfamiliar terrain in the dark, went over the edge of a drop-off into a small quarry. Flynn injured both his knees, the right one more severely, but managed to make it back to the company CP. The next day, in the CP dugout, Flynn's right knee was so swollen he couldn't bend it. Nevertheless, he remained with his unit at the request of his men and managed to get by with some assistance from the company's aid man.

The weather was still extremely cold and wet, and their foxholes filled with water and ice as the foot of snow partially melted then froze again when temperatures dropped below freezing, making it difficult to keep themselves and their weapons dry. Flynn sent several of the enlisted men back to the hospitals to get treatment for frozen feet. Their combat boots had gotten soaking wet in the snow and mud, and in the cold temperatures, their feet had frozen. When the soldiers removed their shoes at night, their feet would often swell up so much that it was difficult to put their boots back on in the morning. Flynn was not immune to the weather and also suffered with frozen toes.

Flynn saw almost all of his men—more than one hundred— killed, wounded, or otherwise disabled before his unit was withdrawn from the Hürtgen Forest. In an interview concerning the Battle of the Bulge six months later, Flynn said the unit of 160 men he commanded several weeks later in Hosingen was almost 100 percent replacements, except for twenty returning to duty from the hospital and his NCOs.

Even though the attack on Raffelsbrand was called off at 2300 on November 11, all battalions continued to receive heavy mortar and artillery fire for two more days, making it impossible to organize into platoons and companies, although there were clearly leaders within each group providing direction. The 110th had done its best but the exhausted and dispirited troops were in no shape for any attack to be a success. "Visiting the 110th regiment on November 13, the assistant division commander, General Davis, caught a glimpse of the depressing situation first hand. What he discovered prompted him to call off all offensive action by the regiment."[2]

November 14-16

Beginning November 14, the U.S. 8th Infantry Division, which had been resting in Hosingen, Luxembourg, moved forward and relieved the 28th, while under continued artillery and mortar fire.

---

2   Scorpio's Web site, The Battle of the Hürtgen Forest, http://www.Hürtgenforest.be/ (Dec. 29, 2009).

"At 1300 on November 15, officers and guides from the 3rd Battalion, 13th Infantry Regiment, 8th Infantry Division arrived at the 110th CP. They were met by officers of the 110th, oriented on the positions they would occupy and the mechanics of the relief worked out. During the afternoon and night, the 110th was relieved and moved into a rear assembly area in preparation to move to the vicinity of Wiltz, Luxembourg. The relief was completed by 2300." [3]

On November 16, 1944, Flynn was finally able to have his knee injuries and frostbite treated at the 42nd Evac Hospital. His injuries were considered serious enough that they sent him to the 3rd Battalion, 110th Infantry Aid Station, where they had a better medical facility and medicine to aid in his recovery.

Battle Summary

During the first eight days of the attack in the Hürtgen Forest, the 28th Infantry Division reported 2,631 casualties with an additional 2,328 casualties over the five subsequent days of operation, for a total of 4,939. Of these casualties, the great majority (4,238) were infantrymen.

Half of those casualties can be attributed to the 110th Infantry Regiment, whose original strength was 3,202 men. The regiment saw sixty-five men killed in action, 1,624 wounded in action, 253 taken as prisoners of war, 288 missing in action, and eighty-six men with non-battle related casualties, totaling 2,316 casualties. As mentioned before, K Company's casualty rates were among the highest within the regiment with twenty-one of the regiment's sixty-five KIA during November 2 to 12, 1944; eleven the first week and ten the second week under Flynn's command.

Nine thousand overshoes arrived for the 28th Division just as it withdrew from the Hürtgen fighting.

---

3 Col. Hurley E. Fuller, Unit Report No. 5–110th Infantry Regiment, 28th Infantry Division; 01Nov44-30Nov44, (Consthum, Luxembourg), 4.

K Company killed in Hürtgen Forest: November 2-14:

- Pvt. Harry C. Scheible — 11/2/1944
- 1st Sgt. Floyd F. Zehr — 11/2/1944
- Pfc Otto A. Bendinelli, Jr. — 11/5/1944
- Pfc Stanley J. Bobzin — 11/5/1944
- Pfc Lawrence Gentry* — 11/5/1944
- Pfc Eugene Harris* — 11/5/1944
- Pfc Charles G. Huskey, Jr. — 11/5/1944
- Sgt. Edger Moore, Jr.* — 11/5/1944
- 2nd Lt. John M. Semanik, Jr. — 11/5/1944
- Pfc Walter C. Smoot — 11/5/1944
- 1st Lt. Ernest L. Templer — 11/5/1944
- Pvt. William M. Bolen — 11/9/1944
- Pfc Philip Falcone — 11/9/1944
- S/Sgt. Woodrow F. Gerdes — 11/9/1944
- 1st Lt. Lawrence L. Love — 11/9/1944
- Pfc John F. Milbrandt — 11/9/1944
- Pfc Herbert H. Neu — 11/9/1944
- Pfc Edward J. Ricci — 11/9/1944
- Pfc William J. Rogowski — 11/9/1944
- Pfc Frederick A. Smith — 11/9/1944
- Pvt. John W. Scott — 11/12/1944

* Member of the original K Company, 110th Infantry Regiment, 28th Infantry Division that landed on Omaha Beach July 25, 1944.

CHAPTER 3

Hosingen, Luxembourg:
November 15–December 15, 1944

After four days at the 3rd Battalion, 110th Infantry Aid Station, Flynn rejoined the men of K Company on November 20, in Hosingen, Luxembourg, about sixty miles south of the Hürtgen Forest. The company's new assignment was to rest and recuperate in this "quiet sector"–the Ardennes Forest. The 28th would be taking up a defensive position for the first time since landing in Normandy in July. The 8th Infantry Division, which had previously occupied the town, was now taking its turn in the Hürtgen Forest.

K Company's commanding officer, Captain Frederick C. Feiker, age 34, who had been injured prior to the Hürtgen Forest action, was not yet able to return to active duty, and therefore, rebuilding the unit and preparing the company for its next combat assignment initially fell on Flynn's shoulders as the executive officer. Flynn was well prepared, having been in charge of training infantry units in the States for several years. His original training at Fort Benning as a Weapons Platoon Sergeant and commanding officer of the anti-tank unit at Camp Carson in Colorado Springs would also prove invaluable, given his expertise with all the equipment and weapons available.

Upon entering Hosingen, Flynn was very pleased to discover that the town had sustained little damage during the war and that the civilian water and electrical systems were still intact. The Americans had liberated Luxembourg on September 19, after four long years under German control, and in general, the locals were supportive and friendly.

Defensive Positioning and Strategy

Along with K Company, the entire 28th Infantry Division had been repositioned along a twenty-five-mile stretch of the Our River. Even though this vicinity was considered a quiet sector, it still bordered Germany and was a critical frontline position. It was also more than three times the area an infantry division was typically expected to defend. The 112th Infantry Regiment protected five miles on the Division's left flank, the 109th covered nine miles on the southern flank, and the 110th Infantry Regiment was responsible for more than a ten and a half mile section in the middle of the Division's frontage.

The 1st and 3rd Battalions of the 110th were spread along one of the best-paved highways in the Ardennes, nicknamed "Skyline Drive" by the 28th Division. This north-south highway ran parallel to the Luxembourg-German border, along the ridge top between the Our and Clerf rivers, reminding the men from Pennsylvania of Skyline Drive in the Blue Ridge Mountains back home. The road was also a supply route referred to as the "Red Ball Highway" as the Army had installed signs displaying a "red ball" for the English speaking troops to follow.

General Cota's Division CP was located in Wiltz, halfway between the frontline and the crossroads town of Bastogne.

Even though the ten and a half mile front defended by the 110th comprised more than twice the territory that an entire regiment would normally be expected to defend, General Cota made the decision to maintain the 2nd Battalion as the division's only infantry reserve. This left the 1st and 3rd Battalions spread so thinly along the sector that they were only able to maintain five company-sized strong points in critical towns along Skyline Drive. The strong points primarily provided coverage for the four main east-west roads that crossed the 110th's sector, along which any German attack would have to pass.

In November, the five strong points and the company and commanders that held them, were as follows, from north to south (see map *Bastogne corridor held by the 110th Infantry Regiment during the Battle of the Bulge*).

- A Company held Heinerscheid with Col. Donald Paul's 1st Battalion Command Post at Urspelt;
- **Dasbürg-Clervaux-Bastogne route**; B Company and a platoon from the 630th Tank Destroyer Battalion held Marnach; Colonel Fuller's 110th Command Post was in Clervaux;
- **Ober Eisenbach-Hosingen-Drauffelt route**; K Company and 2nd and 3rd Platoons of M Company (heavy weapons company) held Hosingen ;
- **Gemund-Holzthum-Wilwerwiltz route**; Companies L and M (platoons not at Hosingen) held Holzthum; Major Harold F. Milton's 3rd Battalion Command Post was located in Consthum;
- **Stolzembourg-Hoscheid-Kautenbach route**; I Company held Weiler.

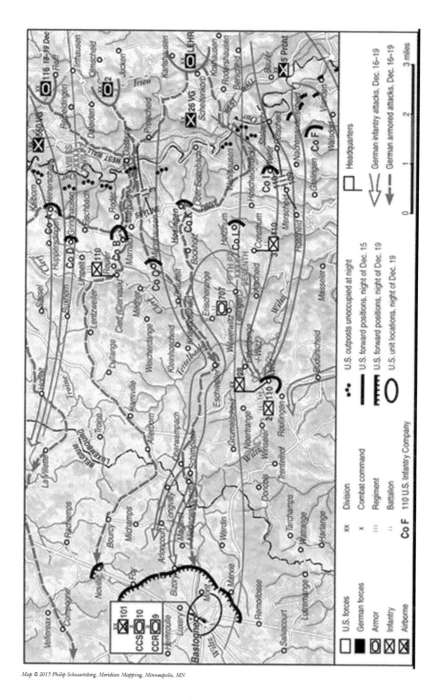

Map © 2015 Philip Schwartzberg, Meridian Mapping, Minneapolis, MN

Map: Bastogne corridor held by 110th Infantry Regiment's during Battle of the Bulge

Units of the 28th Infantry Division during the Battle of the Bulge included the following:

Units of the 28th Infantry Division During Battle of the Bulge*
Commanded by Maj. Gen. Norman D. Cota; Gen. George A. Davis, assistant commander
• Composed of the 109th, 110th, and 112th Infantry Regiments
• 109th and 687th Field Artillery Battalions
• 103rd Combat Engineer Battalion (road and bridge maintenance, set and clear mine fields)
• 707th Tank Battalion
• 630th Tank Destroyer Battalion
• 447th Anti-Aircraft Artillery Battalion
• 103rd Medical Battalion

*Action Report, Col. Daniel B. Strickler[4]

---

4   Col. Daniel B. Strickler, 110th Infantry Action Report of the German Ardennes Breakthrough, As I Saw It from 16 Dec. 1944 -2 Jan. 1945, http://history.amedd.army.mil/booksdocs/wwii/bulge/110thInfRegt/Strickler%20AAR%20Bulge.html (Dec. 29, 2009).

110th Infantry Regiment's Defensive Positioning Summary

110th Infantry Regiment, Col. Hurley Fuller's command post was in Clervaux; executive officer was Col. Daniel B. Strickler

1st Battalion held the northern section with Col. Donald Paul's command post at Urspelt:
- Company A held Heinerscheid.
- Company B held Marnach.
- Company C was in "reserve" in Munshausen.
- Company D held Grindhausen with three machine-gun crews detached to Reuler.

2nd Battalion, in reserve:
- Companies E, F, G, and H were held behind the lines at Donnange and Wiltz, where they served as the division's only reserve.
- General Cota's 28th Infantry Division command post was in Wiltz.

3rd Battalion held the southern section with Maj. Harold Milton's command post at Consthum:
- I Company held Weiler-les-Putscheid.
- K Company held Hosingen; Attachments: B Company, 103rd Engineer Battalion (125 men), 2nd and 3rd Platoons of M Company, 2nd platoon of 630th Tank Destroyer Battalion (30 men), and twenty men from a "Raider" unit (organization unknown)
- Companies L and M held Holzthum (just south of Hosingen).
- M Company and A Company, 447th Anti-Aircraft Artillery, were in Consthum.

Notes:
- Companies C and L, 110th, were the "reserve" companies for their respective battalions.
- Companies D and M, 110th, were the heavy weapons companies; each had spread their men and weapons among the strong points of their battalion.

Also operating in the area of the 110th Infantry Regiment:
- 707th Tank Battalion was at Wilwerwiltz.
- 630th Tank Destroyer Battalion (57-mm anti-tank guns) and 447th Anti-Aircraft Artillery Battalion had also spread their men and weapons among the strong points of each battalion.

Hosingen was at the midpoint of the 110th's ten and a half mile section, along the Ober-Eisenbach-Hosingen-Drauffelt route and directly on the crucial road to Bastogne to the west. The "road" from Ober Eisenbach to Hosingen was a four-mile, unpaved road through terrain cut by ridges and a draw running east-west, making direct observation of the Our River impossible from the town's observation posts. The banks of the Our River were extremely steep, and the access road wound sharply upward with hairpin turns. From Hosingen, the road continued down the west side of the ridge to the town of Bockholtz, where the road then split to cross the bridges over the Clerf River at Drauffelt and Wilwerwiltz. The town of Hosingen, therefore, controlled the main approach from Luxembourg to both critical bridges.

Major Harold F. Milton, who had appointed Flynn as executive officer of K Company on November 8, during the Hürtgen Forest battle, remained commanding officer of the 3rd Battalion, 110th Infantry Regiment, having relieved Captain Howdy Rumbaugh.

With the relocation to the Ardennes, the 28th Infantry Division was transferred to VIII Corps, commanded by Gen. Troy Middleton. Following the Hürtgen Forest action, many of the officers of the division were also replacements and each regiment of the 28th once again began to absorb replacement troops. With so few combat veterans still able to fight, the 28th no longer looked like the Pennsylvania National Guard unit that had once been.

At the suggestion of Gen. Troy Middleton, on November 24, General Cota named Col. Hurley Fuller as commanding officer of the 110th Infantry Regiment after Lt. Col. Seely was wounded by shrapnel in the Hürtgen Forest. Colonel Fuller set up his CP in Clervaux.

Given the strained resources of the Army in late November, General Middleton and his commanding officers realized it would be impossible to effectively cover the eighty-mile section of the frontline to the south of the Hürtgen Forest now occupied by the 106th, 28th, and the 4th Infantry Divisions, the 14th Cavalry Group, and 9th Armored Division, without adding additional units. They knew it was a calculated risk and justified their decision to leave this area more thinly defended than other areas based on the belief that the Germans were not capable of putting together a substantive counterattack. Even if they did attack, they believed it was unlikely the Germans would come through the Ardennes Forest. Middleton also believed that if the 28th was attacked, it could easily fall back into rear positions while reinforcements were moved into place.

As Flynn's K Company made defensive preparations in and around Hosingen, they took into consideration that General Cota favored a defensive pattern of dug-in positions extending well outside each strong point. However, given the less than optimal number of men available in each location now defended by the 110th and the distance between each strong point, that simply was not possible. Instead, each battalion was to establish five squad-strength outposts along the west bank of the Our River across from the enemy's main positions to the east. These outposts were only maintained during the day, as General Cota allowed the troops to withdraw to the villages and warm sleeping quarters at night.

During the hours of darkness, night patrols worked between company strong points and east to the Our River. German patrols typically made their river crossings at night and operated from small towns on the west bank of the river during the day. During the night, the area between the ridge and the river became a no man's land, with German and American patrols stalking each other.

During late November and the first half of December, the Americans had many warnings of a pending German attack in the Ardennes from German POWs, deserters, and locals who were first hand witnesses to the massive German build-up of men and equipment on the German side of the Our River. Unfortunately, most of these reports were not deemed reliable by those officers not on the front line, and the farther up the chain of command each report went, the less seriously it was taken.

The foggy weather, mixed with rain and snow, typical of the Ardennes Forest in winter, helped conceal the build-up of these German forces from American pilots. American intelligence reports also indicated that the German units on the east side of the river were recovering from extensive fighting and were too battered to launch an attack. Due to these factors, the 28th did not rate the fighting capabilities of the German forces in the area very high. One of the last S-2 intelligence reports that K Company read in mid-December rated the enemy's capabilities closest to Hosingen as that of strong patrolling only.

Preparing Hosingen
The Men

Upon arrival in Hosingen, Flynn immediately began to assess the situation. Most of the NCOs of K Company were men who had also been a part of the 41st Replacement Battalion and seen action in the Hürtgen Forest along with Flynn. For the most part, he had selected them on the basis of their visible abilities and the fact that he was already familiar with their qualifications. About twenty-five of the men in Hosingen had just returned to duty (RTD) after recovering from previous injuries. Sergeant Arbella, Pfc Harry Seidel and Staff Sergeant Shanabarger were just three of the six men from K Company that had miraculously survived every battle since July. Due to the heavy losses in the Hürtgen Forest, the balance of K Company's strength of about 160 men now based in Hosingen was nearly 100 percent replacements. There were still a few mild cases of frozen feet that were healing, including Flynn's, but on the whole, the men were in good physical condition.

The 2nd and 3rd Platoons of M Company, the battalion's heavy weapons company, had been moved into Hosingen for support of K Company. For additional support, the 2nd Platoon (thirty men) of the division's 630th Tank Destroyer Battalion was located here as well, with three 57-mm anti-tank guns and three .50-caliber machine guns guarding the crossroads south of Hosingen on Steinmauer Hill.

Also in the town were 125 men with Captain William Jarrett's B Company, 103rd Engineer Battalion. These engineers were responsible for the maintenance of about fifteen miles of Skyline Drive, the secondary road to the west and the muddy road that led east to Eisenbach. It was the combat engineers' job to get the units where they needed to go; from building bridges, to destroying German pillboxes, laying or removing minefields, or just keeping the roads free of snow. In the first two weeks of December it had snowed or rained almost every day so the engineers' kept busy clearing the roads of snow and icy slush. Lastly, there was a group of twenty men from a "Raider" unit (organization unknown), who had come in for specialized training in scouting and patrolling. Neither of the latter two units was originally involved in the defensive strategy employed to protect the town, although the engineers had eight to ten .50-caliber machine guns mounted on their trucks that were utilized after the early stages of battle. Altogether, there were "387 enlisted men and 13 officers"[5] assigned to the Hosingen garrison.

The Setting

The village had suffered little damage from the war thus far, and the houses, shops, and hotels still had electricity and running water. This made the town a comfortable place to rest and train new troops, although Flynn got the impression that the 8th Infantry Division had considered the town a rest center rather than a defensive position. Given their recent action in the Hürtgen Forest, Flynn and his officers deemed the 8th Division's defensive preparations unsatisfactory and set about improving them.

---

5   Excerpt from Capt. William H. Jarrett's Wartime Log, pgs 27- 67, covering 16 Dec 1944–17 March 1945, p.45

In Flynn's opinion, overall, the defensive pattern established by the 8th Infantry Division seemed to have been designed and executed to meet the approval of inspecting officers rather than for a tactical defensive situation. Foxholes had been dug around the town and the approaches had been mined and booby-trapped. However, the minefields and booby-traps seemed to present more danger to friendly troops than to the enemy. Flynn worked with the engineers to establish a better defensive plan, relocating potentially dangerous mines, building additional minefields along potential lines of attack, and planting a minefield on the Eisenbach road.

Ammunition and Supplies

Ammunition was of great concern to Flynn and K Company officers, as only one day's supply was available from day to day. Although K Company advocated having on hand a three-day supply, just a single daily issue was brought up from the rear each afternoon to cover the following day's needs, leaving little in reserve should the daily supply run be disrupted. The supply sergeant picked up extra ammunition and other supplies when he could, but only in small amounts. Some quartermaster supplies (general supplies, clothing, equipment, food, and rations), ordnance supplies (mortars, rifles, machine guns, and replacement parts) and signal equipment also had slowly been coming in. On occasion, a patrol had to borrow the battalion compass to continue its training, as the forest in the area was dense and the men needed to be able to successfully perform their training exercises and return to Hosingen as ordered.

Communications

Flynn coordinated with Major Milton's 3rd Battalion CP in Consthum to make sure reliable primary and backup communication systems were in place through the battalion switchboard at Bockholtz. As a result, K Company believed its communications systems to be in excellent condition. There were twenty-four lines from the company switchboard that established wire contact with the engineers, each platoon CP, north and south observation posts, the flanking cavalry units, artillery forward observers, and 3rd Battalion headquarters. Through the 3rd Battalion switchboard, they could also reach other companies as well as Colonel Fuller's 110th Regiment headquarters in Clervaux.

There were two SCR-300 Backpack Radios in the K Company CP, one used solely for 3rd Battalion contact and the other radio tied in with SCR-300 radios in the 1st and 2nd Platoon CPs. Since K Company had only four SCR-300 radios, 1st Lt. Barrett Weaver's 3rd Platoon CP, south of Hosingen, had to rely solely on wired communications through the battalion switchboard.

The Motorola SCR-300 was a portable, waterproof, battery-powered FM voice receiver/transmitter intended for field use by infantry units. It weighed thirty-five pounds so a soldier could carry it on his back. It had a reliable range of three miles.

Training the Replacement Troops

K Company was responsible for guarding a two-mile section of Skyline Drive around Hosingen and the area just south of it, blocking the Ober Eisenbach-Hosingen-Drauffelt road. At Hosingen, the Our River was four miles to the east of Skyline Drive. The Germans patrolled along the east side of the river and maintained several outposts overlooking K Company's positions.

Flynn followed the strict regimental and divisional directives for training the replacement troops in scouting and patrolling, sniping, and observation. A prescribed number of hours was required for each soldier in "on the spot" practical work. The usual method was to send out patrols with an officer and a combination force of six to nine men – infantry, engineers and mortar crewmen – using routes selected by Battalion Headquarters. The men were alternated and the patrols were gradually extended to the Our River; however, no patrols were allowed to cross the river.

These patrol missions offered the only opportunities for replacement troops to test-fire their mortars and new Model A-6 .30-caliber light machine guns (LMGs). Because no shooting was allowed on the west side of the river, the weapons had to be hand carried close enough that when fired, the mortar rounds and bullets would land on the east bank.

It was typical for patrols to launch mortar rounds into towns where there was a German garrison, with machine guns set up to shoot the German soldiers when they ran for cover.

There were several clashes with the enemy west of the river and in one instance, a patrol ran into a German outpost. One German was killed and one was wounded in the skirmish. The following night, the 3rd Battalion CP directed that one patrol was to go out and destroy the German outpost using a 60-mm mortar. As the officers of K Company feared, the patrol was ambushed. Although there were no casualties, the mortar was abandoned. A third patrol sent to retrieve the weapon the next day, found that it, as well as the Germans, were gone. The mortar was never replaced.

S-2 intelligence reports were made to 3rd Battalion headquarters in Consthum every two hours during the day and every hour after dark. Positive reports were written and negative reports were phoned in.

Defensive Strategy

Flynn carefully studied and implemented a defensive strategy in and around the town to protect Hosingen should the Germans attack. He established K Company's CP in the pharmacy building a block to the south of the 12th Century church in the center of town. Captain Jarrett established the Engineer's CP in the Hotel

Schmitz, a two-story building just to the north of the church. As mentioned previously, General Cota's defensive plan favored a defensive pattern of dug-in positions extending well outside the town; however, K Company estimated that a unit of battalion strength would be required to defend properly its entire zone in this manner. Instead, K Company planned a defense within the town. Because no armored units were available to K Company when making the initial plans, the defense was established considering only the defensive capabilities of K Company. Because there was snow on the ground for most of the month, Flynn used white sheets from the villagers to camouflage their defensive positions; with luck, they would blend in with the snow.

On the south end of town, Lt. Porter's 2nd Platoon (thirty men) and three 57-mm antitank guns from the division's 630th Tank Destroyer Battalion guarded the intersection of Skyline Drive with the east-west road from Eisenbach to Bockholtz. This intersection was located just 200 meters to the south of the village.

Another 1.5 km farther south, along Skyline Drive, .30-caliber machine gunners, Privates Dale Gustafson and Ernest Gallego, and the rest of M Company's 2nd Platoon, with its three .50-caliber machine guns, reinforced K Company's 3rd Platoon position under the command of 1st Lt. Barrett Weaver at the Hosingen-Barrière intersection. The two units occupied neighboring farm houses on either side of the intersection, just 75 meters apart. Both farms had a clear view of the large meadow on the east side of the road that extended down the hill to a grove of trees. From there, they could see any movement coming up the draw from the Our River once it left the cover of the woods. To defend their position, the GIs had constructed four well-fortified, timber pillboxes, positioned in a large arc which enabled them to cover both houses with interlocking fields of fire.

The rest of the 2nd Platoon of M Company and its .50-caliber machine guns supported the 2nd Platoon of K Company in the south part of town covering the south and southeast approaches. One section of 81-mm mortars was set up behind a building in the center of town.

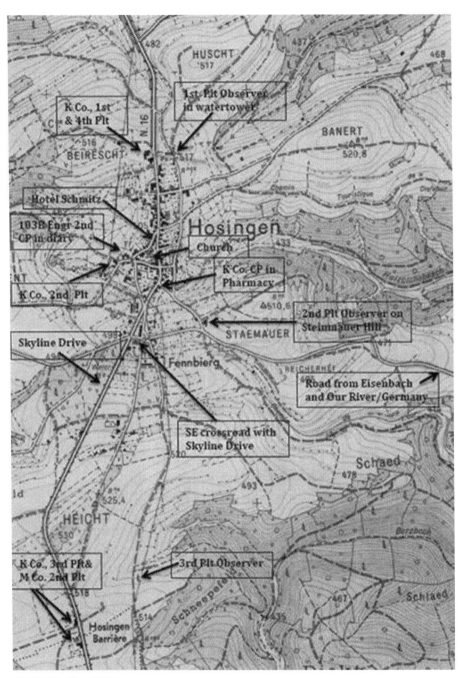

Map © Alice Flynn 2015

Map: Positions of K Co. and 103rd Combat Engr, B Co. in Hosingen

Eight men from K Company's 4th (Weapons) Platoon were stationed in the north end of town, with LMGs and Private Gracie's bazooka, covering Skyline Drive to the north. The platoon's 60-mm mortars were set up in a courtyard (minus one that had been lost during the patrol to the river). Fourth Platoon was prepared to hold their position with two men in each of the four foxholes that formed a defensive arc in front of the house they were using for shelter. The 1st Platoon of K Company was originally positioned at the north end of town on the main road when Flynn first arrived, but, this unit was relieved by an armored cavalry unit on December 12 and Captain Feiker, who had returned to active duty on December 5, directed them to withdraw to the northern edge of town, as well.

M Company officer, Lt. Morse was glad when Capt. Feiker rejoined K company as they had become good friends since the division had started training in the states. Morse had frequently supported K Company with 81 mm mortar fire and when no artillery observer was present, directed artillery fire. Morse had the utmost respect for the man, describing him as "a fine gentleman, capable, cool under fire and very intelligent; an exceptional company commander".[6]

Single-squad observation posts (OPs) were maintained on high ground overlooking the Our River valley, with the hills of Germany in the distance. With the tallest structure in town close to his 1st Platoon CP, Flynn's utilized the water tower in the northeast corner of town as their lookout tower. Lt. Porter's 2nd Platoon maintained an outpost in two farmhouses on the crown of Steinmauer Hill located about 200 meters southeast of the village. Unfortunately, the Our River (and German front line) could not be seen from either OP due to intervening high ground.

To the north, a platoon of B Company, the 32 Cavalry Squadron, maintained a screen from K Company's 1st Platoon on the north edge of Hosingen to the next unit to the north. Another cavalry unit maintained similar contact between the K Company's 3rd Platoon,

---

6   Lt. James D. Morse, Interview given to Al Price, August 16, 1996.

located south of the road junction, and elements of Company I, 110th Infantry Regiment, whose command post was in Weiler, south of Hosingen on the main road. This pattern of alternating cavalry units and infantry companies had been followed up and down the line.

The artillery forward observer had laid out defensive fire plans on the draws and approaches to Hosingen. However, a Division order prohibited actual adjustment of these fire plans.

Because of how spread out K Company's defensive positions were, they relied heavily on .30-caliber Browning Automatic Rifles (BARs) and M1 rifle fire to cover draws and high ground, adjusting the company's mortars to cover the low spots that the riflemen could not see. The .30-caliber M1 Garand semi-automatic rifle, with an eight round clip had a maximum range of 500 yards. The BAR, with its standard 20-round magazine, was capable of firing 450 rounds a minute and could be fired from the shoulder or hip, or mounted on a bipod, usually in short bursts.

Letters from Home

On Thanksgiving Day, November 23, 1944, the men were fed a nice Thanksgiving meal. In addition, mail from home finally started to arrive and the men were also able to catch up on some correspondence. Regardless of how the GIs actually felt, many of the combat veterans did not want their families to worry about them so they downplayed the intense fighting the unit had been through.

Something's Not Right

In general, the mood of many of the men and officers of the 28th was all too relaxed going into the month of December. Hollywood movie star Marlene Dietrich and her USO troupe were making the rounds throughout the Ardennes, entertaining the American troops. Those lucky enough to get at least a two-day pass often went to Clervaux. Clervaux was a picturesque resort town boasting hot-spring spas, mud baths, German *brauhauses*, theaters, and best of all, women. Some men, with enough days off to allow it, headed to Paris.

Those who stayed behind, however, observed many signs that something was going on east of the Our River. K Company patrols saw increased German patrols on the west bank of the Our River and increasingly heard sounds of moving vehicles and equipment. K Company even obtained a report from a German deserter, who walked out of the woods one day with his hands in the air to surrender. The soldier, in his late twenties, was a teacher and had had enough fighting. He warned the K Company riflemen he surrendered to that there was going to be a big push before Christmas. The riflemen had him taken to Captain Feiker for interrogation, but there is no record that this warning was taken seriously by those further up the chain of command.

K Company officers did their best to prepare the town and men for an attack. They were convinced something was about to happen; they just didn't know when. With every new piece of evidence, they became more convinced that the Germans were not going to sit quietly across the Our River for the winter, regardless of whether their superiors agreed with this belief. Much to Flynn's frustration, even Major Milton at 3rd Battalion headquarters in Consthum didn't think the topic worth discussing when Captain Feiker and Flynn visited his command post in early December.

Unfortunately, official scouting reports did not relay the detailed information that company-level troops were observing in the area. Those in command, therefore, were skeptical that the German army would consider or be capable of pulling off the large-scale invasion that was rumored. Both Gen. Omar Bradley and Gen. Dwight Eisenhower knew that the Allies could not be strong everywhere and called the weakly held Ardennes sector a calculated risk, as some portions of the 200-mile front had to be deemphasized. Not remembering or considering what had happened during WWI and 1940, they felt the Ardennes was the safest place to take that risk. This also meant that they saw no reason to order reconnaissance into the German sector in the area, either by ground or by air. Even the weather helped to hide what was going on, as the cloudy, foggy conditions remained bad enough to ground the planes that would have flown routine surveillance missions.

Eventually though, by mid-December, persistent compelling evidence of the pending danger finally convinced Colonel Fuller of a pending attack. General Cota, however, was unimpressed and disregarded Fuller's concerns. Even if General Cota had agreed, it was already too late, as the German attack was poised to come right through the middle of his division.

Hitler's Last Offensive

On the other side of the Our River, preparations were indeed well advanced. Hitler's forces had put together an amazingly detailed plan to launch a massive counter-offensive against the Allied army in an attempt to split their forces in two, isolate the British 21st Army Group, retake the ocean port of Antwerp, and thereby force the Allies into a negotiated peace. Hitler knew he had to lay it all on the line; his empire had steadily crumbled before his eyes since the Allies' initial assault on D-Day. General Hasso von Manteuffel was appointed commander of the 5th Panzer Army, the unit that ultimately led the assault on the 110th through the Ardennes.

All that fall, Hitler had been busy moving his scattered armies into the Ardennes region, rebuilding battered units with replacements troops, pulling soldiers from other military branches, and refitting them all with new equipment. By winter, Hitler had accumulated "an army of 250,000 men, hundreds of tanks, hundreds of self-propelled weapons, thousands of trucks, half-tracks, armored cars, and other vehicles. The Luftwaffe had even assembled one thousand planes for this operation."[7]

---

7   McManus, 29.

In late November, just after the 28th Division arrived in the Ardennes to recover and rebuild from the Hürtgen Forest action, General Hasso von Manteuffel visited the area and saw for himself just how thinly held the Ardennes' border with Germany was. His intelligence reports gave him a clear picture of the status of the battered 28th Infantry Division and he personally observed the Americans withdrawing their patrols to their fortified villages at night.

With this knowledge, Manteuffel was able to persuade Hitler to modify his plans and permit him to infiltrate infantry assault teams across the Our River under the cover of darkness, and maneuver into positions around the American-held garrisons. The assault would get underway just before dawn, with a surprise artillery bombardment against the American-held towns. Manteuffel's engineers would then begin to build a series of bridges over the Our River to allow the mechanized units to cross. Once the sleepy towns were seized and the bridges were built, the tanks would roll through to Bastogne and on to Antwerp. This attack would hit three American infantry divisions across an 80-mile front: the 106th at the north end in the Schnee Eifel region, the 28th in the Bastogne corridor and the 4th to the south. If all went according to plan, the German panzer battalions would be across the Clerf River by the end of the first day and on their way to Bastogne.

Bastogne was the critical point of this attack and speed was of the essence. Hitler and Manteuffel agreed that Bastogne had to fall on the second day of the assault, before the Americans had time to send reinforcements to defend it. Bastogne, with seven major roads running through it, provided critical access for the supplies that Hitler would need to finalize his assault on Antwerp. Without it, the entire offensive would be in jeopardy and any delay or deviation from their precise timetable would certainly put the success of the offensive in jeopardy.

The primary unit of Manteuffel's 5th Panzer Army that would attack through the 110th Infantry Regiment's sector, was General Heinrich von Lüttwitz's XLVII Panzer Corps. The unit was made up entirely of army divisions: the 2nd Panzer, Panzer Lehr and

26th Volksgrenadier Divisions (VGD), which included 27,000 infantrymen and 216 tanks, assault guns or tank destroyers, compared with the 5,000 men of the 110th Infantry Regiment.

Hitler considered Von Lüttwitz's 26th VGD to be the best infantry division of Manteuffel's 5th Panzer Army. Twelve thousand men strong and under the command of Maj. Gen. Heinz Kokott, they were to capture the towns held by the 110th from Marnach to Weiler, seize control of the bridges over the Clerf River and then swiftly move into Bastogne by the end of the second day. Lüttwitz was specific about how many men he needed in order to capture each town—ordering squads, platoons, or company-size units to surround each town and village. But in Hosingens' case, Lüttwitz committed an entire battalion to the assault as one of the key bridges to be emplaced on the Our was to be located near Eisenbach. As the German command would soon find out, it would take much more than that to get Hosingen to fall. Before the men in Hosingen would fire their last shots, the battle would involve the 304th Panzergrenadier Regiment from the 2nd Panzer Division and the 39th and 77th Volksgrenadiers from the 26th VGD, in addition to the 78th Panzergrenadiers initially held in reserve.

Friday, December 15, 1944

At 1800 on December 15, after the daily patrol had returned to Hosingen, activity was heard along the Our River and Flynn quickly went to 2nd Platoon's southern observation post to see if he could help identify or pinpoint any specific noise. Due to the distance between Hosingen and the river (approximately four miles) and the winding, wooded draws in between, the sounds were quite distorted, making identification or location by compass bearings impossible. However, Flynn believed that it was probably German motorcycles used by couriers. Eventually, the noises ended and the area was quiet once again. No patrols were due to go out until 0530 the next morning and so the customary precautions were taken and K Company stayed on 50 percent alert with men in buildings that had observation posts on the top floors or on high ground.

As a precautionary measure, the officers of K Company also decided to change the location of their mortars, which would prove to be an extremely important, tactical decision.

Shortly thereafter, between 2200 and 2300 hours, Flynn and the men in Hosingen observed the Germans shining searchlights into the night sky, the reflections from which bounced off the low winter clouds, lighting up the entire area almost as brightly as daylight. This was not the first time the Germans had done this at night during the past month, so the American officers did not immediately sound an alarm. No further enemy activities were reported. The men of the 110th were unaware that the reflection of the lights off the low clouds was bright enough to help Manteuffel's army cross the Our River and find its way through the woods on the American-occupied side of the river.

In retrospect, what Flynn had heard was the German troops beginning to cross the Our River and move into position around the towns occupied by the 110th.

CHAPTER 4

The Battle of the Bulge Begins: Saturday, December 16, 1944

The Predawn Hours

Around 0300 on December 16, elements of the 304th Panzergrenadier Regiment of the 2nd Panzer Division and the 39th and 77th Volksgrenadiers of the 26th VGD began quietly crossing the twenty-yard span of the Our River in small rubber boats, their movements hidden by a thick fog blanketing the river. As each group disembarked on the west bank, it quickly moved up the wooded hills through the snow-covered forest into pre-planned positions. The 77th Grenadier Regiment, 26th VGD, assembled in the woods just 300 yards from Hosingen. Their mission was to bypass Hosingen to the north and head straight towards Drauffelt in order to seize the bridges over the Clerf River for the Panzer Lehr Division to pass later in the day.

Throughout the area, all the American defenses were quietly being surrounded as the Germans skillfully approached to within striking distance of the towns of Marnach, Hosingen, Holzthum, Consthum, Weiler, and Munshausen. Once in place, some of the impatient German infantry began quietly attacking foxholes and outposts. However, most of the German units waited for the first rounds of the artillery bombardment that would signal the beginning of the attack as they had been ordered.

Even as Lüttwitz's 77ᵗʰ Regiment was still crossing the Our River for the initial assault, the regiment's engineers had begun working on bridges at Gemünd and Ober Eisenbach, with a third bridge under construction farther north at Dasbürg. At these crossings, the river was narrow and not very deep, although extremely steep banks made bridges a necessity to enable tanks to cross. Lüttwitz had hoped to have the three bridges operational by noon so his tanks could follow closely behind his 26ᵗʰ VGD in case his infantry ran into heavy resistance moving through the Bastogne corridor. This would also help Lüttwitz meet the strict timetable Manteuffel required to satisfy Hitler. Lüttwitz's panzers needed to reach the Clerf River by nightfall on December 16, if they were to take Bastogne the following day. He could not afford any major delays.

At 0530 on December 16, a cold Saturday morning, two young GIs from 1ˢᵗ Platoon who had been stationed all night in the OP atop the town's water tower had called to report to Captain Feiker at the K Company CP, when the area east of the Our River suddenly became filled with "pinpoints of light." Before the young GI could finish describing what he saw German artillery and mortar fire began to land in Hosingen and all around, severing all wire communications. What they had witnessed were the muzzle flashes of over 2,000 German artillery pieces aimed at Hosingen and American positions along the front.

The screaming shells were deafening, instantly waking everyone that may have still been asleep. Private Gracie and his platoon scrambled out of bed, grabbing their weapons as they ran out of the house they had occupied; anxious to get to their assigned positions. Their foxholes, near 1st Platoon's northern outpost, were not far away, but snowmelt had left them partially filled with water, topped by a ¼-inch of ice. Wide awake, armed and ready, they waited for the German assault.

An artillery shell scored a direct hit on a three-story building just down the street from the water tower where aidmen, 2ⁿᵈ Lt. Danny R. Mc Bride, Sgt. George McKnight, Pvt. Robert Tucker and T/4 Wayne Erickson, had been working, setting fire to the building. They gathered what medical supplies they could carry and made it across the small town square to a former hotel, noticing along the way that Erickson's jeep had also been hit–three flat tires and a punctured radiator. Lieutenant Mc Bride, a male nurse, in charge of the four-man group from the 103rd Medical Battalion, was new to the front, but the men had already nicknamed him, "Doc" since his initials were "D.R.". The medics set up a new aid station in the basement.

Another shell landed on the top floor of the building where Staff Sgt. William Freeman and thirteen other men from 2nd platoon of 630th Tank Destroyer Battalion were housed. Fortunately the men were all located on the lower floor and in the basement and no injuries resulted.

During the artillery barrage, every man in K Company was sent into his prepared defensive positions. The war had suddenly become very personal and their hearts pounded with the sudden adrenaline rush. Flynn immediately went to the north end of town to monitor the 1st Platoon situation and Lieutenant Porter went to the south end with 2nd Platoon. Flynn jumped into a foxhole with two of his machine gunners, standing behind their LMGs and kept a watchful eye on Skyline Drive. By now, five buildings were on fire and the artillery shells kept coming down. "The town was pretty well lit up," Flynn recalled, illuminating the whole ridge top, but fortunately, there had been no casualties. He and Captain Feiker had no idea of the scope of the attack that was taking place, but they knew they should be prepared for a full-scale enemy assault.

Captain Jarrett, B Company Engineers, sent a runner to Captain Feiker's CP to set up a '500' channel on their radios for communication. After they spoke, they agreed upon a channel over which they would all keep in contact since the shelling had cut all their phone lines. At this point, the men in Hosingen were unaware that artillery shells were also hitting every American-held position of the division—including Colonel Fuller's 110th regimental command post in Clervaux. It was obvious that the Germans were well prepared as their artillery barrages hit their marks, taking down all phone lines within the entire division. Even the radio reception from companies to their battalion headquarters and to regimental headquarters was intermittent at best, as the Germans also jammed reception to prevent communication between and within units. Captains Feiker and Jarrett would have to change their radio frequency eight times over the next two days as the Germans disrupted their communications.

The heavy artillery barrage lasted forty-five minutes and by the end of the shelling a total of seven buildings had been set on fire, and the town's electrical and water systems were severely damaged. When the shelling ended, the men of K Company observed the German artillery shells had fallen on every position in town where the mortars had been located just a few hours before. They would have been destroyed had not Captain Feiker paid attention to the signs of a pending attack and had his men move them.

During the bombardment, trucks were moved to sheltered areas and the upper floors of all buildings were vacated. Then Engineers' Lt. Cary Hutter and 1st Platoon took up positions at the rear of town, established a road block, and provided small arms protection for Lieutenant Morse's mortar section, positioned just inside the town. Lt. John Pickering and 2nd Platoon helped cover the southern half of the town supporting Captain Feiker's command post and the south roadblock. The 3rd Platoon under Lt. Charles Devlin strategically positioned themselves along the northeast edge of town to provide fire support to Flynn's 1st Platoon, helping cover both the north roadblock and the men from K Company in the water tower. Jarrett's men, assigned to his command post, prepared to defend the center of town by covering the draw and the fields to the northwest. Each team was then responsible for adding mines on all roads that entered the town.

After they had taken up their positions and the shelling had ended, the men of the garrison that were able, quickly ate a breakfast of hot cakes and coffee, one or two men at a time, while the kitchen was still operational.

Here Comes the Sun

Between 0615 and 0715, K Company could hear the enemy moving up a draw and crossing the road to bypass the town to the north.

But it was still too dark to actually see the Germans. When the sun finally rose, around 0730, the intensity of the fighting quickly escalated. Through the smoke, morning fog, and low-hanging clouds, K Company's 1st Platoon could begin to make out shadows moving in the distance and Flynn ordered his men to open fire with everything they had. BARs and M1 rifles cut the Germans down as they attempted to cross Skyline Drive, interfering with their westward movement. Flynn had trained his men well over the past month and they were well disciplined; they didn't fire unless they were sure of their target. They all knew that with only a day's ammunition on hand, they didn't have any to waste.

At the same time, Sergeant Arbella, a 60-mm mortar section leader from K Company's weapons platoon, quickly climbed into the water tower and joined the two GIs from Flynn's 1st Platoon stationed as lookouts and gave his mortar crew directions as to where to aim their mortars along the Skyline Drive. One of their 60-mm mortars had a damaged bipod from an artillery shell, but was still functional, so Arbella's men carried it up behind the light mortar battery in the courtyard on the north end of town. From this new location, they were able to continue firing to help pin down the enemy. Locations for the other 60-mm mortars and the 81-mm mortars was relayed by walkie-talkie from units around Hosingen.

The lookouts posted in the water tower continued to scan the area around the town diligently, and as the fog lifted, they observed an entire company of white-clad German soldiers from the 77th Grenadier Regiment charging their northern outpost from across an open field to the east, trying to force their way into the town. Despite the lookouts' surprise, they alerted their fellow GIs on the ground in time to stop this direct assault.

Contrary to Manteuffel's orders, two of his companies attempted an assault from the east. Pvt. Edward Gasper, positioned in the large foxhole with Flynn on the north end of town, was covering the area outside the barn where they had slept for several weeks. Gasper was pointing his M1 rifle to the north, covering that approach, while his two friends, Privates Fox and Melvin Epstein, covered the east, with Flynn positioned behind them: "This

German…jumped up right in front of the foxhole. Private Epstein hit him with a BAR. He was dead before he hit the ground. Private Gasper spotted two other enemy soldiers crawling up towards the farmhouse. They weren't more than thirty or forty feet from me. I saw 'em and I shot 'em. To the left, two more Germans were walking down the main road that led into Hosingen. Before Gasper could shoot them, another rifleman, nicknamed Tennessee, shot them down. The five dead enemy soldiers lay in defeated heaps."[8] Flynn relayed information of the assault to Captain Feiker and he immediately passed the report to Major Milton that the enemy had entered the outer edge of the town at about 0730.

Arbella quickly called out new target positions to his mortar team. The combination of mortar shells, BAR, machine gun, and rifle fire, shattered the advancing enemy companies, stopping the attack. It had only taken a few minutes for K Company's 1st Platoon, Lt. Devlin's engineers, and M Company on the north end of town to force the Germans to retreat to the shelter of the woods as scores of German soldiers now lay dead or wounded all across the open field.

While Flynn and his riflemen were busy on the north end, the 77th Grenadier Regiment was also converging on Hosingen from the east and south. Captain Jarrett, B Company Engineers, had gone up to the town's church tower, and by 0705 hours, could clearly see the Germans about 1300 meters away. He observed Germans moving along the Ober Eisenbach-Hosingen-Drauffelt road and crossing Skyline Drive to the south of town. Radio contact with 3rd Platoon and 2nd Platoon of M Company having been severed during the initial artillery barrage, Captains Feiker and Jarrett were under the impression that their position at Hosingen-Barrière, and the 630th Tank Destroyer Battalion guarding the crossroads south of Hosingen from Steinmauer Hill, had already been overrun. No contact was regained with the men in these units while K Company still controlled Hosingen and therefore,

---

8   McManus, 67.

the much needed support of the 630th's three 57-mm guns and three .50-caliber machine guns was lost.

Despite their inability to communicate with Captain Feiker, the GIs defending the southern outpost at Hosingen-Barrière were still very much a fighting unit as the initial German artillery barrage had missed its target. Expecting little resistance from the outpost, the grenadiers in the dawn attack on their position were in for a surprise. Anxiously the GIs watched the grenadiers come out from the cover of the nearby grove into the open meadow, climbing the steep hill towards their position. Once they were six to seven meters away from the American positions, Privates Gustafson and Gallego and their fellow soldiers opened fire. They managed to repel this initial assault, but the fighting continued throughout the day and into the night, with tracer rounds honing in on their positions all night long.

At some point during the day, they captured three German officers and Private Gustafson was ordered to guard the prisoners in the barn attached to the farmhouse.

Back in Hosingen, Captain Jarrett could see the steady stream of German infantry on foot, on bicycles, and on horse-drawn artillery caissons cutting across Skyline Drive to the south of Hosingen, so he contacted 1st Lt. James Morse, an M Company officer who controlled a section of 81-mm mortars on that end of town, and told him what he had seen. Jarrett's information was exactly what Morse needed and his mortars pounded the Germans, halting their movement for almost two hours.

Captain Feiker contacted Captain Jarrett and had his radio operator, Pfc Jay Stone, call for artillery fire, providing both coordinates and concentration numbers to their supporting artillery unit, Battery C, 109th Field Artillery Battalion, which was located directly to the west of the ridge. Battery C could not respond to his request, however, as it was also under attack by the German infantry that had bypassed Hosingen earlier that morning. Artillery fire was critically needed to stop the constant flow of Germans, but as Flynn noted, "Not one round of artillery was ever fired." Since the initial barrage had severed all phone communications and kept Captain Feiker from contacting any other units, the only support K Company had was from its own mortars.

During the initial artillery barrage, German troops had managed to enter the southern outskirts of Hosingen and Lieutenant Porter's men were involved in fierce house-to-house fighting. But K Company was able to hold them off and contain their progress. During this brief skirmish, 2nd Platoon captured three grenadiers as well as a German officer who carried a 1:25000 map outlining Lüttwitz's XLVII Panzer Corps attack plan all the way to Bastogne. Recognizing the significance of the map and that the attack was actually part of a large counteroffensive, Captain Feiker attempted to have a runner carry the map back to the regimental command post at Clervaux. Unfortunately, by then there were already too many Germans between the two towns, and the runner only made it a mile out of Hosingen before returning with the map.

Flynn contacted Major Milton at battalion headquarters to keep him informed of the situation and to let him know that it had become impossible to get the map to Colonel Fuller in Clervaux. At that point, Major Milton told Flynn to hold the position and promised that L Company, waiting in reserve at the 3rd Battalion command post, would come forward to help and bring more ammunition. But the time Milton was able to order L Company to Hosingen, the unit became involved in its own battle and never made it there.

Jarrett's and Feiker's transmissions were being overheard at the 110th Infantry Regiment headquarters in Clervaux but there was nothing that could be done. The 110th was still too scattered and confused by the sudden attack to mount a counterthrust. Before long, it seemed to be too late to help K Company, for at 0750 a radio operator in Holzthum intercepted a report by the executive officer of Battery C, 109th Field Artillery Battalion that reported Hosingen as quiet; this gave the false impression that the Germans had completely overrun the village and that resistance there had ceased. In fact, the silence was due to the fact that the attacking grenadiers had pulled back from Hosingen and ceased to cross the Skyline

Drive within sight of the town. Having gained a new respect for the firepower commanded by the little garrison, they continued crossing the highway farther north and south, out of range of the American machine guns and mortars.[9]

Enough information had gotten through to Colonel Fuller and General Cota by this time for them to realize that the 110th's frontline companies at Hosingen, Weiler, Holzthum, and Marnach were in the middle of a massive German assault and that most of his company positions were now surrounded or cut off. Fuller tried to convince General Cota to release his 2nd Battalion in reserve to bolster up his own defensive line around Clervaux, but Cota didn't want to commit his key reserves so early in battle. However, at 0700, General Cota alerted the 707th Tank Battalion to be ready to counterattack and by 0900, Major R. S. Garner and sixteen Sherman tanks of the 707th's A and B Companies moved out from their camps at Drauffelt and Wilwerwiltz, headed for Clervaux to support the 110th. This was all General Cota felt he could do.

Not knowing what had happened to the units on Steinmauer Hill and at Hosingen-Barrière, Captain Feiker needed all the help he could get to defend the town. By 0800, Captain Jarrett and the officers of K Company believed that the enemy might now attack the town from the west, so eight men from the 103rd Engineers gathered up their gear and set up in two adjoining farms on the western edge of town, several blocks to the northwest of the church. Their assistance was now essential to establishing a perimeter defense. Six of the men from Lieutenant Hutter's 1st Platoon were assigned this duty – Sgt. Darrell Doyen, Pfc Jacob Sterk, Pvt. Joseph Butler, Pvt. Leland Julien, Cpl. George Stevenson and Pvt. Bill King, in addition to Pvt. Frank Kosick, who was armed with a bazooka, and a sergeant from M Company with an 81mm mortar.

They dismounted the .50-caliber machine gun from one of the vehicles and set it up on a pipe mount in front of the barn

---

9   Allyn R. Vannoy, Jay Karamales, Against the Panzers, United States Infantry versus German Tanks, 1944-1945, (North Carolina: McFarland & Company, Inc., 1996), 203.

along with the 81mm mortar. With these two weapons facing the road, a defensive line was established which would impede enemy movement across the area by paired machine guns firing as an interlocked barrier. However, should a tank make it past their defenses, Sergeant Doyen and Corporal Stevenson had a surprise waiting for it. They had strung eight landmines together on a daisy chain and ran it across the street, hoping to snag onto the first tank to enter from the west. Private Kosick was sent up to the church steeple with his bazooka to help guard against a tank attack.

K Company was already beginning to run low on ammunition, so Jarrett's engineers shared the 3,000 rounds each of .30-caliber and .50-caliber ammunition they had. Even that would not last long once the enemy resumed their attack. The engineers also coordinated their defense with the mortar men of M Company so they could call for fire. Contact was maintained with the engineer teams by radio.

Moving outside of the range of the Hosingen weaponry, the German infantrymen continued to bypass the town to the north and the south as best they could through the forest and the cultivated fields. The GIs in Hosingen could do nothing to stop them. This situation continued throughout the day. At 0830, seeing a lull in the action, Captain Jarrett decided to prepare for the evacuation of his unit, which he believed to be imminent. He knew Hosingen was being cut off and he wanted to be ready when the order to move out came. His unit had too much engineering equipment in Hosingen to allow it to fall into German hands. The German artillery barrage had destroyed the tires on seven of his twenty trucks and Staff Sgt. Harry Brander and his men went to work replacing the tires and loading everything of value, such as barbed wire, food, and packs; leaving their mines, TNT, machine guns, demolition charges, and ammunition available for use, if needed. Jarrett's staff also began destroying the unit's maps and any critical papers that might be of value to the Germans. He planned to wait until the very last minute to remount the six .50-caliber and six .30-caliber machine guns that were dispersed around Hosingen.

Having just bolstered the perimeter with Jarrett's men, Captain Feiker tried to convince Jarrett to stay, that K Company needed their help. Jarrett was not swayed, so Captain Feiker called Major Milton at battalion headquarters. Milton ordered Jarrett and B Company, 103rd Engineers, to stay in Hosingen and support Captain Feiker's unit. He also told Jarrett not to evacuate anything or anyone without Captain Feiker's approval. Milton signed off by promising again that help was on the way.

Jarrett's men dismounted from their trucks and retook their positions on the western edge of town, where he and Feiker feared the Germans might soon attack. Together, the two captains inspected the defensive perimeter around Hosingen, talking with the men and making adjustment to squads and weapons positions where they deemed it necessary in order to give the best all-around coverage. Since the units were short on bazookas and anti-tank guns, they were thankful they hadn't seen any German tanks yet. They estimated they only had enough drinking water to last the men about 48 hours.

Engineer Corporal Stevenson, positioned in the barn on the western edge of town, helped the mortar crew haul the shells for the mortar and drag sandbags from their trucks to place around his machine gun. When everything was set up the way they wanted it, they settled down to watch and wait, as did all the other men in Hosingen. It was clear that there was not much chance of breaking through the German lines, and they had received orders from General Cota to "hold and fight it out at all costs", [10] but the men held out hope that the reinforcements promised by Major Milton would be able to break through to them.

Throughout the morning, they heard the sounds of fighting all around them, but except for the one large scale attack earlier in the day, they were left pretty much alone. However, small scale attacks happened about every half hour so all units were instructed to use infiltration methods when moving from house to house.

---

10   Strickler, 110th Infantry Action Report of the German Ardennes Breakthrough, As I Saw It from 16 Dec. 1944 -2 Jan. 1945.

On the southern end of town, some of the GIs decided to test their skills, and sitting cross-legged in the middle of the Skyline Drive, spent the afternoon sniping with rifles and .50-cal machine guns at any Germans foolhardy enough to try to dash across the highway within range. A few GIs from 2nd Platoon also ventured out to reoccupy the outpost in the farmhouse on Steinmauer Hill that had been captured earlier that day. They, too, kept the Germans at bay, killing about thirty-five and destroying some of their horse-drawn artillery before once again having to surrender the position early the next morning.

The Tanks Are On Their Way

When the tanks of the 707th Tank Battalion got to Clervaux, Colonel Fuller split the tanks into platoons and sent them out to help the different frontline companies. The Shermans of the 1st Platoon of B Company, 707th Tank Battalion, made their way along a winding trail up the west slope of the ridge from Wilwerwiltz to Bockholtz. When they reached the fork in the road at Bockholtz around noon, the first four tanks came to the rescue of Battery C of the 109th Field Artillery, which was under attack for the second time that day. Together, they drove off the attacking German infantry and recaptured one artillery piece that had been lost earlier in the morning, stalling Lüttwitz's 77th Regiment's drive to the Clerf for half a day. The rest of the tanks in B Company took the left fork and headed north to Munshausen and Marnach.

Once things settled down, the tanks took to the road again and fought their way through the German infantry to the edge of Hosingen. These tanks were loaded with ammunition that could have replenished the supply of the men in Hosingen, but when they reached the south edge of Hosingen around 1300, they weren't sure what to do. They had heard reports that Hosingen may have fallen so they took up a defensive position instead and stayed there for two hours, not attempting to contact anyone in the town.

Armed with *panzerfausts* and small-arms, the 77th Grenadier Regiment finally counterattacked, forcing the Sherman tankers to button up and the platoon leader to call for help over his radio. In response, 1st Lt. Richard H. Payne led the 3rd Platoon of A Company of the 707th south along Skyline Drive from Marnach, three miles away. With machine guns blazing down the length of Skyline Drive, Payne's tanks entered the northern end of Hosingen an hour later to the cheers of the GIs in the town. Help had finally arrived! Based on those same radio reports heard earlier that day, Lieutenant Payne and his men were surprised to find the town still under the control of K Company. Unfortunately, the heavy fighting en route to Hosingen resulted in Payne's unit expending most of their large caliber ammunition along the way, leaving primarily .30 caliber for their machine guns and the defense of Hosingen.

At about the same time as Lieutenant Payne's tanks arrived, the four Shermans of the 1st Platoon, B Company, that had taken up position at the south end of town suddenly pulled up stakes and headed south down Skyline Drive toward Hoscheid accompanied by two more tanks of their outfit that had just come up from Bockholtz, taking the extra ammunition with them. With these tanks leaving, Lieutenant Payne scrambled to get his tanks into defensive positions before dark. Three tanks, accompanied by a few of Captain Feiker's infantry, were sent to help defend 2nd Platoon's recaptured outpost southeast of town and slow the enemy traffic coming up the east-west Ober Eisenbach road. Lieutenant Payne remained in town and moved his own tank to cover the road to the south. Another tank strategically positioned itself between buildings that shielded it from the view of the enemy in the northern part of town and covered Skyline Drive to the north.

Captain Feiker, while relieved that he now had tanks to help defend the town, was disappointed that Lieutenant Payne's tanks had arrived without the ammunition that Major Milton had promised. He contacted Major Milton on the radio. Milton told him he had intended for L Company to break through to Hosingen, supplying them with additional men and ammunition, but L Company had gotten caught in its own battles. Milton said that he would try to find someone else to bring more ammunition to Hosingen, but his hands were full in Consthum.

At 1600, Lüttwitz's engineers finally finished construction on the bridges at Gemünd and Dasbürg, and the 600th Pioneer Battalion had completed the bridge at Ober Eisenbach, which finally allowed the German tanks to cross the Our River. The engineers had experienced several unexpected obstacles that delayed the bridges' completion, stalling the tanks' forward movement for most of the day. The initial delay affecting construction at Gemünd and Ober Eisenbach for several hours was the result of a miscommunication between the engineers and the troops manning that section of the West Wall. The engineers also had to deal with a higher water level than normal due to recent heavy snowmelt, making the initial phase of construction much more difficult than anticipated. The bridges themselves presented challenges, as they had to be built in such a way as to allow access up the extremely steep banks on the west side of the river so that the armored vehicles could maneuver them successfully. Lastly, on the western side of the river, the roads were dotted with large craters from bombs and mines. The craters had to be filled in before the armored vehicles could get through the area. The teams also had to move obstacles that had been placed by retreating German troops a few months earlier to block the road. Once all this was achieved, the tanks still had to maneuver around tight curves alongside sharp drops that made the going slow and dangerous. Despite all this, Lüttwitz's 216 tanks, assault guns, and tank destroyers finally moved forward, though at a snail's pace, and headed up the forest roads that led west to the stubborn American-held garrisons.

The delay in the bridges' construction was already causing major problems in Manteuffel's timetable. The tanks, assault guns, and tank destroyers would now be needed to help the grenadiers capture the towns still held by the 110th, instead of making a fifteen-minute drive to the captured bridges over the Clerf, as originally planned.

Lüttwitz desperately needed to eliminate the stubborn American position in Hosingen, regain valuable lost time, and clear the 26th VGD's main supply route. So, at 1700, three Mark IVs and elements of the 26th VGD attacked Hosingen once again. Gen. Heinz Kokott of the 26th VGD had already called upon his division reserve, the 78th Grenadier Regiment, to help eliminate the defenders at Hosingen. Armed with several flamethrowers and assault guns, I Battalion took position two kilometers south of Hosingen near the GIs still holding out at Hosingen-Barriere, while II Battalion bypassed the town and headed for the Clerf, crossing at Wilwerwiltz. Two German tanks moved up to the high ground on Steinmauer Hill southeast of Hosingen and fired on the three Sherman tanks that were covering the road. The Shermans withdrew from their untenable position on the hill and instead set up inside Hosingen near 2nd Platoon of K Company to cover the southern approaches into town. K Company infantry, which had covered the tanks, worked their way back into town as well, except for the few GIs who continued to stay in the outpost. The German advance resumed on the Ober Eisenbach-Bockholtz road after the three Sherman tanks were no longer blocking the road and a steady flow of German traffic continued past Hosingen throughout the night. Lieutenant Payne's crew spent the evening sneaking out of their defilade positions, lobbing a few shells at the German positions, and then racing back to cover.

Despite many hours of continuous fighting, Captain Jarrett reported the morale of the men remained very high.

Captain Feiker ordered his men to run north-south patrols through town all night while the Germans continued to fire semi-automatic and automatic weapons at Hosingen off and on, from the west, north, and south. Lt. Morse's crew set fire to a few select buildings on the outer edges of town to provide enough light to continue to defend the town throughout the night. Small German patrols were noticed moving in closer to town in preparation for another assault in the morning, but most the German effort appeared to be directed at the north part of town, where Flynn and the 1st Platoon were, near the water tower. The Germans continued to push forward, regardless of their losses, and eventually the Germans captured a few houses on the northern outskirts of the village. Vicious and often hand-to-hand fighting continued until around 2200. Flynn became involved in one of these skirmishes, in which he killed a German officer. Flynn quickly searched the officer's body and discovered a document that provided detailed information on all American dispositions along the frontlines. Flynn called the report in to Captain Feiker as soon as he was able.

One of Flynn's squad leaders, Sgt. John Forsell, watched enemy artillery pound the water tower. But the GIs stayed put in the tower so they could continue to call down mortar fire. To the west of the tower, Sergeant Forsell saw another squad from 1st Platoon lay down devastating fire with well-sighted .30- and .50-caliber machine guns from the eight buildings on either side of the road, but the enemy kept coming. The GIs did a lot of damage and temporarily held most of the grenadiers at bay.

Corporal Stevenson, with the 103rd Engineers, was still on watch in the barn nearby with several other soldiers, when they spotted a small group of Germans about forty yards away. Lying on his stomach, Stevenson pointed his rifle out the window and fired a full clip. Several Germans fell and the rest scattered behind a nearby haystack. The men in the tower called down the position of the haystack to the mortar team and shortly afterwards Stevenson heard the sound of an 81-mm mortar shell being placed down its tube. Within seconds, the shell exploded on the haystack, killing most of the Germans hiding there.

Captain Feiker evaluated their situation. During the day, the Germans had so far been able to capture only a few houses on the edge of Hosingen. The fighting had died down, although German patrols continued to work their way to the edge of town. Incredibly, there had only been a few American casualties so far. Hot meals had continued to be served all day to men who came to the kitchen by ones and twos, although food and ammo were both running very low. Most importantly, K Company and the Engineers still controlled Hosingen, causing as much interruption as they could to the movement of German supplies to Bastogne along the roads north and south of the town.

Captain Feiker had heard reports throughout the day of Germans donning American uniforms and driving American vehicles, and in addition to already severe communication issues, this added to the confusion within the 28th Division. In some cases, German infiltrators had switched road signs at crossroads, sending troops in the wrong direction. Others had blocked off key roads with white tape, (erroneously indicating a warning of minefields ahead), and told many outlandish stories to the American troops intended to cause panic and fear. Only nine enemy teams had infiltrated through the American lines but they caused enough damage to have the Americans questioning everyone they met. Stories of "false" Americans spread like wildfire through the division. Feiker passed the word among his officers to beware.

What the men of Hosingen did not know at the time was how significant their accomplishments for the day were in the context of the broader German offensive. Their actions had considerably slowed the German advance and wreaked havoc on their strict timetable. Their spirited defense of Hosingen also forced many more German troops and resources to be used to take the town than Manteuffel had planned. In fact, the 300 men who were left in Hosingen after the initial assault had held up an entire regiment (approximately 5,000 men) from the 26th VGD.

General Manteuffel had a difficult time trying to put a positive twist on the situation when he reported to Hitler that evening. None of his units has reached the Clerf River. Manteuffel reported that while the Americans definitely had been caught off guard by the attack, all units had put forth stubborn resistance, thereby delaying the German movements with skillful combat tactics— especially the men of Hosingen.

By the end of the day, enough information had reached General Middleton that he was finally realizing the Germans were attacking along his entire eighty-mile front and that his four and a half divisions were facing four times that number of German divisions. The commanding officers' calculated risk to have minimal coverage of the area had backfired on them. Middleton knew the only option was to delay the Germans as long as possible to allow Eisenhower and Bradley time to move reinforcements into the Ardennes, and particularly into Bastogne. Middleton reiterated the same orders to General Cota that the regiments of the 28th had already been told several times that day, to "hold at all costs." General Cota once again feared that his unit would be sacrificed for the greater cause, in particular the 110th, as it was the only major unit directly between the Germans and Bastogne, a unit now in terrible trouble.

As the day ended, the fighting gradually tapered off and Hosingen prepared for another assault in the morning. The men could all see two towns to the north and northwest burning brightly during the night and considerable search light activity was still observed; reflecting light off the clouds to provide light for the German operations on the east side of Our River. There were still thousands of German soldiers and their equipment waiting to join the battle. Horse drawn convoys continued to move west.

So far there were just two wounded from K Company and they were being taken care in the chapel on the south side of the town. Lieutenant Mc Bride held the flashlight while his aidman, Tech 4 Erickson, worked on one of the badly wounded soldiers. New to the stress of working on the front lines, the lieutenant fainted in the middle of the procedure.

CHAPTER 5

Hold At All Costs:
Sunday, December 17, 1944

On the night of December 16, 1944, neither the Germans nor the Americans got much sleep, if any. K Company and the Engineers kept a watchful eye in case more German patrols tried to work their way into the town. There had been no casualties during the night and morale remained high. "K" and "D" rations were available for breakfast with hot coffee to anyone that could make it to the kitchen.

Just before dawn on December 17, small groups of Germans from the 78th moved up to the high ground of Steinmauer Hill southeast of town and began to fire semi-automatic and automatic weapons into K Company's southern-most positions in Hosingen. The GIs in 2nd Platoon's outpost southeast of town heard the shooting. Guessing that there were more Germans than they could handle on their own, they decided it was finally time to withdraw. Somehow, they managed to maneuver through the flow of Germans moving over the ridge and make it safely into town, thankful that it was still dark. Their training patrols for the last month had paid off. Captain Feiker had the men dig in 90 meters south of his command post.

The German snipers firing on Hosingen had little effect on the Americans in the town, as the GIs were too well dug in. When the sun finally started to rise, revealing the sniper positions to Lt. Porter's 2nd Platoon, the machine gunners and riflemen opened fire and quickly cut the German snipers down. Any survivors capable of moving quickly escaped back to the east side of the big hill and out of sight. No other threatening enemy activity was observed on the south end of town, but gunfire had now been replaced by the faint sound of tanks and trucks. The Americans thought the sounds were likely the 2nd Panzer Division bypassing the town to the north, but they could not determine the exact identity and location of the vehicles.

Captain Jarrett started to prepare for the inevitable, gathering all maps, minefield sketches, documents and secret papers, which he burned using gasoline. The engineers placed more mines on the "road" to the left of Hotel Schmitz and made up several dozen bottles of gas and oil with caps for his men to throw from the upper floors of buildings along the route of approach he anticipated that tanks might take.

General von Lüttwitz was growing impatient. As long as the Americans occupied Hosingen, they blocked the 26th VGD's supply route, restricting the flow of supplies to the units in the front attempting to cross the Clerf River. If the seizure of this crossing continued to be delayed, the Americans might well win the race to Bastogne. Lüttwitz therefore made the decision to divert several Panthers and Mark IVs from the 2nd Panzer Division and moved them south to help the II Battalion, 78th Grenadier Regiment, exert more firepower on the Americans who were still holding out in Hosingen.

The daylight brought with it a renewed attack on 3rd Platoon's position at Hosingen-Barrière by Company Nr. 5 of Fusilier Regiment 39, 26th VGD, now that German tanks were finally making their way up from the Our River. A shell from one of the tanks blew a hole through the wall of the barn where Private Gustafson was guarding the German officers, knocking him down. Somewhat shaken by the blast, he was just coming to his feet again when a second blast caused a heavy iron cauldron from the fireplace to be hurled at his head, knocking him unconscious. By the time he awoke, his platoon had been captured and their position was now under German control. The German officers, whom Private Gustafson had been guarding, ordered the grenadiers not to kill the Americans that had been captured because they had been so well treated.

About 0900, with Lüttwitz's additional tanks and grenadiers now in place, he was ready to attack once again. Flynn's 1st Platoon was bracing for the next assault as eight tanks and eight armored cars were headed their way from the north.

Artillery began to rain down on Hosingen for the second time in two days. Once again, the town was set ablaze with half of the buildings set on fire. The weather had been bad enough to keep American fighter planes grounded since the start of the assault, but a spotter plane finally managed to make a reconnaissance flight over the area about this time. The crew relayed back to its command post the intensity of the artillery barrage it observed falling on the town.

During this bombardment, a 150-mm shell, with a delay fuse, came through the wall of the Hotel Schmitz and lodged itself about five inches into the ground floor before exploding. Fortunately, Jarrett and his radio operators had just gone into the hotel's wine cellar to wait out the shelling, but as the last one in line, Jarret was hit in the heel with shell fragments and masonry. Luckily no one else was injured. Cpl. John Putz, B Company aidman, bandaged Captain Jarrett's foot with a sulpha dressing so that he could still hobble around. With the hotel in ruins and on fire, Captain Jarrett moved his command post to the basement of a nearby dairy just southwest of the church, which, to his satisfaction, was built of concrete and steel. That combination seemed to be protecting the men in the water tower just fine.

As the artillery fell on the town, turning the beautiful old buildings into piles of rubble, German tanks and infantry once again began another assault, advancing toward Hosingen from their concealed locations in the forest surrounding most of the town. The GIs continued to fight back, their mortars taking out three tanks with two more on fire. Small arms fire continued throughout the town. Anti-tank mines exploded as the Germans wandered into a well laid minefield. Many fallen grenadiers that had not yet been removed from the battlefield were crushed under the tank tracks as the Germans made their way towards the edge of town.

Captain Jarrett took up a position behind one of the machine guns that had been set up in the dairy's basement window. A German soldier moved in close enough to the building that he was able to fire his machine pistol into the window, striking Sgt. Lawrence Gronefeld in the upper thigh near the groin as he tried to shift the machine gun to shoot the German. Jarrett quickly put a tourniquet on Gronefeld's leg to stop the bleeding and dressing to cover his shattered thigh bone, which was protruding from the back of his leg. Medical supplies were getting scarce, but Jarrett managed to locate two units of plasma, which were given him over the course of the rest of the day and night. He came out of shock after a while and Corporal Putz rigged a splint for his leg.

The Americans' already depleted ammunition supply was beginning to run out. Captain Feiker got a radio call through to Major Milton, once again asking for artillery fire to break up the tank attack. But Major Milton informed him that the same elements that had been attacking Hosingen and Milton's own battalion command post two miles south in Consthum had forced supporting artillery batteries to retreat across the Clerf River. They held two of the few remaining American positions and both were now in the same perilous situation.

The assault lasted for another hour, but the Germans remained unsuccessful at dislodging K Company, the Engineers, and Lieutenant Payne's Shermans from Hosingen. Once again, the Germans suffered heavy casualties. Lüttwitz realized this new attack plan was not working, and began pulling his units back to their starting positions around 1000 hours, leaving the ground strewn with more wounded and dead. The artillery had significantly damaged communications and infrastructure, but like before, it had not inflicted many casualties on the Americans. The Americans all agreed that the Germans must have believed the town to be lightly held since they only made small-scale attacks time after time.

Thanks to the support of Lieutenant Payne's five tanks, Lüttwitz had failed once again to break through and capture Hosingen, so Lüttwitz resorted to trickery. Sometime around 1100 hours, two halftracks were observed moving rapidly down Skyline Drive from the north, as if coming from Monarch. Flynn and his 1st Platoon in the northern part of town and the Sherman crewmembers in the area could tell that the lead vehicle was an American halftrack, but no one could make out the second vehicle clearly enough to make a positive identification. It didn't seem possible that an American vehicle had made it through the German defenses and that K Company had heard no shots fired. They were also suspicious after Captain Feiker's warning the day before of German impersonators using captured uniforms, equipment, and vehicles.

Flynn had his men and Lieutenant Payne hold their fire to see what would happen next. Lieutenant Payne cautiously kept his tank in its defilade position, awaiting further developments. When the half-tracks were about 1,000 yards from town, the two vehicles quickly wheeled about and sped back up the road. The Sherman crew identified the second halftrack as German. Still suspicious of what the Germans were up to, K Company kept a vigilant watch and shortly thereafter, the lookouts still manning the water tower, sighted two tanks hiding northwest of town in a position from which they could have blasted the American's Sherman tank had it revealed its location by firing on the halftracks. Thanks to their patience, Lieutenant Payne's tank had not been spotted and fired upon.

Lüttwitz and his officers were growing increasingly annoyed at the impact the water tower observation post was having on their attempts to overrun the town as mortars had destroyed five of his tanks. At 1300, the tanks opened fire directly on the water tower, which took several direct hits but the Americans still maintained their position. The tower's unusual construction of concrete outside walls supported by a steel column and circular steel inner stairway had deflected any shrapnel from the shells that managed to penetrate the concrete walls. However, this last round had cut the telephone line leaving K Company with no communication with the GIs in the tower. Flynn found out later that the Germans had offered a substantial reward to anyone who could infiltrate into town and destroy the tower by demolition.

Before long, six more tanks, Panthers and Mark IVs from the 2nd Panzer Division, had been pulled from their position three miles north in Marnach to join the two tanks there. As they fired away at Hosingen, German small-arms fire once again increased from the woods to the north and west, and enemy semi-automatic and automatic weapons fire from the north prevented Private Gracie and his bazooka team from getting in position to engage the tanks. Up to twenty tanks were reported throughout the day, surrounding Hosingen on all sides. It was very obvious to all that this was the beginning of a major assault on the town.

The fighting continued all afternoon. The eight German tanks in the north began to work their way closer to the north edge of town behind their infantry, wary of the Sherman tanks and bazooka teams, with four more tanks covering their advance with cannon and machine-gun fire. The houses, shops, and hotels in town were slowly and methodically being reduced to rubble as the tanks blasted hole after hole in their walls until the structures collapsed.

Lieutenant Payne proceeded to move the Shermans from the southern part of town to the north and west to engage the enemy tanks, but they were not having much luck against them. Flynn's 1st Platoon machine gunners and riflemen once again opened fire on the attacking grenadiers and mortar shells, still directed by observers in the tower, pinned the enemy down north of town. Flying rocks and masonry added to the devastating impact of each explosion. The Americans continued inflicting significant casualties, but more grenadiers just kept coming from the west.

Contact had to be restored with the water tower, so Sgt. Lloyd Everson, located a few hundred yards to the south of the water tower, climbed out the window of the building where he had a good connection to Captain Feiker's command post, with a phone wire in one hand and his rifle in the other. About halfway to the tower, he was spotted by the Germans, who did their best to stop him. Fortunately the distance was too great for effective fire on a moving target, but close enough that their bullets frequently kicked up the snow beside him as he ran. When Sergeant Everson finally made it to the tower, he discovered the wire had been cut about fifteen or twenty feet from the door of the structure. He was then able to connect the new wire to the existing phone line and went inside to check and see if the phone was live.

Enemy infantry continued to work in from the north as well as from the west. There were just too many to stop them all. The Germans were finally successful in taking out both of 1st Platoon's machine guns covering Skyline Drive to the north and a .50-caliber machine gun. Eventually, all the 60-mm mortars either ran out of ammunition or were destroyed and even rifle ammunition began to run out.

Once inside the water tower, Sergeant Everson found a lieutenant and two or three men. Most of the GIs had already managed to get out and had worked their way south through the town. "The lieutenant had a bad looking wound on his forehead so he told the men to bandage him and check the phone to see if it was working. He knew that they would make their last stand in the tower. Climbing the stairs, he looked out the window–it looked bad for them. The enemy was moving in, infantry supported by tanks. Some of those walking were moving in groups as if they were on a field trip. Sergeant Everson began exchanging fire with them. He observed some of them stopped moving so they must have gotten hit. Some of their bullets had passed by his face so close he could feel their heat and some sizzled in the snow on the floor."[11]

A tank then fired two rounds at the tower and both exploded outside. Not satisfied with the results it was getting, it moved to a position a little farther away, turned and swung its main gun to bear on the tower. Sergeant Everson continued to fire at the German soldiers, watching the tank out of the corner of his eye.

---

11   Sgt. Lloyd Everson letter to Robert Phillips written in 1994.

The tank reared back as it expelled the next shell at the tower just as the empty clip flew from Sergeant Everson's rifle. The impact of the exploding shell blew him down the tower stairs.

Once his body came to rest, he lay stunned on the floor and could not see or hear, but felt the concussion of the next shell hit. His mouth was filled with the taste of cordite. He popped his eardrums so he could hear by blowing his nose while holding it shut with his hand and rubbed his eyes, forcing tears, so that he could see. At that point, he was able to focus on a German pointing a machine pistol at him. Behind the German were three more grenadiers along with a Panther tank. The scene was very tense so he was lucky that a medic was with them. The medic bandaged the wounded lieutenant and they loaded him on the back of the tank. Sergeant Everson's face and hands were bleeding along with his mouth so the medic bandaged his cuts with paper that looked like crepe paper used for decorating. Two of the Germans then left with the tank. The other two marched the remaining GIs about a hundred yards away–hands over their heads–then motioned for them to sit down. Sergeant Everson looked at his watch a few minutes later when they were ordered to their feet again–it was 1615 hours.

Flynn's 1st Platoon command post in the northern most farm on the edge of Hosingen, had a clear line of sight to what was unfolding at the water tower, but Flynn's men were dealing with their own problems. In the middle of all the chaos, Flynn discovered that his radio in the 1st Platoon command post from which he had been reporting for almost two days had been shaken by the concussion of an exploding shell and would no longer transmit, although it could still receive transmissions. At his point, Captain Feiker had no eyes or ears on what was happening from this location with both the water tower phone line down and Flynn's radio malfunctioning. Flynn needed to report 1st Platoon's situation and the enemy attack on the north edge of town to Captain Feiker, so he ran the gauntlet from his position 650 meters to Captain Feiker's command post, dashing from cover to cover through the rubble-strewn streets of Hosingen, even crawling on his hands and knees at times behind stone walls. One of the German tanks spotted Flynn and started shooting directly at him, but its position did not enable it to lower its aim enough to hit him. Flynn thought it somewhat humorous as they continued to shoot over him. He dodged the German gunfire and shell bursts all the way to Captain Feiker's company command post in the pharmacy building in the southern part of town, where he discovered the Germans had also begun moving past the southern end of town again.

It was almost dusk and more Germans had reached the north edge of town, armed with rifles, machine pistols, and panzerfausts. Enemy sniper and bazooka teams began taking houses one at a time and the Engineers and Flynn's 1st Platoon, located in the outlying buildings, became engaged in hand-to-hand combat. With 1st Platoon command post overrun, the GIs continued to fire from the houses they occupied as long as possible, then, after setting booby-traps with their hand grenades for the Germans soldiers entering from the front, escaped out the back door. Not only did this inflict more casualties on the enemy, but setting all the buildings on fire or blowing them up prevented the Germans from using them for cover. The fires also helped light up the fields that surrounded the town, exposing any German advance to American fire. But despite the GIs' efforts, the Germans pressed forward and their numbers in the village grew.

In a farmhouse not far from the vacated water tower, 1st Platoon's 19-year-old rifleman Private Gasper, cornered an attacking German with the help of his buddies. The man wasn't wearing a helmet and appeared to be an officer, but when he reached for his pistol at his side, the GIs instinctively shot him. The GIs weren't sure if he was reaching for his pistol to shoot them or to surrender, but after two days of intense combat, they weren't taking any chances.

Gradually, most of the men from 1st and 2nd Platoons of K Company, Lieutenant Payne's Sherman crews, and the Engineer's 3rd Platoon under Lieutenant Devlin worked their way back to the vicinity of the Hotel Schmitz. However, the Engineer's 1st Platoon under Lieutenant Hutter's were now isolated in a small pocket on the west side of the town, Flynn's 1st Platoon had a few small groups of men cut off in the north, and Lieutenant Pickering's 2nd

Platoon had individuals and groups of two or three still scattered throughout the town.

Despite being cut off from the rest of their unit, Lieutenant Hutter's platoon continued to put up a fight. Shortly after dark a German patrol of eight men entered the street near their position and began to search for GIs house by house. Corporal Stevenson threw a hand grenade at the doorway, but missed, his grenade knocking the shingles off the porch roof instead. Having left his rifle with his unit, Kosick had to resort to shooting a German soldier through the chest with his bazooka when he wandered across the street from his position.

Lieutenant Payne's five Shermans were restricted to movement on the main street, and finally worked into a perimeter defense of Feiker's command post. No dispersion was possible. Lieutenant Payne's radio was now either out of order or his 3rd Battalion command post had moved back out of radio range, as he got no response from them. One tank eventually got knocked out and one other was lost, probably hit by another panzerfaust, but Flynn never found out for sure.

That night, Captain Feiker once again assessed the situation with his officers. Small pockets of his and Jarrett's men were cut off from their units, their ammunition was almost gone, and three of his machine-gun nests had been destroyed along with one of his 60-mm mortars. K Company's kitchen had continued to provide hot meals throughout the day as best it could, but the power was now out, there was no running water, and the cooks were running out of food. The GIs were melting snow for drinking and cooking water. Lieutenant Payne was down to three tanks to use against the German arsenal surrounding the town. There would be no artillery support or relief force coming.

It was the end of the second day, and now only Hosingen and Consthum remained under the control of the Americans. They had followed the explicit orders from General Middleton and General Cota for two days to "Hold at all costs!" Hopefully, their efforts had bought enough time for the American forces to defend Bastogne and halt the German advance.

CHAPTER 6

We'll Make 'em Pay: Monday, December 18, 1944

Monday, December 18, was going to be another cold, cloudy, hell of a day with the temperature just above freezing. Small pockets of fighting had continued all night long.

In one way, the men in Hosingen had been very lucky. Despite the extensive damage the Germans had inflicted on the town over the last two days, the Americans had experienced relatively few wounded or killed, although the medics' supplies had become just as scarce as everything else had and K Company was still under orders to "hold at all costs."

At 0200 hours, sixteen grenadiers with two machine guns assaulted Captain Jarrett's command post in the dairy. But Captain Jarrett, Lt. Theodore Slobodzian, Sergeant Winchester, and a few others were waiting for them and managed to stop their advance with the assistance of Tommy guns and grenades. With three causalities, the German patrol withdrew. After the Germans retreated, Jarrett decided to adjust his positions, sending Lieutenant Slobodzian to check on 3rd Platoon's machine-gun position in one of the houses behind the hotel where their command post had been, while he went to check on 1st Platoon's position in the town.

Unfortunately, when Lieutenant Slobodzian attempted to enter 3rd Platoon's position, he had not responded with the correct password and was shot by his own men in the left arm and left leg.

Several men carried him to the aid station in the town church where his best friend, Corporal Putz, did his best to take care of him and keep him alive, but he had lost a lot of blood. Corporal Putz applied a turnicut to stem the bleeding and administered morphine, but Slobodzian was already in a state of shock. Captain Jarret had one of his men run through the German-held streets to get plasma from Feiker's company, but K Company was out as well.

It was now 0300 hours and Lieutenant Slobodzian was sinking fast. Without the proper medical attention, neither he nor a badly wounded Sergeant Groenfeld would last much longer. Captain Jarrett was empathetic to Corporal Putz's request to go for help, but he didn't want to risk sending out a jeep and risk more lives.

The fight continued and enemy fire was now being directed at the windows of the church where the wounded were. Captain Jarrett had his men cover him from both floors of the dairy while he worked his way close enough to throw a hand grenade over the side street wall where the shots were coming from.

By now, the majority of the buildings in the town were on fire and the heat was almost unbearable. Most of the American vehicles had already been destroyed.

At 0430 on December 18, Captain Feiker spoke once again to Major Milton, explaining K Company's situation and asking for instructions. Much the same situation prevailed in Consthum, and Major Milton finally gave the order for the men in Hosingen to infiltrate westward through the German lines in small groups while it was still dark. Captain Feiker said it was too late for that but proclaimed, "We can't get out, but these Krauts are going to pay a stiff price if they try to get in."[12] Feiker's several attempts to send runners out of Hosingen for help over the past two days had been unsuccessful. There were just too many German troops in every direction around his position, and escape was highly improbable. Feiker knew that by now Hosingen was as much as eighteen miles behind enemy lines, if the Germans had made it to Bastogne.

---

12   "To Save Bastogne" by Robert F. Phillips, p. 160.

Major Milton told Captain Feiker and his men to do whatever they saw fit.

Captain Feiker promptly called a meeting with his officers to discuss the situation. After a quick assessment, K Company determined that it only had two rounds of smoke ammunition left for the 81-mm mortars, the last 60-mm mortar had been knocked out, and rifle ammunition was so low the men were sharing each other's supplies. The mission of delaying the enemy had been carried out, but they were now entirely surrounded and were no longer delaying the German advance. They each agreed with Captain Feiker that there was little chance of escaping back through German lines. Major Milton was contacted again and he left the final decision to Captain Feiker, signing off by saying, "You have done your job well. Good-bye and God Bless You."

As the officers' discussion ensued, 24-year old Flynn recommended, as executive officer of K Company, that they surrender so the men would have a better chance of survival. There was nothing else they could do. Captain Feiker conceded and the other officers all agreed. Captain Feiker spoke with Captain Jarrett, briefed him on the situation, and asked for his help with the demolitions. Captain Feiker then issued the order that all remaining weapons and materials that would be of any value to the enemy were to be destroyed. In response, Flynn removed his personal weapon, a .45-caliber Smith and Wesson revolver, from its holster and destroyed it while the other officers watched. He then laid the useless revolver on the table, turned, and left the room to get started on the rest of the demolition.

The Demolition

Feiker called Major Milton to tell him of their decision. In the meantime, Jarrett's engineers went to work and supplied the infantry and Lieutenant Payne's crews with handmade grenades made of one quarter pound blocks of TNT and fuses from their own supplies. All of the engineer trucks and road equipment not already destroyed were burned and tires were shot out and cut. All K Company vehicles and their garage were set on fire and the tanks were rendered useless. The men demolished their personal weapons and all functioning rifles and machine guns making sure to break the same parts on each weapon to prevent making any repairs possible. M Company buried any remaining mortars after firing pins were removed from each tube base and broken. Those who had extra clothes nearby put on extra layers under their coats. Bulk rations, mail, and other papers were soaked with gasoline and burned. Field ranges and supplies were destroyed. All men who were able to get to the kitchen were issued one K ration and one D ration until the supply ran out. After handing out the rest of the food, the cooks destroyed all the kitchen equipment. The only items not destroyed by the engineers were items lost to the Germans during battle the day before.

"Unfortunately the company records (morning reports, rosters, etc., covering a period of several months) fell into the hands of the enemy. These records had been prepared for burning with military police grenades. Shortly before these records were to be destroyed, the aid station next door to the command post caught on fire. The aid station was then moved into the basement of the command post, and as there were wounded still there at the time of the surrender, it was impossible to start a fire of the records which were there."[13]

The Last Hoorah

While the demolition was still taking place, men continued to guard the perimeter. Around 0700, Lieutenant Hutter made his way out to his 1st Platoon engineers still stationed in the barn on the western edge of Hosingen, and told them to take their last shots with their .50-caliber machine gun at the German wagon

---

13   1st Lt. Thomas J. Flynn interview, K Company, 110th Infantry Regiment, 28th Infantry Division, National Archives, Record Group 407.

trains as soon as the fog lifted. As the morning sun was coming up, they could make out several German horse-drawn ammunitions supply wagons traveling on the east-west road about 400 yards southwest of Hosingen. Gunners Butler and Sterk opened fire, pouring several hundred rounds right into the wagons, setting them afire. The engineers could hear the Germans cussing all the way from the barn as they cut the horses loose from the wagons. Captain Jarrett saw it happen and called it, "a grand sight."

Captains Jarrett and Feiker finally gave their permission to Corporal Putz to try and slip through the German lines to get blood plasma and a medical officer after Pfc Frank Smith volunteered to go along. Unarmed and wearing Red Cross arm bands, they left on foot at 0650. They made it less than a mile before they were spotted and captured by a German patrol.

Both Lieutenant Slobodzian and Sergeant Gronefeld died from their injuries about one hour later.

Surrender

Sometime between 0800 and 0900 hours, the German snipers and tanks once again began to fire on Hosingen. In order to prevent additional American casualties, Captains Feiker and Jarrett had a white flag hung from a building on the north end of town and from the church steeple, as well as having white panels hung on the tanks. Feiker also had one of his men that spoke German advise the handful of prisoners they had captured during the fighting of his plan to surrender under a white flag. They were then released and sent out in all directions, to advise the German units of the American's plan and to ask those units to cease fire, which they did immediately. Carrying a white piece of cloth, Captains Feiker and Jarrett then headed across the 1,000 yards of open ground between the two armies. Jarrett was still hobbling from his wounded foot, and this delay gave the soldiers a little bit more time to complete their demolition work.

When Feiker and Jarrett reached the German soldiers, they were thoroughly searched and one of the Germans removed Captain Jarrett's dentures from his pocket and kept them. A German private also took Jarrett's cigarettes, gloves, socks, and watch. They were taken to the German command post of 5th Company, 76th Grenadier Regiment, 26th VGD, where they met with the ranking German officer on the scene, a staff colonel, and began to discuss surrender arrangements. This took about an hour.

Just before 1000 hours, Lieutenant Morse radioed news of the surrender to Major Milton's command post. "We're down to our last grenades. We've blown up everything there is to blow up except the radio and it goes next." What sounded like a sob came over the radio, but after a brief paused to compose himself, he continued, "I don't mind dying and I don't mind taking a beating, but I'll be damned if we'll give up to these bastards." Then the radio went dead.[14] Lt. Morse had ended the conversation by shooting the radio with his .45 caliber pistol.

At 1000, Captains Feiker and Jarrett returned at gunpoint, accompanied by German officers and troops. They gave their men one last order and told them to come out of their buildings in a column of threes with their hands on their helmets. German soldiers were now all over the place rounding up prisoners.

The Battle of the Bulge, as the Americans would come to call it, lasted until January 28, 1945, but for the Americans in Hosingen, their next mission was simply to survive.

Summary of the Battle

Flynn summarized the casualties of the battle in Hosingen as follows:

> *"There were initially about 300 men, including the engineer company, which had been cut off west of town, and odd men*

---

14 Phillips, p. 160

who had been captured individually and eight officers. Three of the officers were from K Company (the 1ˢᵗ and 3ʳᵈ platoon leaders were missing and the 2ⁿᵈ Platoon had been commanded by a T/ sergeant. Lieutenant Flynn later learned that the 1ˢᵗ Platoon leader had been wounded in the water tower OP and had been evacuated by the Germans with other wounded.) The other officers were a tank platoon leader, and four engineer officers. Known casualties with the town were seven killed, ten wounded, (two seriously), and none missing."[15]

In defense of Hosingen, the brave defenders left an estimated 2000 Germans lying dead or wounded in the open fields that surrounded the village, killing more than 300. They were often outnumbered more than ten to one and were provided no artillery support during the entire two and a half days of battle.

They had done exactly as General Middleton and General Cota had ordered and held their position at all costs, buying the precious time that the 101ˢᵗ Airborne and other units needed to arrive at and defend Bastogne. The title of John C. McManus's book on the battle, *Alamo in the Ardennes*, sums it up.

The Germans were extremely surprised when all of the Americans gathered in the street as they could hardly believe that such a small group of men had put up such a tenacious fight, at times against 5,000 Germans, suffering so few casualties, while inflicting such enormous damage on their own forces.

Killed in Hosingen, Luxembourg during December 17-18 (reported by the US Army as December 20, 1944):

K Company, 110th Infantry Regiment:

- Pfc. Merritt McGlashen   12/20/1944
- Pvt. Philip P. Glick   12/20/1944
- Pvt. Alvin P. Skovbo   12/20/1944

---

15   Flynn National Archives interview

B Company, 103rd Engineers:

- Lt. Theodore Slobodzian   12/20/1944
- Sgt. Lawrence Gronefeld   12/20/1944
- Pfc. Kenneth E. Grady   12/20/1944
- Pvt. William B. Hawn (unconfirmed
  at the time of surrender)   12/20/1944

C Company, 110th Infantry Regiment:

- Unnamed T/4 (Medic)   12/20/1944

World War II era photos of Hosingen, Luxembourg: 1940–1945

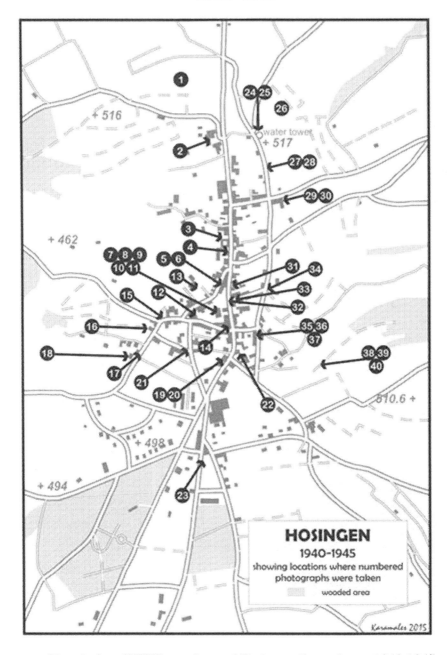

Photo index of WWII era photos of Hosingen, Luxembourg 1940-1945

Photo 1: NW view from Hosingen water tower in the direction of Dorscheid (prior to 1944). Skyline Drive runs through the lower half of the photo–
K Co.'s 1ˢᵗ platoon CP in the farmhouse was just to the left of the photo.

Photo 2: NW view from Hosingen water tower.
Overlooks K Co.'s 1st platoon CP on north end of Hosingen–
Café Beyrisch and barn Heutz-Arend (about 1944)
Photos courtesy of Archives of Hosingen, Luxembourg

Photo 3: An der éweschter Gâss (street) – view towards the church.
Courtesy of Archives of Hosingen, Luxembourg

Photo 4: An der éweschter Gâss (street) – House Nic. Oberlinkels
Courtesy of Archives of Hosingen, Luxembourg

Photo 5: Postcard of Hotel Schmitz prior to 1940
Courtesy of Archives of Hosingen, Luxembourg

Photo 6: Hotel Schmitz in 1945 – sandbags still in the windows
Courtesy of Archives of Hosingen, Luxembourg

*Photo 7: Postcard of Hosingen's main square prior to 1930–
Hosingen 12th century church & Hotel Schmitz shown.
Courtesy of Yves Rasqui*

*Photo 8: Interior of Hosingen's church before WWII.
Courtesy of Archives of Hosingen, Luxembourg*

Photo 9: Hosingen's main square in 1945–
Hosingen 12th century church & Hotel Schmitz in ruins.
Courtesy of Archives of Hosingen, Luxembourg

Photo 10: Northern section of the church known as the 'sister house', 1945
Courtesy of Archives of Hosingen, Luxembourg

Photo 11: The interior of the church looking toward the exit, June 1945.
Courtesy of Archives of Hosingen, Luxembourg

Photo 12: Kraeizgaass (street) – building of the fire brigade
and farm Berscheid, after 1944
Courtesy of Archives of Hosingen, Luxembourg

Photo 13: Kraeizgaass (street) – view from Hotel Schmitz
Courtesy of Archives of Hosingen, Luxembourg

Photo 14: Main street looking in the direction of the main square
Courtesy of Archives of Hosingen, Luxembourg

Photo 15: Kraeizgaass (street) – view of the main street in 1945
Courtesy of Archives of Hosingen, Luxembourg

Photo 16: Kraeizgaass (street) – house Dohm-Atten, post-war it is house #22.
Courtesy of Archives of Hosingen, Luxembourg

Photo 17: Kraeizgaass (street) – farm Rodesch
Courtesy of Archives of Hosingen, Luxembourg

Photo 18: An der Méilchen; farm Hoscheid-Weiler, post-war it is house #21
Courtesy of Archives of Hosingen, Luxembourg

Photo 19: Postcard of Hotel Hippert at intersection of
Haaptstrooss & Holzbicht, after 1920
Courtesy of Archives of Hosingen, Luxembourg

Photo 20: Hotel Hippert in 1945 – K Co. CP directly across the street (intersection of
Haaptstrooss & Holzbicht)
Courtesy of Archives of Hosingen, Luxembourg

Photo 21: Kraeizgaass (street) – farm Peters, post-war it is house #32
Courtesy of Archives of Hosingen, Luxembourg

Photo 22: Main street house Kaiser-Kipgen by Oberlinkels J.P.
Courtesy of Archives of Hosingen, Luxembourg

Photo 23: Chapel–cemetery in SE Hosingen in 1945
Courtesy of Archives of Hosingen, Luxembourg

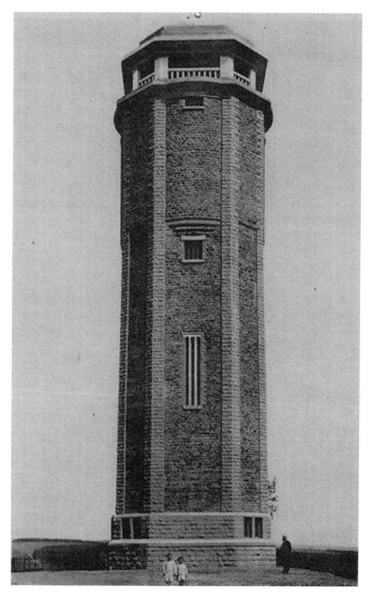

Photo 24: Hosingen water town used as K Co.'s 1ˢᵗ Platoon's
northern observation post; pre-WWII photo
Courtesy of Yves Rasqui

Photo 25: Hosingen water tower in ruins, 1945
Courtesy of Archives of Hosingen, Luxembourg

Photo 26: NE view from Hosingen water tower prior to 1944.
Our River valley looking east towards Grovenbérg Fallbich and Preischeid
with Germany in the far background
Courtesy of Archives of Hosingen, Luxembourg

Photo 27: Looking south from the water tower on to the street below
Courtesy of Archives of Hosingen, Luxembourg

Photo 28: Op dem Knupp (street) looking down the street south of the water tower. You
can see destroyed houses, left house Schmitz, right house Kaiser.
Courtesy of Archives of Hosingen, Luxembourg

Photo 29: Haus Schmitz, prior to 1944
Courtesy of Archives of Hosingen, Luxembourg

Photo 30: Op dem Knupp (street)–Haus Schmitz after 1945,
viewed from direction of Graaf
Courtesy of Archives of Hosingen, Luxembourg

Photo 31: Café de la Post, today Café des Sports, #42
Courtesy of Archives of Hosingen, Luxembourg

Photo 32: Main street in direction Duurchfaart (street), after 1944
Courtesy of Archives of Hosingen, Luxembourg

Photo 33: Durchfaart (street) – view east from main street by Hotel Schmitz
Courtesy of Archives of Hosingen, Luxembourg

Photo 34: Durchfaart (street) – view west from house
Meyer Anton in the direction of the main street
Courtesy of Archives of Hosingen, Luxembourg

Photo 35: Holzbicht (street) – House Ludwig
Courtesy of Archives of Hosingen, Luxembourg

Photo 36: Holzbicht (street) – House Ludwig
Courtesy of Archives of Hosingen, Luxembourg

Photo 37: Holzbicht (street)–House Welter-Weydert
Courtesy of Archives of Hosingen, Luxembourg

Photo 38: Pre-WWII view of Hosingen from Steinmauer Hill–
water tower is seen in the top right corner, approximately 1 km away.
Courtesy of Archives of Hosingen, Luxembourg

*Photo 39: Pre-WWII postcard view of Hosingen from Steinmauer Hill–
church steeples are in the center
Courtesy of Archives of Hosingen, Luxembourg*

*Photo 40: Post war view of Hosingen from Steinmauer Hill–
church steeples in the center were destroyed
Courtesy of Archives of Hosingen, Luxembourg*

CHAPTER 7

German Prisoners of War: December 18, 1944

Prisoners of War—December 18, 1944

Unfortunately, word of surrender and the order to destroy their weapons was not relayed to all the men around Hosingen as quickly as it should have been. Sergeant Arbella, the 60-mm mortar section leader, had received minimal communication from Captain Feiker over the past two and a half days, so when he saw the other men from his unit coming out of the buildings with their hands on their heads, a buddy had to clue him in on what was happening. He nodded in agreement and headed to their garage to make sure his jeeps had been set on fire. He then gathered the rest of his soldiers and prepared to surrender.

As he did so, he ran into eight of the mysterious Rangers who had been in the town this entire time. Those who had witnessed the Rangers in action for the past few days all agreed they really knew how to fight. Their commander asked Arbella if the surrender order was true. Arbella confirmed that it was, so it was no surprise that the Ranger responded that they were not giving up. He and his men took off west out of Hosingen, never to be seen again. Arbella watched them go and then he and his men joined the other American soldiers lined up on Hosingen's main street.

Pvt. Edward Gasper heard the grenadiers coming closer, as there was no longer any need for the Germans to be quiet. He took a deep breath and prepared to give up. He slammed his rifle down, venting his frustration and anger at the same time, breaking the stock and throwing the parts away. He then opened the door, put his hands up in the air, and joined the others falling in line. The Germans searched him thoroughly, taking anything of value, including his watch, cigarettes, and K rations.

K Company's Staff Sergeant Norman Guenther, and Master Sergeant Joe Winchester's Engineers were hesitant to come out into the open after spending the last two and half days protecting the wounded in the old church and small chapel on the southeast corner of town. As the men headed out the massive church doors to join their unit already forming a column in front of the church, Pvt. William Hawn fainted in the church building and his unit was not allowed to help him. Once the Germans entered the building, the GIs heard his screams. No one saw Private Hawn after that.

Surrounded by the dead bodies of twenty-eight Germans soldiers, all but one shot in the head, one of the high-ranking German officers confronted Medic Erickson and demanded to know where all the rest of the Americans who had defended the town were. Erickson told him that he was looking at all of them. The German officer clearly was surprised at his response and told the medic he was not telling the truth, but Erickson reiterated, "This is it and there are no more." After a few moments, the German officer decided he was telling the truth and commented, "Nice shooting," to which Erickson agreed with a simple, "Yah." This was the second time since the 28th had started fighting in Europe that Erickson was a prisoner. His first capture occurred while his unit fought its way through France. He had just been reunited with K Company in December.

The German officer was not the only one who was confused and angry. The grenadiers had watched many of their comrades be killed or wounded over the past two and a half days and many of them still lay unattended in the fields surrounding the town. Needless to say, the mood was very tense. All the American officers could do was watch in silence as their men were yelled at, slapped around, searched, and stripped of their valuables. Unfortunately for the enlisted men, many of them were also forced to give up their combat shoes and/or galoshes in exchange for the inferior German boots of the soldier doing the trading. In most cases, the German boots did not fit very well and a number of the GIs found themselves with shoes that were to cause them nothing but problems in the months to follow.

The officers and enlisted men were allowed to keep their helmets and gas masks, and any toiletry items that they had brought with them.

While the exchanges were going on, one of the German officers was intently questioning the enlisted men to find out who was responsible for killing one of his medics. First Lt. Bernie Porter had shot the weapon-carrying medic in self-defense and he knew he would be executed on the spot if anyone gave him up. The enlisted men also were aware that Lt. Porter would be punished if discovered, so everyone kept quiet and acted as if he didn't know what the German officer was talking about.

Another group of Germans were busy mounting two MG42 machine guns, one on a trailer and the other on the ground just twenty-five yards away, pointed directly at the America POWs. All eyes were fixed on the weapons when a German soldier accidentally tripped the trigger letting off a burst of bullets, seriously injuring Pfc Kenneth Grady and killing a T/4 from C Company, that had been in the town since the fighting started. Pvt. John Wnek was also wounded in the forearm. Private Grady would later die at Stalag 4B at Mühlberg.

Cpl. Sam Miller, who was standing right next to them, had avoided being shot by jumping behind the blade of a bulldozer parked nearby, but had not escaped danger as another German soldier quickly had a gun pointed at his head to force him back into the line-up. As Miller got back in line, he couldn't help but stare at the lifeless bodies of his two buddies lying on the ground; the pools blood slowly growing larger underneath them. He assumed they were dead.

The German captain in charge reprimanded the machine gunner responsible for the shooting, and made a move to strike him with his pistol for his carelessness, but controlled his urge to do so. Captain Jarrett later reflected that the German captain had saved many GIs' lives that day by stopping the potential massacre.

The ranking German officer then ordered his men to take the American officers to an isolated house at the south end of Hosingen. There they were crowded into a small room, searched, and interrogated. One by one, each officer was required to empty his pockets into his helmet so a German officer could inspect each item. For some reason, no physical search was made of their clothing. During this investigation, some of the officers were forced to destroy maps and papers which they had decided to keep or hadn't thought to get rid of before capture. Lt. Flynn was glad he spoke German so he could help the other officers understand what the Germans wanted.

The interrogation took approximately an hour as the Germans were primarily concerned with details about the locations of minefields and booby-traps. The officers of K Company spoke only of the minefield the Germans had already discovered the previous day during one of their attacks. The Germans threatened to march the prisoners cross-country to detonate possible mines, but fortunately, this threat was not carried out. At least there was some satisfaction in the possibility that the Engineers' other minefields would still be wreaking havoc on the Germans long after the POWs were gone.

Once the officers were separated from the enlisted men, a disgruntled German sergeant separated Corporal Miller, along with a number of the other GIs from his unit, and marched them around the corner and out of view. He then had the GIs line up in a nearby drainage ditch, machine guns located at each end of the column and two bulldozers waiting nearby on the field above where they stood. They all knew what was going to happen–they were going to be executed and buried right where they stood.

As fate would have it, or by divine intervention, a German staff car drove up. The staff officer could see what was about to happen and stood up and angrily yelled at the German sergeant to get the prisoners out of the ditch–yelling, "Macht schnell!" Everyone could see the sergeant's frustration as it was clear he wanted to kill the Americans, but he followed orders and allowed the prisoners to climb up onto the road. For the second time that day, a level headed German officer had saved their lives and they were relieved to be marching down the road to a field where they would wait for the rest of the prisoners to join them.

Happy to still be alive, Sergeant Winchester whispered to his buddy, Corporal Miller, "We put on a heck of a show, didn't we?"

The rest of the enlisted men had been moved out into the open fields around the town to tally and search through the dead and wounded while the officers were being interrogated.

Medic Erickson was one of the men who was forced to help bury the three hundred dead German and American soldiers. He was told it was the German medics' job to bury the dead and now that he was a POW, it was his job. Once the dead were all buried, the medics were ordered to help take care of the wounded, both German and the POWs from Hosingen, until transportation could be arranged for them to a prison hospital.

The remaining officers and enlisted men were corralled into a fenced-in area where they were held for several hours until the Germans could get confirmation as to what they should do with the prisoners. The POWs were exhausted, hungry, and cold and most of the enlisted men with ill-fitting boots already had problems with their feet. There was nowhere in the field to sit that wasn't wet, muddy, or snowy. They wondered what would happen to them and whether they would make it through the rest of this war alive. Their survival would depend on the mercy of these German soldiers, who obviously hated them.

While the weather conditions had been bad enough to ground most planes over the past few days, the spotter plane's report of the intense shelling at Hosingen the day before had prompted several American fighter planes to finally be sent to the area for air support to help defend the town. Unaware that the men of Hosingen had surrendered that morning, the American planes flew in from out of nowhere in an attempt to attack the German infantry, which the pilot had observed gathered on the ground below. He didn't realize that he was targeting the American POWs from Hosingen.

German planes weren't far behind and the prisoners witnessed a dogfight directly overhead, with German and American fighter planes shooting at each other. One of the American planes was hit and set afire, but despite the plane's rapid decent en route to a crash landing, the machine guns were still firing and some of the prisoners in the field were killed. The man next to Corporal Miller was hit, but once again he miraculously escaped injury for the third time that day. The plane crashed and exploded into flames close enough to the men for them to observe that no one made it out of the plane alive. The POWs assumed the pilot probably thought that they were Germans.

Around 1500 hours, with evening fast approaching, the POWs were finally moved out in columns, with the enlisted men leading in one group and thirteen officers following behind in the second group. As it had been for more than a month, the weather was rainy, the ground was wet and muddy, and the patches of snow that lay all around reminded the men of the winter weather still to come. As the POWs moved out, leaving the Germans in possession of Hosingen, the Germans still could not believe that so few Americans had put up such an amazing fight.

The POWs were marched to Eisenbach just four miles away on the Ober Eisenbach-Hosingen-Drauffelt road, along the German's main supply route south. Even after three days, it was still jammed with westbound traffic in support of the massive German offensive. The POWs had to maneuver their way using the truck headlights that were shining right in their eyes. Because the road was very narrow they frequently had to move into the muddy ditches to permit the passing of motorized and horse drawn vehicles. The POWs were surprised to observe so many trucks towing two or three other trucks, as reserve vehicles.

It was 1600 hours when the POWs arrived at Eisenbach and the exhausted, hungry men were jammed into a small church, where they lay tightly packed together on the floor and pews with only straw to cover them. Captain Jarrett, selected as senior officer of the group, was removed by the Germans and marched off for further interrogation.

The cold and wet conditions had already caused frostbite to appear on some of the men's feet. The Germans had promised a hot meal when they got to Eisenbach but that did not happen. Those who still had their K and D rations shared them with their buddies. At least they were now sheltered inside a building and able to rest, as most had not slept for almost three days since before the fighting began. They tried to get some sleep. The next day promised to be another long and miserable one.

Photo: Church in Eisenbach, Luxembourg where many of the GIs who'd fought in Hosingen spent their first night as POWs – 18 December 1944. Courtesy of Yves Rasqui

CHAPTER 8

Individual POW Stories

It is at this point that the GIs stories begin to vary as the separation of the men headed to the prisoner of war camps seemed to occur at random as the German Army struggled to process the massive intake of prisoners they had captured during the first week of their attack.

The POW stories that follow clearly show that most of the men who followed the "Hold at all cost" order in Hosingen, suffered greatly at the hands of their captors. For those that survived, it would be an ordeal they would struggle to overcome the rest of their lives–both physically and mentally–many living their remaining days with what has been identified as Post Traumatic Stress Disorder in soldiers of subsequent wars.

MIA-POW Service Medal

It wasn't until November 8, 1985, the United States military created the MIA-POW Service Medal that was retroactive for all military personnel back to April 5, 1917. It had taken forty years for the military to finally acknowledged that time spent as a prisoner of war was above the call of duty. The medal reads: "For Honorable Service While a Prisoner of War," "United States of America" –a recognition that was long overdue.

T/4 Wayne V. Erickson
Medic (Technician, 4th Grade) –
103rd Medical Battalion assigned to K Company

Excerpt from *My Part of Time* by Wayne V. Erickson

After capture we medics were separated from the line men and stayed with our wounded and had to help with some of the German wounded too. (*S/Sgt. William Freeman and the other wounded were also part of this group.*) We also had to bury some of the dead. We buried twenty-eight Germans in one grave and most of them were shot through the head. A high ranking German officer came over to look at them and then told me, "Good shooting". I just said, "Yah". He wondered how we had killed so many Germans when we were so few.

We kept our wounded in a small church on the south side of the town and when they had all been evacuated on German trucks, we were marched down the road and into Germany.

We were given only one piece of bread for the first four days and we were marching as far as forty miles a day. On January 10th, 1945, we reached Stalag IVB at Mühlberg, Germany and were interrogated and registered as POW's. (*The group, including Sgt. George McKnight, had been marched 700 km in 24 days*). We were allowed to send a card from there and it arrived home almost four months later. We were loaded in box cars after a two day stay here but our fighter planes strafed and bombed the train and we were taken off. Many were killed or wounded.

Our next march was to Stalag VIIIA at Görlitz near the Polish border (*another 166 km*). We spent a few of the nights in barns or other buildings but most of the time we were just out in the open. This was in the middle of winter and the weather was very cold. I had a short drivers coat but no blanket. Our shoes and stockings were wearing out.

Several of the fellows would drop out every day and it was impossible for us to help in any way because of being in such poor condition ourselves. We never had any German medical aid and we didn't know what became of the fellows that dropped along the way.

Our battalion doctor had just given me an extra pair of paratrooper boots that he had and I was wearing them when we were captured. I had frozen my feet while we were up in the Hürtgen Forest but they improved when we got down to Luxembourg and could stay indoors. I also got a small shell fragment in my lower left leg while in Hosingen and this was painful while marching.

We hadn't been in Stalag VIIIA very many days when the Russian Army started moving in our direction. When they got close enough that we could hear their artillery, we had to start marching again back into Germany. (*It was February 14, 1945.*)

Our food at this time consisted of a cup of luke warm, odd tasting tea in the morning and a bit of grass soup when we stopped for the night. They would fire on any of us who tried to pick frozen vegetables out of the fields or gardens along the roads without permission. However, we managed to pick a few beets or potatoes whenever we had the chance. We drank water from the ditches. We didn't receive any Red Cross parcels and few were the times that we got any bread, meat or cheese. Everyone had lice and other body insects despite the fact we tried to kill them. There were no showers or places to clean up.

A German officer rode in a horse drawn wagon leading the march and German Army guards with police dogs were all around us. Many were bitten by the dogs and some were shot by the guards when they tried to escape. We were freezing our hands and feet repeatedly and during the last part of the march, our hands, faces, and joints were swelling to twice their normal sizes and movement was very painful. We were growing weaker and thinner and couldn't walk very far each day. If a person stumbled and fell it was very difficult to get back up. Those that just couldn't walk any farther were just left along the road. We don't know what happened to them.

We reached the city of Braunschweig, Germany a month later. They were going to put us to work on the railroad but we refused and a German doctor looked at us and said that there wasn't anyone in our group that was fit to work. (*The 635 km route, freezing temperatures and starvation had taken its toll.*) We were kept in a brickyard enclosure there for about a week and it was while there that I traded a Waltham wrist watch for three loaves of bread. I did this trading with one of the German guards in the middle of the night. I shared this bread with a couple of the fellows that I knew – S. Sgt. Edward Anderson from Barron, WI and Sgt. George Knight of Amsterdam, N.Y. We had to carry it inside of our shirts so others couldn't see it.

During the third day of our stop here, we started to hear artillery from the Americans ahead of us, so we started marching in the direction of Berlin.

A couple of days and another 66km later, we stopped in a farm yard and during the night, elements of the 2nd Armored Division bypassed us and our guards took off. We stopped at this farm on April 12th, 1945 – the day that President Roosevelt died and we were found and liberated close to the town of Horsingen, Germany, which name is almost the same as Hosingen, Luxembourg where we were captured. There were 483 of us in the group that was left from about 2000 that were there when we left Stalag VIIIA on Valentine's Day 1945 and about 80 were taken out on stretchers. The rest of us were picked up in trucks and taken to a nearby landing strip where C47 planes picked us up a few days later and brought us to Camp Lucky Strike on the coast of France. The first food we were given after liberation was K rations which were no good for us but was all that was available. We had dysentery and were vomiting almost every time that we tried to eat.

When we arrived at Camp Lucky Strike they put a walking plank up to the door of the plane and when I came walking down, there was a one star General there to greet us. I remember his words "you're looking fine there, soldier". I knew better.

The first thing that we did after landing was to look for the shower tent. We left our clothes in a pile when we went in and picked up anything that fit us on the way out. I took my aid pouch and paratrooper boots with me.

We received very few instructions as we were some of the first liberated POW's to arrive and there were very few around to help us. We slept on some cots in tents that night and in the morning I reported to the Medics. A doctor there took one look at me and sent me by ambulance to the 77th Evacuation Hospital where I stayed for about three weeks. I had weighted about 190 pounds before being captured and when I was discharged from this hospital, I weighed 106 pounds and was running a temperature of 103 degrees.

The doctors didn't know what to do with me. Malnutrition seemed to be something that they had had very little practice in. They treated me with penicillin and sulpha drugs and put me on a soft diet and I soon began to feel better. Just before I left, one of the doctors with the rank of Major came in and asked me if we could talk for a few minutes and I said "Sure". He asked me if I knew whether I was coming or going on the day that I came into the hospital and I said, "Yes", I thought that I did. Then he said that he didn't have any ideas of what to do for me and then spent several minutes apologizing for his lack of knowledge in the treatment of malnutrition.

I was discharged from the hospital there when the good news came that the war was over in Germany – that was May 8, 1945. Every plane in the area was up in the air, trucks and jeeps were running around the camp and we were all a pretty happy bunch.

A group of us POW's were staying together in a staging area waiting for transportation back to the states. They wanted to put us on a hospital ship but there were none available. We told them to just get us on a boat with a few Medics and some good food and we would take care of ourselves. On May 13th, which was Mother's Day, we were put on a liberty ship, the SS George Washington Carver, also known as USAT Hospital Dogwood, at Le Havre, France and we started for home. There were about 300 of us.

I received my honorable discharge from the U.S. Army on September 4, 1945. At the time, I was still suffering from the effects of malnutrition. My main distress was the swelling in my joints, and my feet and back were also causing me a great deal of discomfort so I filed them all in a claim and also mentioned my shell fragment wound. They recorded a bullet wound in my left leg, but recognized nothing else.

Sgt. George Mc Knight is the only fellow that I can name who was with me throughout the four campaigns of Normandy, Northern France, Rhineland and the Ardennes, and who was also with me through the torture as a prisoner of war in Germany.

Sgt. Lloyd C. Everson
K Company, 110th Infantry Regiment

Excerpt from a letter written in 1984 to 110th veteran
and author of *To Save Bastogne*, Robert Phillips

17 December 1944, Hosingen, Luxembourg

(captured when the water tower fell)

After going through the trees we came to a road that it had been used a great deal lately along with a small bridge across the river. The stream was narrow at this point. The bridge was newly constructed of logs and looked capable of handling a Panther tank. A farm house stood very near the river and bridge; in the yard was a German field kitchen and a German Army truck.

We were given a can of sausage to be shared. With my mouth still bleeding along the lingering taste of cordite, I passed it up. They then moved us into the house. Inside sitting at a table were several Germans and a lady washing dishes. Apparently they had just finished eating. She appeared to be very nervous and afraid. On the table was a military type radio, some papers, maps and a briefcase. We were put in a room where they guarded us all night. It was this group that took all of our cigarettes and chocolate. They were very arrogant, mostly motions and grunts. The one that seemed to be in charge tried to act tough. He reminded me of little puppies that had just learned how to bark and growl. We spoke very little to each other. We had been trained not to speak freely around the enemy. In any case we had very little to talk about. Prisoners are often treated badly by rear-echelon troops who try to act tough or brave. The feeling one gets from being a prisoner is unexplainable. Hard to understand how it could have happened. In battle for some reason many times you are alone fighting a war. You feel that no one could help and you are the only one who can do anything.

18 December 1944, Hosingen, Luxembourg

In the morning we were given a piece of dark bread and sausage. Then we were loaded into a truck that looked as if it had been converted to use charcoal or wood. They took us a short distance, probably only a couple of miles. We came to a building that was made of stone blocks; I think that it was yellow. We were interrogated at this point. They asked for our name, rank and serial number. "We need nothing else because your officers told us everything." To me the statement was stupid–who in this area had any high level information. It was said probably to hurt morale. We were issued POW identification tags and a piece of string. Our money and various other items were taken away. I lost my watch, three French scrip notes and my lucky silver dollar. They gave us a piece of scrap paper as a receipt that they initialled. They did allow me to keep a small pen-knife which was to be very valuable to me later.

19 December 1944
We were roused out early in the morning, given a piece of dark bread and moved out again. We walked all day. At one place they stopped us in an orchard for a break. There were some apples lying on the ground, others still hanging on the trees. We gathered them up–they were frozen and some were partially spoiled. During all of the marches the only water we had was from the snow. Evening came and we were put in a barn with some cows. Later a lady came and milked the cows, returning later with a pail of potato soup. We shared the soup, drinking from the pail. It was no doubt the best potato soup I had ever tasted. That night we slept on the hay with a full stomach. Many times I have thought about the lady and the pail of soup. We checked the guards and found them to be very alert.

20 December 1944
We started out again in the morning. Many times crossing fields, other times following the roads. As we moved along other groups of prisoners joined us. Some of the guards rode horses and moved us at a faster pace. Some of the prisoners were so tired and weak they only stumbled along.

In the late afternoon we entered a town and were loaded into boxcars. I am told that these cars were called "40 or 8"; that is forty men or eight horses. I think that there were more than forty men in our car. We took turns at sitting and standing as we travelled, stop and go throughout the night. The entire country was blacked out. In the front corner there was a small hole about eight by eight inches. This small opening was covered with heavy screen. A few peeks out showed dimly lit signs in the stations. The names of the towns meant nothing without a map or knowledge of the area. Sometimes we let other trains pass us. When men had to urinate, the only place to go was against the large side doors. The door had a space of about an inch between it and the floor. The urine rained down to the road bed until it froze over. With the number of us in the car, it was warm; the smell horrible. We came to a city, pulled into the yards and stopped. The train had hardly come to a stop when air raid sirens went off. Germans ran for cover in all directions. The planes had a field day. It was a moon-lit night giving the bombers a good target. They flew over us and then turned. I could see their reserve tanks and they were now turning. It was not hard to figure out the drop zone. The Germans were firing a great deal of anti-aircraft shells. This time fear did set in; locked in a boxcar during a bombing. When the bombing was over they unloaded us. We had been lucky as several of the other cars had been hit. It was tough not being able to help the men who were hurt. We do not even know the number of casualties. It looked like all of the bombers got away. I did not see any of them go down. I am sure they were British. They sure tore up that rail yard.

21 December 1944
Unloaded and walking again. As we walked through the town, kids yelled and threw rocks and snow at us. Many of the adults just stood by the side of the road. They looked very tired and sad. We walked along some more, the column moving much slower than the first few days. At last we arrived at Bad Orb, Stalag IXB. We were put in barracks, issued half of a blanket and a can or a pan to eat out of. No silverware, you had to make do. We would remain here until the first part of January.

These incidents happened during my internment. I am not sure as to which camp they happened in. These things happened, as I said before, fifty years ago. At the time some of the incidents did not seem so important. Many of us never thought we would live through it. I think for that reason some of the things were forgotten. The incidents I recall here seem unforgettable.

- A visit by the Red Cross – They never spoke to any of us. They looked at us as if we were pigs in a sty.
- During evening service someone stole the Chaplains bread ration. I never heard if the thief was ever caught or not.
- A black GI tried escaping but failed. He made no secret of what he intended to do. That night there was a single shot. In the morning they lined us up to view the body.
- The shoes were usually taken from Russian troops leaving them bare footed. In the winter this was especially harsh, as they were forced to walk in the snow.
- Once they dropped off a load of wooden shoes at our barracks and gave instructions that we were to have our leather shoes ready to turn in, in the morning. We kept the stove hot all night and burned them. The Germans came the next day but did not know which barracks had gotten the wooden shoes.
- I slipped a hoop off a rain barrel that was near the rear door. By bending it back and forth, it was broken into two pieces. Having done this in a way that the riveted part was in the center of one part. Rubbing it on the back step, it soon separated. I now had two pieces of strap iron, each with two holes in one end. By bending and rubbing on the step a rough knife was finally formed. The other part was given to another man, who used it to make a knife for himself.
- We were shown a movie, part of which was about the good life. I believe it was filmed in the Alps. It showed people having a good time. Tables loaded with food and drink. The other part showed a small gauge rail line. A man took his seat in a sled that was similar to a bobsled. The rear was

shaped like what we now know as the back of a rocket. They fired it and it took off at a tremendous speed. I think they introduced us to jet propulsion of aircraft.

- We were given a shower and our clothes were deloused, they must have used sulphur as our clothes smelled of it. Being naked in that shower room with no soap, we washed the best we could. The water temperature was good. Many times I think about those people who were taken in rooms much the same but were gassed.

Based on facts from Sgt. Everson's story and what is known about the transfer of prisoners to other camps, he was most likely relocated to Stalag IXA at Ziegenhain, Germany on January 25, 1945 along with Cpl. Miller and over 1200 other non-commissioned officers from Stalag IXB.

Executive Officer, 1ˢᵗ Lt. Thomas J. Flynn
K Company, 110ᵗʰ Infantry Regiment
On the Move—Days 2-7

Based on National Archives interviews conducted
at Moosburg Stalag VIIA by Army Field Historian Capt.
William K. Dunkerly on May 1 and 2, 1945, and Flynn's
Medical Application for V.A. Medical Benefits in 1982

*Lt. Flynn is one of the officers from Hosingen that were first shipped to
Stalag IXB at Bad Orb. Flynn, along with Capt. Feiker, Lieutenants
Porter, Morse, Payne, Hutter, Pickering, Devlin and Mc Bride were then
later relocated to the officer's camp located at Hammelburg's Oflag XIIIB
on January 25, 1945. An allied escape attempt of Oflag XIIIB by Task
Force Baum failed on March 27, 1945 and all the POWs that survived
and were recaptured were disbursed to other camps. Capt. Feiker and Lt.
Devlin died while prisoners of war.*

After the GIs had all assembled outside the church, a German officer
led the captured officers to an isolated house south of Hosingen
where they were crowded into a small room. They were searched
and interrogated. Each officer was required to empty the content
of his pockets into his helmet. These items were inspected by a
German officer but no search was made of the persons' clothing.
During this investigation some officers destroyed some maps and
papers which were still in their possession. The interrogation was
brief and the Germans were primarily interested in the location
of mine fields and booby traps. The officers of Company K spoke
only of a mine field which had already been discovered by the
Germans after one of their vehicles had already be disabled by one
of the mines. The Germans threatened to march the prisoners
across country to detonate possible mines, but this threat was not
carried out.

While the officers were being searched, the enlisted men were
lined up in a field, tallying and searching. The men were not as
fortunate as the officers. They were stripped of their personal
belongings, and many were forced to give up their combat shoes

and/or galoshes and made to take German boots in exchange. All of this "bartering" was done by individual Germans and as a consequence the enlisted men found themselves with shoes which did not fit properly.

The officers and enlisted men had been allowed to take toilet articles with them. At the time of this first search, helmets were retained as well as gas masks. Each man had with him a minimum of one K ration and one D ration which had been issued just before capture.

From the site of capture, they were then marched into a holding area in now German territory (fenced in but open area). While so penned in, an American fighter plan came in to attack, but a German plane came in behind him and shot him down. He crashed and burned in the immediate area. No one got out of the plane. The pilot probably thought that they were Germans.

The group of approximately 300 officers and enlisted men were left in this area for four or five hours.

After that time the prisoners were moved out in column, with the enlisted men leading in one group and the officers in the second group. The weather was rainy, the ground wet and muddy. Patches of snow reminded the men of the winter ahead as they moved north and then east back over the German main supply route (MSR) south to Hosingen.

On the foot march to the Our River, the MSR was jammed with westbound traffic and the men frequently moved into the ditches to permit the passing of numerous horse drawn vehicles. The men saw trucks which were towing two or three other trucks.

At Eisenbach, a small town on the west bank of the Our River, the men were jammed into a small church. Once inside the church, the men did not receive the hot meal which had been promised. They lay tightly packed with only straw to cover them. Their ill-fitting and inferior German shoes had irritated their feet and the cold had caused the appearance of frostbit in some cases.

The next morning only a little hot coffee was served. As only a few guards could be seen, the men were tempted to escape but they did not know how far they were from the American lines.

Already they could see heavy artillery moving up the road from the south on the west side of this river.

The prisoners crossed the Our River over a footbridge and moved by foot to Prum (Germany). During the two and half days which followed, the only food received was from civilian supplies procured along the road by the *feldwebel* (sergeant) in charge of the column.

Before Prum was reached, an attempt was made to relive the enlisted men of their money for "safekeeping". Captain Fieker, Commanding Officer, Company K, protested to a German NCO that this was prohibited by the Geneva Convention. Finally, after a German officer had been contacted, the men were allowed to keep their money. However, in spite of protests, each man was allowed to keep only his field jacket or overcoat, whichever he chose. Most of the men kept overcoats.

At Prum other prisoners from miscellaneous units were added to the column, bringing the total to approximately 500. Many of the men which joined the group were from the 3rd platoon of Company K which had been overrun on the afternoon of December 17 south of Hosingen.

The next move was a foot march to Gerolstein. No ratios were issued and many of the men were suffering from frozen feet due to colder weather and inadequate footgear. At Gerolstein the men were locked in an ice house where they were joined by other prisoners. Lt. Flynn observed many reunions taking place between the men from other outfits. However, no new members of his Division were seen, and the men of Company K were instructed to speak to no one whom they had not known previously.

Some straw was issued and a limited amount of hot soup was furnished upon arrival. During the stay at this camp, rations were insufficient. A two day ration was issued for the next move, which consisted of a fair sized can of cheese per six men, and two packages of German field biscuits per man.

The prisoners were loaded onto a train, about 50 men per boxcar, and locked in. Individual cars were not guarded, the guards riding in separate cars and dismounting to patrol whenever the train stopped, as trains carrying supplies to the frontlines took priority on the railroad tracks. The men were let out only occasionally to relieve themselves, but on the whole Lt. Flynn did not observe that there was a latrine problem in his boxcar because of the small amount of food being consumed.

The train pulled into the Frankfurt train yards later that day, December 22, but the POWs remained locked inside and no food was issued. Water and brief bathroom breaks were the only things they received frequently.

On Christmas Eve all hell broke loose and the group "sweated out" a Royal Air Force (R.A.F.) bombing raid. As the air-raid sirens in Frankfurt went off, bombs began exploding all over the city, including in the Frankfurt train yard. A number of boxcars exploded several rails away from where Lt. Flynn's car was sitting, sending shock waves and shrapnel everywhere. One man tried to escape out the small window in the boxcar but was immediately shot and killed by a German guard. Fortunately, there were several other parked trains between Flynn's boxcar and the strike area to absorb and hold back any shrapnel coming their way.

The next day was Christmas Day, and the men were given one Red Cross parcel per five men to share in lieu of German rations. On December 26, the train finally headed northeast out of Frankfurt for Bad Orb, Germany.

Stalag IXB at Bad Orb, Germany—Days 10-24 (Fifteen days)

That same day, Lt. Flynn's train pulled into Bad Orb and he, along with hundreds of other GIs captured on the Western Front, were organized into columns and marched three miles up the mountain road to the POW camp, Stalag IXB.

Once inside the compound gates, they were processed and issued numbered, metal prisoner ID tags. The prisoners were de-loused and allowed to have hot baths and then the officers and enlisted men once again were separated. The Americans were

packed into sixteen of the dilapidated barracks. Lt. Flynn was one
of 250 officers jammed into a single barracks.

The conditions in this camp were terrible. There were only outside
latrines and the use of these was denied during the darkness.
Toilet paper was scarce and there was no hot water or soap. The
men had to make do with just the one or two taps of cold water
that were in each room.

Most of the men were issued only one German blanket, many
of which were worn and threadbare. Some men had no blankets
and many had to sleep crowded on the bare wood floors in rooms
that lacked bunk beds. In addition, one fifth of the men did not
have an overcoat since many had been forced to give them up to
the German soldiers.

The food consisted of ersatz coffee for breakfast. Some type
of vegetable soup was served at noon. It usually consisted of field
beets but sometimes five or six potatoes were added, although
overcooking usually made them unrecognizable. On a good day,
some form of black bread or sugar was included to supplement
their diet. Occasionally, a dead horse would be dragged through
the camp, meaning the prisoners might find a piece of meat in the
soup. Even a dead bug in the soup was deemed acceptable, as it
was just another form of protein to the starving POWs. Late in the
afternoon, each man received one-sixth of a loaf of bread, a small
portion of margarine, and occasionally, a little cheese or meat
(horsemeat). Many of the soldiers had to use their steel helmets
as eating bowls. Lt. Flynn never saw a Red Cross parcel distributed
while he was at this camp

By this time, many of the men were in a rundown condition
and were suffering from intestinal problems. The POWs were
losing weight rapidly and their strength seemed to ebb every day.
It didn't take long for some of the heavier-built POWs to become
too weak to leave their bunks, so Flynn and the lighter-built men
managed to get around and help take care of them.

Contact was made with other officers from the 28th Infantry
Division while at Stalag IXB. Due to the terms of the Geneva
Convention, the officers were separated from enlisted men,

but because of a lack of space, they were not kept in solitary confinement. Officers were not allowed on work details outside of camp, which meant there were no additional opportunities to supplement the minimal rations they were given, nor chances to gather firewood for the stoves in their barracks. This would be the case throughout their captivity.

Lt. Flynn remained at Bad Orb for about two weeks until he and the officers were moved to Oflag XIIIB at Hammelburg.

Move to Oflag XIIIB at Hammelburg, Germany—Days 25-26 (Two days)

The Germans also divided their POW camps into two types. Stalags were for the enlisted men and oflags were meant for officers. On January 11, 1945, Flynn and 452 officers, twelve non-commissioned officers and eighteen privates were marched back down the mountain road, where they were loaded once again into boxcars and transported to Oflag XIIIB, thirty-four miles south near Hammelburg.

A partial list of prisoners found at Oflag XIIIB after the war, included the following officers from the 110th with whom Flynn had fought with in Hosingen:

- Capt. Frederick C. Feiker, CO, K Company
- 1st Lt. Bernard V. Porter, 2nd Platoon Leader, K Company
- 1st Lt. James D. Morse, Mortar Section Leader, M Company
- 1st Lt. Richard H. Payne, Platoon Leader, A Company, 707th Tank Battalion
- 1st Lt. Cary H. Hutter, 1st Platoon Leader, B Company, 103rd Engineers
- 2nd Lt. John A. Pickering, 2nd Platoon Leader, B Company, 103rd Engineers
- 2nd Lt. Charles F. Devlin, 3rd Platoon Leader, B Company, 103rd Engineers
- 2nd Lt. Danny R. Mc Bride, 103rd Medical

A three day ration consisted of a one and a half pound can of beef and three quarters of a loaf of bread for each two men was issued for the next move. The train ride to the camp near Hammelburg lasted only two days (11-12 January) and, in anticipation of being fed upon arrival at the Lager, the men finished the rations on hand. However, the men were made to go without rations the first day at Hammelburg because of the previous issue which they had devoured.

Oflag XIIIB at Hammelburg, Germany—Days 27-100 (Seventy-four days)

The Lager at Hammelburg was an old one and no civilian reactions beyond the natural curiosity were noticed as the men marched the three miles from the rail yards to the enclosure. This was the first American officer group to be sent to Hammelburg, but more followed. Former commanding officer of the 110th, Lt. Col. Theodore Seely, also was transferred to this camp in mid-January. By March 1945 there were 1200-1500 Americans in the camp.

The winter of 1944-1945 was one of the coldest on record in Germany and the barrack temperature in the old stone barracks averaged about 20 degrees Fahrenheit throughout most of the winter. There were no washrooms and no hot water due to the fuel shortage so the GIs had to carry water from the kitchen faucets to the wash basins in each room.

Flynn kept his thoughts to himself. Despite the cold weather, his preference was to be outside whenever possible, and he spent his time talking to the Serbian officers in Oflag XIIIA through the fence that separated the two compounds. Flynn developed a friendship with one of the Serbian officers. He believed the Eastern Europeans in the camp were treated worse than the American officers were.

Colonel Goode and the other evacuees from Oflag 64 in Poland arrived in early March 10.

Tension between the American POWs and German personnel was ongoing and treatment of the prisoners by the guards was only fair, at best as several POWs were shot and killed for frivolous reasons.

By the end of March, many officers were in a dangerous condition due to malnutrition. Fortunately, the Serbian officers from Oflag XIIIA shared approximately 1,800 Red Cross packages over the three-month period, but Flynn never received a Red Cross parcel during this time.

Most POWs experienced psychological and physiological issues—some better and some worse. Poor heath, sub-standard living conditions, and the psychological issues POWs experienced lead to a decline in their mental health as well. Flynn and many of the other officers began to believe they had been used as bait in the Ardennes to draw out the German reserves. Flynn also felt that General Patton was not concerned about the welfare of his men.

Ironically, near the end of March, military intelligence had informed General Patton that his son-in-law, Lt. Col. John Waters, who had been captured in the fighting in Tunisia, North Africa, in 1943, had been transferred to Hammelburg. Waters had been imprisoned at Oflag 64 in Szubin, Poland, but arrived at the Hammelburg camp on March 6 with the rest of Col. Paul R. Goode's group.

The Escape from Oflag XIIIB at Hammelburg—Days 101-104 (Four days)

Only sixty miles from the advancing American frontlines, Patton ordered Capt. Abraham Baum, to lead a task force of two companies of Sherman tanks from the 4th Armored Division and 293 men to liberate the American POWs in Oflag XIIIB.

On March 27, the task force of 16 tanks (Shermans and M5A1 Light tanks), 27 half-tracks and assorted other vehicles quickly made their way to the camp, demolishing the camp's guard towers and breaking down the main gate to free the camp. There had been resistance along the way and one-third of the task force had already been lost and the rest were pretty shot up. They planned to head back, carrying as many POW's as they could. Those with some infantry experience with tanks and the artillery fire they draw, did not see how, in their condition, they could make it back to American lines.

The German camp commandant surrendered to Colonel Goode, the ranking U.S. officer prisoner. The Colonel marched the men out of the camp and onto the road with the tanks. It was hoped that transportation for all would be available, but the tanks were the only vehicles there. No radio contact as rear elements of the tank unit had been lost, but the tankers said that some of their elements were in Aschaffenburg. As many of the men as possible climbed onto the tanks, and the Colonel Goode briefed the others and gave the Allied prisoners permission to strike out cross country to try and reach the Allied lines.

About a dozen of the officers decided to try to make to the American line on foot – three groups in all. Flynn and four other officers made plans to head southwest through the hilly and wooded terrain toward Gemunden. Lt. Colonel Thomas Paine Kelly, Captain Aloysius Menke and Lt. Colonel William Scales decided to head north and where they eventually met up with the U.S. Seventh Army. A third group of three men, including Lt. Donald Prell, from the 106th Infantry Division headed west.[16]

---

16   Phone interview with 2nd Lt. Donald Prell on June 9, 2010

Photo: Task Force Baum's Sherman tanks from the 4th Armored Division break down the Hammelburg camp gate March 27, 1945.
Source: U.S. National Archives and Records Administration

Before leaving, Flynn's group canvassed the tank column and took a case of C rations, water and a compass from the Task Force members. Several officers picked up pistols to carry with them but Lt. Flynn expressed his concern that he wished to avoid complications should the group be recaptured.

The men that opted to stay at the camp were hopeful that other American units would be coming soon and they just had to hold on a little bit longer. A total of 550 men left with Colonel Goode and Captain Baum's tanks. As Flynn suspected, the tankers didn't get far before they ran into resistance. Some returned to camp with Colonel Goode, just six miles out, before all hell broke loose.

The Flynn's group moved out to the southwest and a day and half later they came upon a small hut near a stone quarry occupied by an old couple. After some discussion they decided to approach it. A German answered the door and invited them in. Flynn spoke German so he convinced them they meant no harm, and were only trying to get back to their people. The couple had heard of the Armored Force attacks and was afraid but the man was very friendly and the situation seemed to be safe so the officers went in and sat down in the kitchen. A woman gave them coffee and milk and heated some rations for them.

It was learned that the only other German soldiers in the near vicinity were two men guarding some Polish prisoners. It was found that the German couple had interests, such as religion, in common with the five officers, and friendly conversation went on far into the night. The German gave them a military map of the region and pointed out a likely route which the officers decided not to follow. The men had about decided to remain there until night when someone knocked on the door (approximately 28 March 0500). The woman quickly turned off the lights and the man went to answer the door. When he returned, he told the officers that it was another guard from town who was looking for the two guards in that area to tell them that there were SS troops in town.

This incident caused a hasty change in plans and the German volunteered to lead Lt. Flynn and his companions over a back trail before daylight. This was done and the German pointed out a secluded section of woods before leaving them. The officers selected another position and bedded down for the day.

The initial plan was to attempt crossing the Main River at Gemunden. However, this was changed in favor of attempting to cross the Frank Saale River north of Gemunden to avoid having to recross the Main River further west. No move was made on March 28 because the men had decided to move by dark and stay hidden during the day. The men also remained in this hiding place on March 29 because one of their members was sick.

On the night of March 29, two men reconnoitered to the north along the Frank Saale River. The nearest bridge was a motor road in a small town. Here there was observed a Volksstrum guard who spotted the patrol and sounded an alarm. However, the men got back safely. They reported the river to be only 30-40 yards wide but unfordable due to a depth of approximately 8-10 feet. It was decided that due to the cold weather and the below par physical condition of the men that they would risk crossing the bridge and not attempt to swim.

The group worked onto high ground overlooking Gemunden on the day of March 30. The town was full of activity, but a foot bridge was discovered just below their position, so the possibility of crossing here was considered. Two men went out on reconnaissance while the others observed and made notes of German traffic along the road. This was for their own use and U.S. units which they hoped to contact. It was noted that there was a checkpoint at the footbridge, but it was tentatively decided that a crossing would be tried that night. However, the patrol returned late in the afternoon and reported that the Germans were preparing a defensive position between the bridge and where they were hiding. They knew that possibly the Americans were near and that this would not continue to be a safe hiding place.

The group started back to the stone quarry by a different route than the one they had taken initially and were making fair time when, unfortunately, they came into an area where many search parties were out looking for escaped East European prisoners. The search party they ran into was armed youngsters, only 15-18 years of age, and older Home Guard type adults. When Flynn saw his group had been spotted, and as the Germans came toward them, he quickly hid the map under some leaves and loose dirt, to avoid getting the old couple in trouble. He advised the officers with pistols to hide them the same way. Once again, Flynn's proficiency in German came in handy. He explained that they were unarmed POW's turned loose by the "Panzers" and that they were now lost in the woods. They were recaptured on "Good Friday" 1945 after having been loose for about a week.

The young guards were enthusiastic and still felt they were winning the war. They never even searched Flynn's group before putting them in some old trucks to take them back to their camp The five officers were marched a short distance to a small village, where they were given tea and a sandwich. They were then taken to a command post where they were issued German front line rations. They received good treatment during this second capture. That night they were placed in a barn with plenty of straw. The next morning the group was joined by other retaken prisoners and driven back to Hammelburg by horse and wagon. The men noted that the entire area was being prepared for anti-tank defense.

At the same camp at Hammelburg from which they had escaped, it was learned that most of the other men had been recaptured. The tanks had be forced to blaze their way into Germany so unfortunately German resistance to the "Hammelburg Raid" on their return was much stronger than anticipated. The tank column had run into trouble several times and finally the tanks had been knocked out and the entire group had been left on foot. Thirty-two men from the task force were killed in action and only thirty-five made it back to Allied territory, with the remainder being taken prisoner. Most of the fifty-seven tanks, tank destroyers, trucks, and half-tracks were lost.

It was also learned that as a result, evacuation of the camp had been underway for several days; Colonel Goode's contingent and others having left for the Nuremburg on foot. The Germans continued to move prisoners farther into the interior of Germany to keep them away from the advancing American armies.

Captain Feiker and the other men who had stayed in the camp because they were too sick to march were marched anyway to Stalag Luft III at Nuremberg on March 29. Colonel Goode's contingent of men, which had been recaptured, were moved out by train at the request of the Serbian Chief of Staff, as the American tanks were shooting into the Serbian camp due to bad intelligence.

The Serbians who were tending to the POWs still in the camp hospital served Flynn's group a hot meal, and there were suddenly plenty of Red Cross parcels available. Among the POWs left behind was General Patton's son-in-law, Lt. Col. John Waters. Waters had been shot in the lower back and buttocks while he carried a white flag to meet the Shermans by a German corporal hiding just outside the gate. Now partially paralyzed, he was one of only seventy-five wounded and sick Americans who would be liberated from this camp by the American 14th Armored Division within the week.

Ninety-six Miles to Stalag Luft III at Nuremberg, Germany— Days 105-109 (Five days)

The following morning, Flynn and any remaining POWs capable of being moved were loaded into unmarked boxcars once again, en route to Nuremberg. This time, old prison guards were stationed in each car. Approximately 10 kilometers (6.2 miles) outside of Hammelburg, an American P-51 fighter plane strafed their unmarked train. The .50-caliber ammo slamming into the metal roof of the cars was deafening and sounded to Flynn like someone hammering on the roof. The fighters flew up the length of the train to shoot up the engine at the front. As the train slowed to a stop, Flynn and the other POWs convinced the old guards to open the doors before the fighters came back. The guards jumped out first, and the POWs followed, taking cover far away from the train. The fighters returned to rake the train again but the men were far enough away by then to be safe.

The senior U.S. and British officers protested that their men would not ride farther unless the next train was plainly marked as a prisoner train. With the train disabled, they refused to wait for another unmarked train, and talked the guards into continuing by foot. They organized a column and left for Nuremburg on foot. Flynn chose to be a straggler at the end of the column, and he walked as slowly as the guard would let him in order to delay their arrival at the next camp.

When Flynn's group reached Nuremberg and Stalag Luft III, he found out that twenty-six American POWs who had been in the first group to be evacuated from Hammelburg, including Captain Feiker, had been killed during an Allied air raid of Nuremberg on April 5 and 40 were wounded, as their POW column was being marched through the city on their way to their next destination, Moosburg's Stalag VIIA.

Lieutenant Charles F. Devlin also died as a prisoner of war. It is not clear at what point this occurred, whether he was part of the escape attempt with Task Force Baum or during the same air raid as Capt. Feiker was mortally wounded.

Stalag Luft III at Nuremberg, Germany—Days 110-111 (Two days)

By the time that Flynn's group reached Stalag Luft III at Nuremberg, the 14th Armored Division had arrived in full force at Oflag XIIIB in Hammelburg, liberating the camps there for good. The German army continued to fall back towards Berlin and kept moving the prisoners with it.

When Flynn's group arrived at Nuremberg, there wasn't much left as the Allied air raids had severely damaged the city. As a result, the prisoners were held in what was left of a bombed out stadium for just two days.

Once again on foot, Flynn group was marched through the city of Nuremberg en route to Stalag VIIA in Moosburg. By this time, the American fighters and bombers had also destroyed much of Nuremberg and as the POWs were marched through the bombed-out sections of the city, the German civilians were hostile and angry with the American POWs. The Germans were especially angry with the pilots and called them "terror flyers." (Flynn later said the phrase sounded like *tier pfluger*). Flynn understood what they were saying and told all the pilots around him to hide the pilot wings on their uniforms. When a group would press too close to them, Flynn would point to the crossed rifles insignia on his uniform coat and tell them, "*fuss soldaten*" (foot soldiers or infantry). Flynn saved all the pilots in his group from harm in this way, and they made it safely through the city with no injuries. Unfortunately, some of the POWs in other groups were not so lucky and were pelted with stones by the mobs.

Ninety-four-mile March to Stalag VIIA at Moosburg, Germany—Days 112-119 (Eight days)

Near exhaustion, Flynn lost track of time on the march to Moosburg. The prisoners walked as slowly as the German guards would let them in an attempt to prolong the journey. By this time, both the prisoners and guards had to scrounge for food along the way from the Bavarian farmers but the warmer weather allowed them to sleep in the large stacks of hay in the fields at night.

Yet they still were not safe, and once again, Flynn's POW column came under attack by an American fighter plane. This time it was near a railroad overpass. Flynn wasn't sure if they had been the primary or secondary target this time, but some POWs at the front of the column were injured. Flynn remained content to be one of the stragglers at the back of the line.

Stalag VIIA at Moosburg, Germany—Days 120-133 (Fourteen days)

Flynn's POW column arrived at Moosburg Stalag VIIA around April 15, 1945. Once again, the men had to register upon arrival. By mid-April, the camp census had swollen to over 100,000.

With such overcrowding, there was little food and no hot water for cooking or washing. The straw beds were infested with lice and fleas. There was one outdoor latrine for every 2,000 men. At this point in the war, the buildings were old and many were just wooden shells because the POWs had been taking them apart gradually to burn the wood for cooking on their makeshift stoves.

When Flynn and the other POWs were shown where they were to stay, the American and British airmen shared with each of the new arrivals an entire Red Cross package. This was quite the luxury to Flynn, as it was the first time in four months of captivity that he had gotten a package just for himself. The airmen also shared the rumor that Hitler had ordered all American officers in this camp killed, rather than surrendering them to the American Army.

On the April 29, 1945, the 14th Armored Division had reached Moosburg and was fast approaching Stalag VIIA.

The rumour of Hitler's orders to kill the American officers was true and SS troops began to fire their weapons into the camp from the roof of a cheese factory nearby in a last-ditch attempt to carry them out. The POWs were told by the German guards to stay inside with their heads down and "the prison guards and the German Army fought off the Gestapo and SS and saved all the prisoners' lives."[17]

The fighting was over in less than an hour and Flynn could soon feel the vibration of the army tanks headed in their direction. It didn't take long for the sound of the moving Sherman tanks to be drowned out by the sounds of euphoria erupting from every able-bodied man in Stalag VIIA.

The Sherman tanks of the 14th Armored Division soon crashed through the fences of the compound. Each tank was immediately engulfed by the sea of ragged, emaciated, and filthy POWs. Flynn wanted to join the celebration on top of the tanks but there were already so many bodies covering every inch of the tanks that the tanks themselves were no longer visible.

Brigadier Gen. Charles H. Karlstad received an unconditional surrender from the camp commandant and the Americans assumed control of the camp about 1230.

Unbeknownst to Flynn, his wife's youngest brother, Staff Sgt. Magnus B. Bennedsen, had been assigned to the 14th Armored Division's maintenance unit in October 1944 and his maintenance crew was not far behind the tanks that had just crashed through the compound fences. Unfortunately, with all the chaos, neither of them would discover the other was there, and the two men never shared their stories after the war.

At approximately 1300 hours on April 29, 1945, 1st Lt. Martin Allain, a twenty-three-year-old bomber pilot who had been a POW for over two years, revealed the treasured American flag he had been hiding, sewn between his two German blankets to conceal it

---

17   http://www.Moosburg.org/info/stalag/bilder/

Photo: Moosburg Stalag VIIA POWs cover the U.S. tanks in excitement. Photo provided courtesy of U.S. Air Force Academy, USAFA Special Library.

from the guards. Lieutenant Allain now realized what his prized flag was destined to be used for and he shimmied up the German flagpole with Old Glory in hand. The entire camp went silent as Allain replaced the ugly swastika with his beautiful Stars and Stripes; a symbol of freedom for some 100,000 prisoners of over 40 different nationalities, some of whom had been in German prison camps since the dark days of Calais and Dunkirk in 1940. As Old Glory waved in the breeze to the freed prisoners, each and every man immediately came to attention and saluted the American flag, regardless of his nationality. The prisoners were overcome with emotion and almost every eye filled with tears.

General Patton arrived in the camp for a visit on May 1, his entourage driving right past Cpl. Richard J. Berkey; Medic for C Company, 68th AIB, 14th Armored Division. He was seated with his

Photo: Lieutenant Allain's American flag flies over Moosburg. Photo provided courtesy of U.S. Air Force Academy, USAFA Special Library.

men in their half-tracks while the medics waited for the column to move "when Old George (hell raisin") Patton comes tearing up with his four stars, six "peeps", three armored cars, and a couple two-star generals. A prisoner just liberated got in the way of his jeep while he was passing our vehicles. He (Patton) jumps up in his seat and throws up his arms and says, "Get that thing the hell outa' the way!""[18]

---

18   Karen B. Huntsberger, *Waiting for Peace, The Journals & Correspondence of a World War II Medic* (Oregon: Luminar Press, 2015), p. 257.

*Photo: General Patton visits Moosburg. Photo provided courtesy of U.S. Air Force
Academy, USAFA Special Library*

The men of the 14th Armored Division, however, were much more compassionate and the medics gave the GIs about all the food and drink they had with them, including champagne. Cpl. Berkey had trouble holding back the tears seeing the condition of these ex-prisoners.

Standing in his jeep, General Patton spoke briefly to the men, shook a few hands, and then left again. Like Cpl. Berkey, Flynn was not a fan of the general and he wasn't impressed by Patton's gratuitous gesture and short stay. "His blood and our guts," was what Flynn would say about him when his name came up in conversation in the years that followed.

Flynn was one of the first officers to be interviewed at Moosburg by Army Field Historian Capt. William K. Dunkerly on May 1 and 2, 1945, about the Battle of the Bulge and how he and the other POWs were treated during their captivity.

Standing 5 foot 10 inches, Flynn weighed only 125 pounds when he was liberated, a loss of 40 pounds in four and a half months.

Flynn received a general medical exam to attend to immediate issues. No psychological evaluation or emotional assistance was provided. Army personnel did not brief Flynn on any events that had occurred while he was in captivity.

As the Army sorted through all the men in the camp, it made sure they were well fed to build up their strength and prepare them for travel. A field hospital was set up near the Landshut airstrip to provide them with hot showers, soap, delousing, and fresh clothing. The sick and infirm were quickly processed and forwarded on for treatment, as needed. As the men were processed and approved for travel, the ones who were healthy enough would wait near the Landshut airstrip until C-47s landed to resupply the 14th Armored Division with gas and ammunition. Each plane would then be loaded with soldiers for the return trip to the airbase in France. One officer even purchased a couple kegs of beer in town to share with the soldiers while they waited their turn to go home.

Flynn had his first plane ride in the bucket seat of a C-47 on May 7, 1945, en route to the 195th General Hospital outside of Paris for further processing. He was then transported by truck along the back roads into Paris that night, just before the big Victory in Europe Day (V-E Day) celebration on May 8. Flynn would never see or hear from any of the men of the 28th Infantry Division again.

Flynn was released from the 195th General Hospital to Camp Lucky Strike near Le Havre, France on May 8, where he stayed just a few days until he received orders to be shipped home. On May 13 Flynn boarded the U.S. merchant ship, *the John Erisco* and headed for New York. The Army provided the POWs with all the food they could eat on their two-week trip back to the states. Flynn's emaciated body packed on 45 pounds in just three weeks and he weighed 170 pounds when he arrived in New York's harbor.

As the *John Erisco* neared New York City, Flynn could see the familiar Statue of Liberty off in the distance. He watched eagerly as the ship passed all of the familiar landmarks of home, having grown up on the Upper East Side of Manhattan. He couldn't wait to be off the ship and with his family. Flynn also longed to see his wife, Anna, as he hadn't heard from here since he'd left in

September. The few photos in his wallet he had been allowed to keep were all he'd had to hold onto all these months.

Lt. Flynn surprised his family when he walked in the door of their apartment that evening. He left the next day to reunite with Anna at his brother's place in Chicago as he had orders to report to the Palmer House at Ft. Sheridan near the Chicago suburb of Lake Forest. As soon as Anna heard from Tom, she immediately packed her bags and left Minneapolis to meet him without telling anyone or turning in her resignation at the hospital where she worked as a Registered Nurse.

By the time Lt. Flynn arrived at the Chicago apartment of his brother, Bill, on June 4, 1945, Anna was already there waiting for him.

Pvt. William A. Gracie
K Company, 110th Infantry Regiment
Bazooka, 4th Platoon (Heavy Weapons)

Based on letters written by Pvt. Gracie to family and friends;
contributed by his daughter, Anne Gracie

Upon surrender to the Germans, Pvt. Gracie became part of the
group headed for Stalag IVB at Mühlberg. It took several days to
march to the train station where he was then loaded and locked
inside a crowded boxcar. As was the case for every other prisoners
headed from the front lines into Germany, the Allied Air Force
Christmas Eve bombing proved to be a traumatic experience as
bombs exploded all around his boxcar causing panic and fear
for everyone inside. Gracie was hit in the upper back by a small
metallic fragment during the air raid.

Starved not only physically but emotionally, Gracie long for
communication with his loved ones and once settled at Stalag IVB,
he began writing letters to his family back home as soon as he
was allowed. His always positive attitude not only helped his family
deal with his captivity but helped him keep his spirits up, as well as
keep him alive.

With nothing but time on their hands and hunger in their
bellies, Gracie and the other POW frequently talked about food,
dreaming of their favorite meals. Taking their conversations very
serious, Gracie jotted down everyone's ideas in his notebook.

Gracie also grew in his faith in God as he read the entire New
Testament of the Bible while in captivity. He was very proud of
himself for that accomplishment as he rarely had attended Sunday
school while growing up in Cumberland, Maryland.

From Gracie's perspective, "*the German guards were elderly
(relatively) and not at all brutal. Most of the prisoners were British and
friendly. By far the toughest ordeal was starvation on a diet that was mainly
turnip soup. Initially the diet for prisoners had been supplemented by Red
Cross parcels delivered from Switzerland and containing both nutritious
food and cigarettes, which the non-smokers could exchange for additional*

food. But as the number of prisoners grew and deliveries into Germany became more difficult, distribution of the Red Cross parcels diminished and eventually ceased as the Allied bombings of Germany intensified."

Jan 9th '45
Dearest Mother and Daddy,
This is my 2nd letter, and I'm still here at IVB. My 1st letter was written Jan 3rd. Everything here is fine and running smoothly along. It has become very cold, but we spend most of our time indoors cooking our meals.
Love to my wonderful parents,
Billy

Jan 25th '45
Dearest Mother and Daddy,
This is my 3rd letter to you, the other two having been written Jan 3rd and 9th. I'm still at IVB, and consequently have had a swell chance to meet some fine English chaps. The weather is still cold, but I guess it is just as chilly at home. I've been keeping myself in fine health.
All my love,
Billy

Feb 4th '45
Dearest Mother and Daddy,
This is my 4th letter to you; the other three having been sent Jan 3rd, 9th and 25th. I'm still at IVB, and I'm enjoying the same simple and easy life as before. But I have had a chance to do a lot of thinking and planning for the future when I'm repatriated. Believe me Mother and Dad, we're going to see each other a lot more than ever before once we're going to have loads and loads of fun together. Being away like I am now makes me realize more and more that you're the most wonderful parents an unappreciative youth like myself could have. But again believe me; I'll never be unappreciative again.
And now I can fully realize how kind your friends and our family have been to me. The weather is decidedly warmer and everything more pleasant.
Every bit of my love,
Billy

Feb 11ᵗʰ '45

Dearest Mother and Daddy,

This is my 5ᵗʰ letter and finds me in even better health and spirits than before! Since we are given the opportunity of preparing our own meals, I'm becoming an accomplished chef. Spring is here and I'm catching up on my reading. See you soon!

Love & Kisses,

Billy

Feb 26ᵗʰ '45

Dearest Mother and Daddy,

This is my 6ᵗʰ letter and still finds me idling my time away at IVB. A great number of Red Cross packages have been arriving – and consequently my stomach has been kept very filled. The weather remains fine, and I've been spending much time loitering in the sunshine.

Love to everyone,

Billy

By the end of February 1945 and contrary to his optimistic letters, Pvt. Gracie had calculated how many days it would be before he starved to death so he decided to take his fate into his own hands, making plans to escape. His first escape occurred while on a work detail near Dresden when he managed to slip away from the guards. He was recaptured just a few days later and was sentenced to a week of solitary confinement.

Confinement only increased Gracie's desire to be free and just one month later when the camp became crowded with new Russian POWs, he seized an opportunity to slip away again with three other prisoners; this time they continued westward, sometimes assisted by German farmers tired of the war and sympathetic to the starving young GIs. Within a few weeks, they reached the advancing American troops that were moving into the area near the Elbe River. Shortly thereafter, Gracie's renewed his letter writing campaign to his family, which would continue until he returned stateside. He was very concerned about keeping his parents' morale high as he knew they had been very worried about him since he'd left for Europe nine months before.

On April 23, 1945 the Red Army liberated the remaining prisoners at Mühlberg's Stalag IVB.

April 27, 1945
Somewhere in Germany in the hands of the United States Army
Dearest parents,
I am now about the happiest person alive!! On April 24th at 6:30 p.m. we were overtaken by a Yankee "Recon" Outfit" and became free men again. Since then I've been in heaven! I'm now behind the lines and will never be in danger again. Soon I'll be headed for Southern France or England where we'll spend two or three weeks living a life of ease – and then (and I'm not kidding) I'll leave for the wonderful United States!! We're to be stationed as near as possible to our home towns for several more weeks and then we'll all be given a 30 day furlough!!! (and it won't be along after that, that I'll become a permanent civilian).

I'm so happy and excited that I can write no more at this moment and my next letter will probably be postmarked France. This address is just temporary so please don't use it in writing back. I'll write all the details later but right now I just want you to know that I'm ever so well and happy.

All my love,
Billy

April 28 '45
Dearest Mother and Daddy,
I wrote you an Airmail yesterday from an artillery outfit where I was spending the night along with three other ex-POW friends. Everyone has been treating us like kings, and I bet I've answered a million questions about prisoner life inside Germany. I know that you, my parents, will have even more to ask – and it will be a pleasure telling you all about everything. I fear most fellows will want to forget their last five or six months, but personally I want to remember it and tell everyone about it so the people back home will know how to deal with Germany (and this includes the German people as well as their military leaders) – and thus prevent once and for all a recurrence of past barbarities. I was extremely lucky myself and escaped the ill treatment that befell so many thousands of prisoners. Consequently I am now in very fine health and intend to arrive home

with quite a suntan. I can't stop from praising all the Americans around here for their extraordinary kindness. Right now we're living in beautiful German Luftwaffe quarters just waiting but it won't be long now when I can write everyone back home.
    Lotsa love,
    Billy

Transportation deep into Germany was still quite a problem so Gracie and his buddies remained with this unit and rested in former Luftwaffe barracks next to the airdrome near Polsen (a town 23 km from Leipzig) as their bodies recovered from months of starvation. On May 4th, the Quartermaster Corp arrived and they were finally able to get clean clothes and a hot shower. During this time, Gracie gained back nearly all the weight he'd I lost while in Stalag IVB. He estimated he now weighted between 150 and 155. He'd weighed only 148 lbs. when he'd joined the Army.

     When the unit packed up and relocated to the airfield near the large industrial city of Halle, Gracie moved with them and again the ex-POWs were housed in another old Luftwaffe barracks. On May 8th, V-E Day (Victory in Europe Day), the GIs gathered around a "Heinie" radio to listen to Winston Churchill's "Victory Speech". At 2:30 that afternoon, the five whistles (of the town nearby) began screaming in celebration of this great event.

     In a letter to his parents, Gracie commented on his observations of what was going on around him. *"I've been wondering if any rumors are circulating back in the states to the effect that the German people are being treated too leniently. If so, don't believe them, because the German people (and soldiers) are now being taught a lesson that they will never forget. And you can rest assured that the G.I. soldier who performs his duty will be just as strict and harsh as is humanely possible. And as for the people back home who pity these wretches, I have only utter contempt."*

     By his May 19th letters home, Gracie had finally been transported to Camp Lucky Strike, near Le Havre, France. His group was told everyday that they would be leaving for home very soon but they finally were told it would be another 10-15 days before there would be a ship available for them. The camp had grown to 90,000, many of which were wounded and ex-POWs in much worse condition than Gracie, taking priority on the incoming troop and hospital ships returning the veterans home.

Gracie was disappointed with the continued delays but understood the situation. He commented in a letter to his parents that Camp Lucky Strike was a tremendous facility and that the entertainment was first rate. Besides the Red Cross Recreation Center there were five movie houses (tents), several outdoor movies that take place after dark, several camp bands, and four or five USO Shows.

On May 21st, the Army stopped censoring the GIs outgoing mail in the British Isles and Northern France.

May 23 '45
At Camp Lucky Strike (Le Havre, France)
Dear Mr. Nungesser,
What a wonderful feeling it is to be alive again. That five months seemed like five years but perhaps experience even such as that is worth it. I was very, very fortunate while inside Germany and fared 100% better than most of the inmates. Some of the weaker fellows were so shattered that they ended up as unrecognizable creatures. Thank God I took care of myself and suffered only a loss in weight – which thanks to good American food, I've completely regained.

Perhaps I'm looking through rose-colored glass, but my only outlook on life now is one of complete beauty and happiness. It's so easy for me to appreciate things that I had before taken for granted. It might be that this war, as horrible as it is, has helped to pave my way into the future. I'm looking forward to sitting down across the dinner from you at 630 Washington St again (seafood might replace the steak – ha!).

My very best regards,
Bill G.

May 28 & 29 '45
At Camp Lucky Strike
Dearest Mother and Daddy,
We've been quite busy since my letter of the 26th – typhus injections, change of address cards to fill out, a physical examination, interviews

about POW life, and bringing up to date our Army Service records. Now that this 'processing' is completed, there is nothing for us to do except wait for the boats to come into the harbor. I've had my name crossed off the list for that short furlough in England because it is rumored that the fellows going to England will be delayed two or three weeks in getting back to the states. (And I've been delayed enough already.)

.... We were also issued some of our medals – an ETO ribbon with three bronze stars, and two overseas stripes for the sleeve of my left arm. When I get back to the states I'll also be issued the combat Infantry Badge, the Good Conduct ribbon and a Presidential Unit Citation which was awarded our division for fighting in the Ardennes last December (this is wore over the right pocket). (The 110th Infantry Regiment was ultimately denied the Presidential Unit Citation as noted in Allyn Vannoy's foreword.)

Plenty of love,
Billy

Now that Gracie was feeling better, he decided to take advantage of the delay and took several days leave with his friends to Paris from June 2 – 7. They took in all the main sights and Gracie was truly enchanted by the beauty of the city.

By June 11, Camp Lucky Strike only had 10,000 ex-POWs still on the base and Gracie was confident his trip home would be soon. All this waiting had given him nothing but time to think about his future and he began pondering the idea of staying in the Army and applying to Infantry Officer's Candidate School as he more than qualified with an IQ of 135. He also was considering the medical program the Army offered. It was hard to say what his future held though as the Army was planning to do a thorough review of his record and reclassify his status. Shortly thereafter, Gracie finally was shipped stateside. After his discharged, Gracie chose medicine and went on to become a doctor, like his father.

Pvt. Dale L. Gustafson
M Company, 110th Infantry Regiment
Machine Gunner, 2nd Platoon stationed
at Hosingen-Barriere with K Co. 3rd Platoon

Contributed by his son, James Gustafson

Pvt. Dale Gustafson wasn't sure how long he'd been knocked out for after the second tank artillery blast had sent the large metal cauldron across the room, knocking him unconscious, but when he came to, his head throbbed from the blow and he discovered the sharp pain he now felt in his leg was a shrapnel wound. He also quickly realized he was surrounded by the enemy and he was their prisoner.

By then, the German soldiers had rounded up all of the GIs from K and M Company's 2nd and 3rd platoons stationed in the farmhouses at Hosingen-Barriere and had moved one of their trucks with a machine gun mounted on the back in front of the group. They were all preparing to be shot where they stood but fortunately, the wounded German officer that Gustafson had been guarding ordered them to stop. The Americans had treated him well while he'd been a prisoner and he saw no reason to kill them. From there, the prisoners were marched to a train station and loaded on box cars. (According to K Company's Lt. Thomas Flynn's story, the Americans that had fought at Hosingen-Barriere were added to his POW column in Prum, Germany on December 20. They were marched another 12 miles to Gerolstein before being loaded in boxcars the following day, headed for Stalag IXB at Bad Orb, Germany.)

The Germans packed Gustafson's boxcar so tightly with American prisoners that the men that died in transit to the camp, remained standing because there was no room for them to fall. Although not that far away, the train ride to Stalag IXB took several days as supplies being transported to the German troops on the frontlines took priority on the railways. Stuck in the train stations over Christmas, they were sitting ducks when the American bombers began their massive assault on the German train stations and air fields on December 24th, not knowing that there were American prisoners inside the box cars below.

Pvt. Gustafson and his buddy, Pvt. Ernest P. Gallego remained at Stalag IXB for the remainder of the war until the camp was liberated on April 2, 1945 by American forces. Stories of Gustafson's internment and camp conditions which he witnessed and shared with his family are as follows:

- Gustafson's prisoner barracks only contained wooden bunk beds; no mattresses, pillows or blankets were provided. The room didn't seem much warmer than it was outside and as a result, the floor remained slippery from frozen urine for quite some time. To keep warm, Gustafson shared his bunk with Ernie Gallego; they'd put one of their overcoats underneath them and the other on top. More often than not, they laid in there bunk, picking the never ending growing lice off of each other.

- The food typically consisted of one ladle of watery soup, which often contained spiders and blackened, rotten potatoes that had frozen in the fields. They also received a small loaf of bread which had to be shared between several men. Each group would rotate who cut the bread into equal size pieces; whoever cut the bread got the last piece. Gustafson believed there were more vitamins and minerals in the ends of the loaf of bread so he always cut one of the end pieces a little smaller to make sure he got that piece.

- The men were starving but some of those that smoked willingly traded their food for cigarettes. They tried to eat rats, birds or bugs, when possible; anything with protein. Gustafson recalled seeing one prisoner, so weak from hunger that he fell on top of the giant pot where the Germans made the soup. His back landed against the pot and another POW grabbed him by the hair and pulled him off. All of the skin from his back was left stuck to the pot.

- Another POW had a bullet in his head and his wound became infected and swollen. The Germans gave him no medical attention and he died a week before they were liberated.
- One time three POWs bashed the German kitchen guard's head in with an axe in order to steal some bread from the kitchen. The next morning all the prisoners were called outside and forced to stand naked in the freezing cold. Gustafson thought they were going to be killed, but they were not, despite the fact that they all refused to identify the perpetrators.
- Gustafson passed the time by carving things. Although it is unknown how he got a knife, he carved a small two inch sword out of a toothbrush, a wooden spoon with his name on it and a small horse out of a bone from the soup.
- During his captivity, Gustafson's weight dropped from 205 lbs. to 120 lbs. and he developed whooping cough and diphtherial paralysis. Once he could no longer walk, the Germans moved him into a separate barracks where conditions were no better. He still only had a wooden bed and the broken windows did little to keep out the freezing cold temperature. Despite being move, he received no medical attention for his condition. The doctors that attended to the POWs when the camp was liberated estimated that Pvt. Gustafson was about a week away from death.
- Once the German guards realized the American forces were going to liberate the camp, they slipped into their civilian clothes and walked away.
- When the camp was eventually liberated, the American GI's cried at the sight of Pvt. Gustafson and his fellow prisoners. They wanted to offer their rations to help their fellow soldiers but the POWs' stomachs couldn't handle the food.
- Gustafson was eventually put on a plane to England, but the plane was shot down en route. He somehow survived and spent months recovering at an American Hospital,

which is now Birmingham High School in Los Angeles, California.

It took Pvt. Gustafson over a year to be able to walk again and determined to make it on his own, he crawled up the walkway when he was dropped off at his mother's house. He received the Purple Heart for the shrapnel wound to his leg; however, Los Angeles Dorsey High School's 1939 star quarterback's football career was over.

Capt. William H. Jarrett
B Company, 103rd Engineer Battalion

Excerpt from a journal written by Capt. Jarrett from
December 16, 1944 – March 1945. The journal was given
to Robert Phillips.

A WARTIME LOG
(Pages 45–63)

PROPERTY OF CAPT WILLIAM H JARRETT
CORPS OF ENGINEERS
US ARMY, 0-416086

18 December 1944–1400 hour
Arrived at 1600 (at the Eisenbach Church) and then I was selected
as senior officer and taken out of column and started marching
back to Pintsch to 2nd Panzer Division Headquarters. There I
was to be interrogated. The twelve guards marched me as far as
Hosingen where I observed the entire town burning and where I
refused to march any farther, wherefore I was put on a half-track
and rode from Hosingen to Pintsch. At Pintsch I was taken into
a warm room in a priest's house and given some black bread and
where I met Capt. Meisenhelter and his Lt.

After eating we were told to surrender our shoes and we could
sleep on the floor. The German Private was able to talk very good
English. His family owned a bakery shop in New York City for a
period of twelve years. He stated that he was forced to return to
Germany by the Party. He was definitely a Son of the Fatherland.

Colonel Fuller was brought in during the night along with Lt.
Burns.

19 December 1944–
We were fed hot soup at 1300 the next day and this made the first
food I had had since Saturday morning December 16th breakfast.

1400 hour
Loaded in truck and taken as far as Hosingen where we were unloaded and forced to march down to the Our River again, where we were kept in church all night without blankets. Did not sleep all night due to cold. Given one slice of bread.

20 December 1944–0830 hour
One hundred wounded men and aid men and ourselves were started across Our River on wooden footbridge and marched about six miles to a headquarters in the Siegfried Line. Joined Lt. Col Erving and other 28th Infantry Division officers (32 total) and all officers were placed in a pillbox without lights, and given boiled potatoes; about eight apiece. At this time I was taken to a command post where I observed a 1:25,000 map showing four Division boundaries and phase lines from the Our River to Bastogne.

After waiting in the command post for ten minutes, I was taken before a medical officer who examined my foot and removed a small piece of shell fragment. He dressed my wound and said it was be alright. I then went back to the pillbox in the company of a German Lieutenant who had spent eight years in England. He expected the war to be over within three months one way or another. He wanted to go back to Oxford University and finish his education.

21st December 1944–1400 hour
Still in the pillbox and issued another ration of potatoes–no indication of moving. Can hear heavy artillery in distance and can see water tower of Hosingen from top of pillbox in a west direction. Pillbox very cold and we have to take turns cranking machine every fifteen minutes to change air. Colonel Fuller is in bad physical shape.

22nd December 1944–1400 hour
Moving out of box at last. Ground covered with snow and very cold. After assembly in school house awaiting truck transport to Gerolstein, they asked for five officers to fill up a truck almost filled with wounded men; Meisenhelter, his lieutenant, myself,

and two other officers offer to go with and left immediately. After a cold four hours ride, we arrived at Gerolstein, a rail hub and O.M. (Ordnance & Maintenance) depot where we were given a cup of hot coffee (Ersatz), a fifth loaf bread and a quarter can of cheese. We were then formed with about 1100 men and officers of 106th Division and Surgical unit. Marched to railroad siding and placed in box cars; fifty men each. Told us we would move out right away, but we stayed on siding all night. Very cold and British Air craft over all night; flak batteries were firing at least every half hour.

23 December 1944–1100 hour
Still in cars and tracks were strafed and bombed by P-47s 300 yards behind us. Guards left us in cars locked up and ran away to shelters.

1400 hour
Issued half loaf of bread apiece and water and reloaded into other cars on main line. Cars full of manure.

2200 hour
Train started to move and I fell asleep.

24 December 1944–0900 hour
Train has been stopped for two hours and guards say that tracks ahead are bombed, can't move; near the town of Hillesheim.

1300 hour
Bombers and fighters going over by the hundreds, bombing very close; still locked in cars.

1400 hour
Just strafed and bombed by two P-47s. Guards ran away and left us to our fate. Fortunately one man outside of cars opened all doors. Terrible screams and noise. Eighty-five wounded officers and enlisted men; one officer and eight enlisted men killed. What a terrible Christmas Eve. May God help us.

Have asked senior American officer to get permission for us to march to place we are going. Whole countryside is being bombed and our chances look very slim. Our destination is Koblenz where we will be able to get a train to proceed on to stalag. Everyone is weak from hunger and lack of sleep. Only those with sleeping bags are able to sleep any length of time.

1900 hour

Wounded have been evacuated to a German hospital and permission has been granted to start marching at 0600 hour Christmas morning. Half loaf of bread per man and two gallons of molasses per hundred men will be issued before the march. Have 60 miles to march. Expect the march to take five days.

25 December 1944–0600 hour

Christmas morning–nine dead Americans lying cold and stiff on station platform; able men are forming into group of a hundred men each. I hope that I never see such a sad Christmas morning as this again.

Marched all day, rate very slow due to some marching wounded in column, halts every two hour. Reached Boos at 9 PM and slept in barns of town; very cold. German people in town fed us next morning and gave us hundreds of quarts of milk to drink. These people were the only German people who treated us like human beings

26 December 1944 -

Started marching at 0800 hour, marched all day passed through town in Mayen which was badly torn up from our bombing all railroads, roads, and bridges out. Went on to a clay products factory five kilometers further, and slept in sheds. Cold all night long; no food.

27 December 1944–

Started marching for Koblenz at 0800 hour. Entered Koblenz at 1700 hour; town on both sides of Rhine levelled to the ground. No lights or water. Bridges all unusable, except for foot traffic.

Much anti-aircraft defense on east side of river. No concrete forts visible, only open and direct dirt emplacements. Stayed all night at German officers' school on heights, just east of the river. Slept in stables, gave us hot soup at 0300 hour following morning. First food since bread issued on Christmas morning. May now get sick due to over eating. (This place was bombed the following night.)

28 December 1944 -
Started for Montabaur to get train at 0800 hour; 35 kilometer march. Had to leave road several times due to plane activity. Montabaur is a Wehrmacht headquarters. Walked five kilometers further and reached a town with a large clay products factory where all 1100 of us were put inside a large brick building with broken windows and no fires. Very few men slept at all.

29 December 1944 -
Stayed all day, were issued a half loaf of bread and some cheese and two cups ersatz coffee.

Lots of sick men. We were near a railroad siding and expected to be bombed at any moment. Train to take us to stalag due that evening. Arrived at midnight and we were loaded on, fifty to a car, and left almost immediately. Passed through Giessen (large foundry located there and bulk gas plant) and Erfurt and arrived at Mühlberg.

31 December 1944–1900 hours
Marched to Stalag IVB, deloused, showered and given shots and can of hot soup. Put all officers in hot barracks (one building) and had first good night's sleep.

1 January 1945–
Interrogated by German officer; gave no information except name, rank and serial number.

British boys at camp very helpful and we received first Red Cross parcel. Canadian–one per four men. Food was delicious. Morale everyone much improved. Stayed at this camp till 9th of January and then boarded train for Oflag #64, 150 miles east of Berlin. (Our location at Stalag IVB was about ninety miles southwest of Berlin.)

Arrived at Szubin, Poland on 11th January and after turning in papers and being searched, we were led to auditorium to await call for delousing. First man I met was Maj. Hasselet, and then Lt. MacFadden. I was certainly relieved to find MacFadden alive. Found out that his whole detail was alive and that not one man was killed, as suspected.

Had plenty of cigarettes to smoke at last. Assigned barracks in 8A and started to feel like a human being again. Had hot water, cup each morning after apel (roll call). Made coffee or chocolate from Red Cross parcel. Also half bowl of soup at 1130 and potatoes or fish or canned meat at 530 after every apel. Red Cross parcel (Christmas box) issued on first day. Also razor, towel, soap, toothbrush, shower brush, comb, roll of toilet paper, and two thin blankets. Plum pudding, candy, nuts and turkey in parcel was delicious; ate every piece first night. Made some very delicious baskets. Issued Red Cross parcel following week and then started to hear about Red Army advance; all kinds of rumors. Issued another parcel and given orders to be ready to march back into Germany. Due to fractured wrist and left heel, I was sent to infirmary for examination by German doctor.

January 1945 – Pages 57 and 58 are missing due to censoring of written material with details on Russian Army liberation of Oflag #64 at Szubin.

On January 21, 1945, 1,471 POWs left Oflag #64 on foot, headed towards Oflag XIII-B at Hammelburg because of approaching Soviet troops. The 400 mile (640 km) march would take them until March 10 to complete. Captain Jarrett was one of approximately one hundred Americans, sick and medical personnel left behind, along with the men that had hidden in an old escape tunnel. Two days, later, on January 23, 1945, the camp was liberated by the Soviet 61st Army. Russia took the opportunity to barter with the Allies for the release of Russian prisoners of war in exchange for liberated Americans and British soldiers.

Jan 29, 1945 – at Leslaw

Jan 30, 1945 – at Kutno

Jan 31, 1945 –
Kowitsch (Army Headquarters) 31st arrived Warsaw and then Romber Tow' (Polish West Point) early morning of 1st and fed by Russian Army. Warsaw a ruined city with people buried in the streets. Graves all over the place and every house and building burned out completely.

Feb 22, 1945 –
Stayed at Rombertown till 22 Feb during which time I was put in charge of operations designed to keep the former plant for electricity and water in operation and also heating systems in main building and laundry and showers in other buildings. Work was very successful and was commended by Lt. Col Riggs, Division Engr 106th Division. Left for Odessa, Russia by train (box cars, 50), on 23rd Feb arrived at Odessa.

1 March 1945–
City badly damaged but people seem cheerful. Found out that exchange of ships, British transports would arrive with 7000 Russian prisoners about the 4th and we would leave for home on same ships about 8 March.

On maneuvers across Poland and Russian. I was Provost Marshall and saw each building and town burned and levelled to the ground.

7 March 1945–
After an early breakfast we departed from Odessa Barracks about 0800–column of companies; Americans with American flag and British with their flag. After a march of about four kilometers through a portion of the city completely destroyed, the harbor is somewhat bombed but being used by about eight large ships. (All water in Odessa is salt due to breakdown and destruction by Germans.)

On 8 March 1945, Capt. Jarrett boarded the Marenton Bay and headed for home.

Cpl. Samuel L. Miller
B Company, 103rd Engineer Battalion

Excerpt from an interview given in 2003 at the request of his
wife, Dorothy; pages 24-37. Contributed by his son, Hank Miller

We walked about a mile down the road and they put us in a fenced
in cow pasture. We were standing there and all of a sudden there
was a dogfight right above our heads, German and American
planes shooting at one another. One of the American planes got
hit and it was on fire. It was coming down right over our field, like
he was going to crash. Smoke was coming off it and the pilot must
have been dead, but the machine guns were still firing, killing
some of our men. The guy next to me got hit. I was fortunate I
survived that; I didn't get hit.

When we were finally taken out of that field, they put guards
on us and they marched us down the road ten miles. At the end
of the ten miles, there was a truck waiting with guards on it. They
took the guards that were handling us and put them on the truck
and they put fresh guards on us and they marched us another ten
miles. They made us carry their sacks and their packs; anything
they could relieve themselves of, they made us carry. It wasn't
enough that we had to carry ourselves; we had to carry their stuff.
After ten miles, they did the same thing again: there was a truck
waiting with fresh guards, they changed the guards and marched
us another ten miles. And they did that all the day of the 18th, and
into the night, through the night of December 20th. In three days
we'd been forced marched ninety miles.

Man I was tired. If you got exhausted and fell down, they
put a gun to your head and shot you. So I wasn't about to get
too tired and lay down. I kept going. I had no water. There was
water in the ditch, and I took my helmet and scooped some of
that water up. I had a little bottle of water purification tablets
so I put two tables in that water. I didn't know if there was urine
from the animals – I didn't know what was in that water, but I
drank it anyway. I didn't even try to taste it, I just drank it. I was
so thirsty.

And finally after ninety miles, we came to a railhead, and there was a train waiting with boxcars. They were built for eight horses or forty men – and they loaded sixty men in that car. We were jammed into that car like sardines; no sanitation, just a box. And we defecated in that box; everybody had dysentery. The odor was horrible. And we were in that car for five days under those conditions – no food, no water, and everybody sick as a dog.

We arrived in Koblenz, Germany, on the fifth day *[Christmas Day]*, and we were sitting in that box car at 11:30 in the evening. It was dark outside. There was a little opening in the box car up too high to look out of but it was starting to get light outside and so we boosted somebody to see what was going on outside. What was happening was parachutes were coming down with flares on them. The British were up there and the flares were marking their target; the railroad yard we were in. All of a sudden we heard five hundred pound bombs exploding – they were dropping them on that yard. One of them dropped fairly close to our train and the car we were in rocked on its springs. I had nowhere to go. I couldn't get close to the ground. I felt like I wanted to crawl inside my helmet.

The vibrations must have caused the door hinge to come undone as all of a sudden the door on our boxcar flew open. I jumped out of it right away and took off running when I hit the ground. I kept running and running, and I thought my lungs were going to burst. I kept running until I got out of the bombing area. When I stopped, I was trying to catch my breath and I realized I was in the deep forest. I had no water, no food, no ammunition, no weapons, nothing. I knew I was in real bad shape and had to do something about it. The weather was bitter cold and I didn't have sufficient clothing on. So I stood there in the forest trying to figure out what to do.

I knew the train had come east from Luxembourg all the way into Germany and if I was going to go in any direction, I would have to head west toward the Rhine River because I knew our troops were on the other side of the Rhine River. So I remembered to find the North Star to get my direction. I looked up through the trees and I found the Big Dipper because the two bottom stars on the Big Dipper are in line with the North Star. Once I found the North Star, I put it over my right should and I knew I was facing west. Then I'd looked for an object in my line of sight, like a big tree trunk, and I'd walk toward it. When I got to that point, I'd relocate myself by looking up through the trees to find the North Star again, I'd put it over my right should and I head west again. I kept doing that all night long.

Finally it was starting to be daybreak and I knew I was in trouble, being that it was so cold and it was snowing all around. There was a big bush that I saw so I crawled under the bush in the snow and I lay there quietly. I soon heard the Germans beating the bushes nearby, trying to find escaped prisoners, so I kept real quiet. It wasn't long before I was looking up the barrel of a gun and the German said "Herraus, herraus mit uns!" which means, "Get out, hands up!" So that's what I did; I got up and came out with my hands on my head, on my helmet, and they marched me all the way back to the train again.

When I got back to the train I found out thirty-five of our men had been killed that night. We were loaded back in the boxcar and we continued deeper into Germany, finally stopping at a town called Bad Orb, Germany. They unloaded us and marched us up the street and all the way up this hill. On the way up the hill I saw something that seemed out of place as there was this sign on the side of this building that said, "Trink Coca Cola."

When we neared the top of the hill, it levelled off like a plateau and you could see these buildings, which was the prison camp, Stalag IXB. We marched into the camp and the first thing they did was separate us. I was brought into this office where there was a German major and he interrogated me. He said, "I'm not trying to get any information from you; all I want to do is verify what I already have, so you won't be intimidated." But I knew to only answer him one way. Every time he asked me a question, I said, "I'm only authorized to give my name, rank and serial number, Sir." And so he'd try another way, another form of questioning.

The major spoke perfect English and he told me that he was educated at New York University (NYU) in the United States – that was where he got his education – and that he was a major in the German army. He kept trying to intimidate me, so when he realized he wasn't getting anywhere with me, he called the sergeant over and told him to take me outside and make me stand in the cold for a while at attention. And the sergeant took me outside and took off my jacket, and made me stand in my shirt in the bitter cold. Boy, my hands were blue. I couldn't move; I had to stand at attention. And the weather was brutal. It was the worst winter they had in Germany in fifty years, bitter cold. And after about an hour, he brought me back in and I could hardly move.

The officer started to interrogate me some more. He said, "What's your religion?" The guys warned me, "Don't tell them you're Jewish." So I said, "I'm Protestant." I had thrown my dog tags away when we were breaking up our equipment in Hosingen so he had no way of knowing if I was lying so he let it go at that. He didn't go any farther with it. The only time I've ever denied my religion was at this point in time. It was a question of survival. And after several more tries, he finally told the sergeant, "Take him back to the barracks."

They finally gave us our dinner that day – a gourmet dinner which was just a small piece of black bread, about two inches across, and some ersatz tea. I don't know what it was made out of but it was called ersatz tea; the bark of some tree or something. Anyway, that was dinner, the only food we got. And all the meals in the camp were about the same. I started to lose weight right away.

I only stayed in Stalag IXB until January 25, 1945. They singled me out because I was a corporal; I was a non-commissioned officer. In mid-January, they sent me along with 1274 other non-comms to Stalag 9A at Ziegenhain, Germany where I would stay the rest of the three months that I was in prison. I lost 55 pounds during my four months in captivity.

They didn't treat non-commissioned officers much better than privates. We got a little food once a day. Basically, it was a piece of bread and some ersatz tea, whatever ersatz tea was, and makeshift something or other, from the bark of the tree or something.

[Prisoners were often given barely edible bread made with 20%–50% sawdust.]

There was no meat. If they gave us any kind of food, it was like a soup made out of the waste they didn't eat. No nourishment; it was very weak and watery. We didn't get much of it or get it often. We were all suffering from malnutrition. When I came home, I had to reorient myself with food; I couldn't eat right away. It took me a while before I could eat food again.

By the time my prison days were over, I weighed 118 pounds, skinny as a rail like everybody else. My biggest fear while I was a prisoner was disease because guys were dying. We didn't know what from, but guys were dying from all kinds of ailments. I didn't want to get sick and die. That was frightening more than anything, to survive.

The barracks were very cold – no heat, no sanitation. Wooden buildings with only tar paper covering the boards. The floors were wooden with one inch cracks between the boards. There weren't enough bunks for everybody so many of us had to sleep on the floor. I mean, it was cold. The cold air would come up between those boards and hit you in the back, and then your back would ache. You couldn't sleep; it was terrible, you were shivering cold. They had a hole outside; you had to go outside if you had to urinate, or defecate, or whatever you were going to do. You had to straddle over a pit.

We had a barracks sergeant we called Fritz, who was sadistic. He used to come through the barracks in the morning to wake you up and he'd give you a boot in the back. He kicked anybody lying on the floor, including me, and he'd say, "Herraus, herraus!" If that wasn't bad enough, he'd order everybody outside in the bitter cold – we didn't have sufficient clothing. So he would line us up, four abreast, and he'd go down the columns, down the rows, and he would count: "Eins, zwei, drei, vier, funf," and after he got to number five or six, he would play like he forgot his count and he would start all over again. He was sadistic and so he did this half a dozen times, just to keep us out there in the cold. We had no choice but to put up with it until we were liberated.

We spent a lot of our time talking about food trying to pass the time. We talked about all different kinds of foods that we liked – all different meats and how to prepare fish – everything pertaining to food. We were starving and it was on our minds constantly. We were hungry all the time.

Two of our guys tried to escape – one of them Smitty and another guy, Sam Jones. Sam was a black guy, not from our company; from a black unit. Sam Jones and Smitty were motorcycle riders. There was an opening on the outside of the fence on the other side of the latrine so they went down into the shed, climbed in the toilets and they walked through it and got out through the opening in the far wall. They must have smelled real bad, covered in shit. Once outside they jumped into the ditch the guards were to use in case the camp was attacked and they worked their way out to the fence. Jones was spotted and got hit by a large shotgun while in the ditch but Smitty got under the fence and out and escaped temporarily but got caught.

The only escape I ever made was from the train – and I got caught the next morning. That was a bitter experience. We were looking for every possibility to escape, but were unable to do it.

It was early April when a spy plane flew over our camp one day, an artillery spy plane that looked like a Piper Cub. We were all outside walking around in the fenced in field for exercise when we spotted that plane up there and one of the guys said, "Hey let's give them a signal! Take your shirts off!" And we all took our shirts off and laid them on the ground, and we spelled "American POW's" with our shirts. The plane wiggled his wings so we saw that he recognized us and we knew we'd been found. Anyway, the next day, an American Armored Division came in. The Germans guards had run off, including Fritz, but they were soon captured and brought back to our camp as our prisoners.

The tanks came right through the fence, and the guys in the tanks opened the hatch, and they were throwing whatever food they had to us. It was wild. Boy, we were all smiles. We knew we had it made then. As more troops arrived, they brought in equipment and we were kept there in like a hospital for twelve days. They turned the whole place into a hospital, with doctors and everything, because they couldn't take us back yet, because all our troops were moving, chasing the Germans through that area, pushing them further into Germany. But we were liberated; we were in American hands.

After twelve days they put us on trucks and they took us to the airport in Wiesen, Germany where they had C47's waiting for us. They loaded twenty-five guys to a plane and we took off to Le Havre, France, where we landed at a camp called Lucky Strike. We were at Camp Lucky Strike for about two weeks. They had us in a hospital, and the nurses were treating us wonderfully, and would give us good food but I couldn't eat it. I would eat it and throw it up; my stomach wouldn't hold food. It took me a long time before I could retain the food there. Even once I was home.

We then boarded a ship in LeHavre headed for the States. There was a section of that ship where they had war brides and babies that were going to America. They were roped off, and we weren't allowed in that area. And the trip back was not like the trip across as the trip across was stormy weather and took three weeks. We came back in the spring time and it was a five day crossing. We landed on May 5, 1945. The trip back was just as smooth as it could be – it was a very pleasant trip back. The ship landed in New York, around the Statue of Liberty. Boy that was some sight. Everybody ran to the side of the ship where the Statue of Liberty was and the ship listed forty-five degrees. The Captain came over the PA system and said, "Everybody to the starboard side!" And we all went to the other side of the ship. I was standing on the rail, with my arms around an upright so I wouldn't fall in. What a sight that was – Manhattan Island and the Statue of Liberty. We finally made our way into New York Harbor and we docked at 45th Street in Manhattan. It took all day to unload the ship with troops coming off all day. I didn't get off the ship until almost dark. I don't know what time it was in the evening but the Red Cross was still selling coffee and doughnuts for twenty-five cents.

Cpl. John M. Putz
T/5 Surgical Technician, 103rd Medical Battalion, assigned to Company B, 103rd Engineer Battalion

Contributed by his son, Jim Putz

Born and raised in Cincinnati, Ohio, Cpl. John Putz had been assigned to the 103rd Engineer Battalion since he'd left for Europe on New Year's Day 1944. He'd tended the sick and wounded through many bloody battle since landing on Omaha Beach just three days after the D-Day invasion, initiated early about the cold reality of war with the blood and body parts of fallen soldiers still floating in the water. The battle weary medic had seen it all by the time the 28th Infantry Division was relieved in the Hürtgen Forest but watching his best friend, Lieutenant Slobodzian lying there wounded and in shock, knowing that he could do little to save him, was more than he could take. He made a request to Captain Jarrett to allow him to go for help.

Unarmed and wearing Red Cross arm bands, Putz and Pfc Frank Smith, who had volunteered to go with him, left Hosingen on foot at 0650 on December 18, 1944 in an attempt to try and slip through the German lines to get blood plasma and a medical officer for the wounded in the town. They had made it less than a mile before they were spotted and captured by a German patrol. Covered in blood from tending to the wounded, the Germans initially thought Putz was the one badly wounded and laughed when they realized that was not the case. Although he spoke fluent German, he did not let on that he understood what the soldiers were talking about.

It wasn't long before the GIs in Hosingen raised the white flag of surrender later that morning and Putz and Smith most likely were reunited with their Engineer unit while waiting for the Germans to decide what to do with them. The few stories that Putz shared with his family later in life are very similar to stories told by the other veterans that fought in Hosingen and that waited to be sent to the camps.

Putz noted the Germans would take either the Americans rubber boots that covered their army boots or the army boots themselves. Putz opted to give up his rubber boots. Other that gave up their army boots quickly regretted their decision.

Once the group left Hosingen, they were marched for three days in the snow and freezing temperatures, which resulted in Putz' toes being frozen. He recalled, "The treatment wasn't so hot, they marched us through the streets and the women and children booed and spit on us."

During the march one of the German soldiers, in perfect English said, "You American pigs want to see Berlin so bad, now you're going to". This struck Cpl. Putz as funny and he laughed out loud but he quickly regretted the impulse as the guard reacted by striking him hard with his rifle butt between his shoulder blades. Putz never made that mistake again.

After the third day, they were loaded into box cars where they spent the next week. On Christmas Eve, the American planes bombed the marshalling yard where their train was. Somehow the POWs in Putz' box car were able to get a man out to open the box car doors. Putz saw a German soldier running and followed him into a shelter. When the raid ended, they came out of the shelter and Putz observed that their train had not been damaged. After all the POWs were rounded up and loaded back into the boxcar, the train left for Stalag IVB at Mühlberg.

When Putz arrived at the camp, he was quickly befriended by an Irish soldier who had been in captivity for a while. He taught Putz not to sit around. He told him he should get up every day, shave and move. Putz confided in him that he spoke German and he told him never to let anyone know that as anytime something would go wrong, they would come to the men who spoke German first so it was better to avoid those volatile situations.

The Mühlberg camp had quickly become overcrowded so on January 9, 1945, approximately 3000 GIs that had just arrived after their capture on the frontlines, once again were loaded into boxcars. Many were moved to Oflag #64 near Szubin, Poland. Putz remained at Mühlberg.

Stalag IVB was made up of many nationalities. Food was scarce and many of the barracks pooled their rations. According to Putz, one of the British prisoners was suspected of stealing food from the pooled rations in their barracks so they set a trap for him and he got caught. The English prisoners formed a circle and beat the man to death. After Putz witnessed this, he said he hated the English more than the Germans.

There were also Russians in another area of the camp. Putz observed that the Russians were treated worse than the other prisoners. Putz recalled that one day hunger got the better of one of them and the starving man ran after a truck load of potatoes. The Germans shot him and left him lying where he fell. Putz said that when someone was shot or killed in the camp, they were left in the latrines as an example for the others to not make the same mistake.

Putz realized that hunger was the most miserable feeling he'd ever had and he often dreamed of home and his mom's good cooking.

Meanwhile back home, his mom and three sisters anxiously awaited for news from him as they had heard nothing since before the Battle of the Bulge had begun. Finally on April 3, 1945, his parents received a Western Union telegram from the War Department notifying them of their son's MIA status. It was soon followed up on April 19 with a telegram informing them that he had been identified as a POW in one of the German camps. By this time, the war was already close to being over in Europe so they were hopeful he would be returned home to them soon.

On April 23, 1945 Putz and the other POWs woke to discover that all the Germans guards had left the camp as the Red Army was very close by. In fact, they were liberated by a single Russian soldier that rode into camp on a white horse. Corporal Putz didn't want to be there when the rest of the Russian Army showed up so he and two other men cut through the wire fence and left on their own. They found two bicycles and the three men rode the two bikes in search of a place to cross the Elbe River to reach the American lines, which they found out was just to the west of the camp. While riding they came across an elderly German man on a bike. For the first time, in the war, Putz spoke German to the old man, asking how they could get across the river. After he told them, they forced him to give them his bike and they rode off. Putz told his son many years later that taking that man's bike was the only regret he had in the war.

On April 25, 1945, U.S. and Soviet troops met at the Elbe River in Germany, near Mühlberg and Cpl. Putz and his two friends were soon freed by the American forces.

On April 28, 1945 Putz' mother received a letter signed by three of Putz's buddies from the Mühlberg POW camp – Alvin Byrnes, Robert A Vogt, and Julian Verfaillie – letting her know that John had been liberated by the U.S. Army and that he was in good health and feeling fine. They, however, were not with him. The men must have made a pack to contact each other's families when they were liberated to make sure their families knew what had happened to them.

On May 12 Putz sent a Western Union telegram to his Mom for Mother's Day informing her that he was doing well and was waiting in Paris for a convoy of ships from England to arrive that could take the impatient POWs home. He confided in his mom he was tired of blood, war, bombing and strafing and that some of his best buddies had gone crazy as a result of intensive battle fatigue.

Putz finally made it back to the states on June 4, 1945. Before his Honorable Discharge, he was promoted to Technical Sargent, 4th Grade, and among the many medals he was awarded, were three Bronze Stars. Other mementos he would forever carry with him were the damage to his feet, which he would suffer from the rest of his life, and horrific nightmares that would terrorize his sleep.

CHAPTER 9

German POW Camps Where Most of the GIs from Hosingen Were Held

Once Hitler began his invasion of Poland in 1939, the Wehrmacht began to establish numerous prisoner of war camps, separating officers and enlisted men, according to the Geneva Convention. Stalags were meant for non-commissioned personnel, and Oflag were established for officers. By 1944 there were over 250 camps spread across Eastern and Western Europe. Transit camps, such as Bad Orb's Stalag IXB was intended to be, were set up close to the front line to enable the Nazis to easily transfer POWs to other camps within German held territories. Prisoners of war from all nations occupied, or which fought against the German Army, were held captive at Stalags and frequently deployed in forced labour.

Stalag IXB at Bad Orb, Germany
The first Americans had arrived at Stalag IXB on December 25, 1944 after being captured in the Battle of the Bulge. Stalag IXB was supposed to be used to classify POWs and send them to regular camps but the sudden and massive intake of Allied prisoners in December and January did not allow this to happen. Instead, most privates and Pfcs never left. Officers were kept until January 10

when they left for Oflag XIIIB at Hammelburg, Germany and 1275 NCO's were transferred on January 25 to Stalag IXA, Ziegenhain.

However, in mid-January 1945 before the non-commissioned officers left, the camp commandant was given a quota of three hundred fifty prisoner to fill for "special detail" so during the daily line-up, all Jewish prisoners were ordered to step forward. The GIs' dog tags designated their religious affiliation so all of them had gone into battle with dog tags bearing an "H" for Hebrew. Some had already disposed of them when they were captured but not all of them. Word ran through the ranks not to move. The non-Jews told their Jewish comrades they would stand with them. The commandant gave the Jewish GIs until six the next morning to identify themselves. The prisoners were also told that if they discovered any Jews in the barracks after twenty-four hours, they would be shot immediately, as would anyone trying to hide or protect them.

American Jewish soldiers had to decide what to do. After several hours standing in the freezing cold weather, approximately one hundred thirty Jews came forward. To fill out the quota, approximately fifty non-Jewish NCOs from the group were selected, along with those GIs that were considered troublemakers, those the Germans thought looked Jewish or names sounded Jewish and rest were others chosen at random. The Jewish American soldiers were then segregated and placed into separate barracks until the group left Bad Orb on February 8, 1945 headed for Berga Am Elster slave labor camp.

It is unknown whether any of the men from the 110th Infantry Regiment, 28th Infantry Division, who fought in Hosingen and were sent to Stalag IXB were subsequently sent to Berga; however, Cpl. Sam Miller from Company B, 103rd Engineer battalion was one of the Jewish American soldiers that his comrades protected.

On April 2, 1945, Stalag IXB at Bad-Orb, Germany was liberated by a task force comprising the 2nd Battalion, 114th Regiment, U.S. 44th Infantry Division, reinforced with light tanks and armored cars from the 106th Cavalry Group and 776th Tank Destroyer

Battalion. The raid release 6,000 Allied soldiers, 3,364 of which were Americans. The liberators cried at the sight of thousands of emaciated soldiers, some having lost up to 40% their body weight since capture.

The overall condition of Stalag IXB was terrible and it was considered one of the worst German POW camps that held American prisoners. POW doctors and medics ran a hospital in the camp and did the best they could for men needing medical attention, but their supplies and equipment were limited. The International Red Cross was allowed access to the camp but it had little impact on improving the living conditions for the prisoners. Unfortunately for too many POWs, Stalag IXB became a death camp. By the time the prisoners reached the camp, many were already rundown and suffering from unpleasant intestinal conditions. Lack of proper food, medical care, and sanitary conditions wreaked havoc on the POW population and some of the barracks displayed handmade crosses along the outside wall, bearing the names of the POWs who did not survive.

Hygiene was a major problem. The prisoners shared only three very primitive latrine houses and three latrine trenches. At night, the POWs were required to use the one equally primitive latrine in each room of the barracks.

Each barrack had two large rooms fitted with only one small stove meant for heating the space. Many of the rooms had broken windows and the wood or cardboard covering the holes did little to keep the below-freezing temperature outdoors where it belonged. For the most part, the size and poor condition of the stoves really didn't matter, as the coal or wood provided to the prisoners each day produced only a few hours of heat. Lighting was also minimal as each room had only one very dim light bulb to illuminate the entire space during the long winter nights. Lights-out was at 7:30 p.m.

Berga Am Elster – 12 km south of Gera, Germany
Berga Am Elster was a slave labor camp. Together with inmates of the Buchenwald concentration camp, the 350 men that arrived

from Stalag IXB in mid-February 1945 were put to work digging seventeen tunnels for an underground ammunition factory. The Germans would dynamite the slate loose and then the prisoners would be forced back into the mine shafts before the dust could settle to break up the rock and shovel into mining cars. As a result of the inhumane conditions, malnutrition and cold, as well as beatings by brutal civilian overseers, forty-seven prisoners died.

Three hundred surviving American prisoners were marched out of the camp on April 4, 1945 as American troops approached. After a two and a half week forced march, they were finally liberated. During this march another thirty-six Americans died. The fatality rate in Berga, including the march, was the highest of any camp where American POWs were held—nearly twenty percent—and the seventy to seventy-three men who were killed represented approximately six percent of all Americans who perished as POWs during World War II.

Stalag IVB at Mühlberg, Germany
Located on the Elbe River approximately 80 km northwest of Dresden, Stalag IVB at Mühlberg, Germany was one of the largest German prisoner of war camps, operating from 1939-1945. Designed for about 16,000 soldiers, it sometimes held more than 30,000. Approximately 300,000 prisoners from over 33 nations passed through the camp. Due to the bad conditions and maltreatment by the guards about 3,000, most of them Soviet POWs, died there.

The Soviet Union had not signed the Geneva Convention, so as a consequence, the Germans did not allow Soviet POWs to have the often lifesaving Red Cross parcels, in contrast to the treatment of prisoners from other countries.

At the end of December 1944, a massive influx of 7,500 Americans arrived from the Battle of the Bulge instantly putting the camp over capacity. On January 9, 1945, over 3,000 POWs were soon transferred to other camps, including both Stalag VIII-A near

Görlitz and Oflag #64 near Szubin, Poland. On April 23, 1945 the Red Army liberated the camp.

Oflag XIIIB at Hammelburg, Germany
This camp was later made light of by Hollywood in the 1960's television series "Hogan's Heroes".

The POW camp at Hammelburg was quite old and it had been housing Serbian prisoners since 1941. After the capture of so many Allied officers during the Battle of the Bulge, the Germans split this camp into two sections and hastily made some upgrades to the Allied side to make the buildings liveable, although the conditions were still far below acceptable standards. The Serbians were kept in Oflag XIIIA and Allied officers in Oflag XIIIB. In the Allied compound, each of the seven stone barracks had five rooms and was set up with enough stacks of bunk beds to house 200 men—forty per room.

Despite the winter of 1944-1945 being one of the coldest on record in Germany and due to the fuel shortage, the Germans rationed the coal for each stove at a rate of just forty-eight 5-x-3–x-3–inch briquettes per three days, which did little to warm the rooms. It was up to the POWs to ration their heat supply. Although some officers were allowed to search for wood outside the camp to supplement their coal, it still was not enough to keep the soldiers warm. As a result, the barrack temperature averaged about twenty degrees Fahrenheit throughout most of the winter, even though there were 200 bodies in each one.

There were no washrooms and no hot water. The officers had to carry water from the kitchen faucets to the washbasins in each room. Dysentery was a major concern due to the unsterile conditions and lack of hot water to sterilize the kitchen utensils, further weakening many men in the camp.

Ventilation and daylight were adequate in the barracks but each room contained only two 15-watt drop light bulbs to see by once the sun went down.

Within a month after their arrival at Oflag XIIIB, the POWs were allowed to send their first cards home to their families. The camp never received any incoming mail so the POWs never knew if their letters were ever received by their loved ones.

In early March, Colonel Goode and the other evacuees from Oflag 64 in Poland arrived after enduring a 345 mile, ten-week forced march through the often sub-zero winter weather.

Tension between the American POWs and German personnel was ongoing and treatment of the prisoners by the guards was only fair, at best. As a result, three POWs were shot and killed during their two and half months in captivity for no or frivolous reasons.

The only item that was provided in enough quantity during captivity was water. Initially, the men in the camp were given a diet of 1,700 calories a day, but as supplies ran low and the camp population increased, food rations were cut to less than 1,100 calories a day. There were no dairy products, nuts, fish, fruits, grain products, or rice. POWs received just enough broth, with the occasional piece of meat or vegetable, and bread to keep them alive.

The normal daily menu consisted of one-tenth of a loaf of bread, one cup of ersatz coffee, one bowl of barley soup, and one serving of a vegetable per day. About three times a week a small piece of margarine was issued, and occasionally a tablespoon of sugar. Toward the end of March, many officers were in a dangerous condition due to malnutrition and the senior medical officer credited the generosity of the Serbian officers from Oflag XIIIA and the sharing of approximately 1,800 Red Cross packages over the three-month period with the saving of many American lives.

The main topic of conversation was often food, favorite recipes their moms and wives made, and the best restaurants and favorite items on the menu.

The POWs developed their own way of making sure the bread was equally divided for each meal. Each day a different man in each group was responsible for slicing the bread into portions as equal as possible. Crude measuring tools were created and the man who sliced the bread was the last man to get his piece. The process usually took an hour and no bread crumbs were ever brushed onto the floor. Every last morsel was consumed. A rare piece of meat or vegetable in the soup was always cherished and worth bragging about.

After Task Force Baum liberated the camp on March 27, 1945 and the majority of the POWs were either killed or recaptured and moved to other POW camps, only seventy-five American's remained that were in the camp hospital and not healthy enough to travel. Less than one week later, the camp was liberated by Combat Command B of the U.S. 14th Armored Division on April 6, 1945.

Stalag VIIIA at Gorlitz, Germany
Built in the 1930's by Hitler Youth, the camp at Gorlitz, Germany – located 50 miles east of Dresden – was converted into Stalag VIIIA when Hitler began his assault on Poland. The camp had 56 barrack that could each house 500 men. By June 1940, there were 15,000 Polish prisoners that would ultimately be shipped to be used as labourers. By December 1944 the delivery of Red Cross parcels became increasingly scarce until their delivery ceased altogether. The Russian prisoners had no Red Cross organization to support them and so the British shared with them what they could spare from their parcels. By the end of the month, 1,800 US troops arrived from the frontlines but despite the British sharing what they could, there were not near enough to go around.

As the Russian Army continued its advance from the east through German occupied territory, German prisoner camps were evacuated and its occupants forced to march westwards. By February 14, 1945, the Russians were close enough that their artillery could be heard within the camp so the evacuation of Stalag VIIIA began with a large group of US soldiers, which included Hosingen medics, T/4 Wayne Erickson and Sgt. George Mc Knight, S/Sgt. William Freeman, as well as 140 British soldiers. The next day, another 1,200 headed west on foot. Between 700-800 sick prisoners followed on February 17th, headed for Stalag

XIB. However, a few prisoners hid themselves to await the arrival of the Russians.

16,000 Russian prisoners died from disease or malnutrition at Görlitz, and they were buried in mass graves at the rear of the camp.

Oflag 64 at Szubin, Poland

On June 6, 1943, American officers captured in the North Africa Campaign in Tunisia arrived at the camp, included General Patton's son-in-law, Lt. Col. John Waters,

Shortly after their arrival, the American's formed an escape committee and started digging a tunnel which would take them outside the barbed wire fence. It was only a few months later that they received word that about the disastrous escape attempt at Stalag Luft III at Nuremburg, which resulted in the execution of fifty American prisoners, halting their efforts.

Senior American officers captured in the D-Day Invasion joined them in June 1944, followed by officers captured during the Battle of the Bulge in December. By January 21, 1945, there were 1,471 prisoners. Approaching Soviet troops forced the evacuation of all POWs so on January 21, 1945, led by Lieutenant Colonel Paul Goode, all men capable of walking were marched out, en route to Hammelburg's Oflag XIIIB. Approximately two hundred prisoners would escape from the marching column to return to the camp to await the Soviet troops.

Two days, later, on January 23, 1945, the Soviet 61st Army liberated the camp. Capt. William Jarrett, B Company, 103rd Engineer Battalion was among the hundred sick and wounded Americans and medical personnel that had been left behind. There were also a few prisoners that opted to take their chances with the Russians and had hidden in the old escape tunnel.

The column did not reach Oflag XIIIB at Hammelburg until March 10, having marched nearly 400 miles (640 km) during the most severe winter on record. Too weak to march, almost 400 men fell along the way or escaped. A number were shot.

Those that had stayed at the camp and were liberated by the Red Army were temporarily held hostage by the Soviets in exchange for Soviet POWs held behind Allied lines. They were later transported by train to Odessa on February 23. After an exchange of prisoners, they boarded ships headed for the United States on March 8, 1945. Capt. Jarrett boarded the Marenton Bay and others headed for home on the New Zealand ship, HMNZS.

Stalag IXA at Ziegenhain, Germany
Opened in 1939, Stalag IXA at Ziegenhain incarcerated prisoners from all European countries at war with Germany, especially Soviet prisoners of war. By 1944, the camp had grown to over 50,000 prisoners; the majority deployed in the camp's over 3,000 labour commandos, from manufacturing weapons and ammunition to road, construction and field labor. Soviet prisoners of war and Italians, who were considered traitors, were in a separate part of the camp in which the conditions were much harsher than those of other prisoner groups. Numerous executions took place in the labour commandos of Stalag IXA. Two nearby cemeteries are filled with victims of Nazi abuse.

On January 25, 1945, 1275 American non-commissioned officers captured in the Battle of the Bulge arrived from Stalag IXB, including Cpl. Sam Miller and Cpl. George Imhof from B Company, 103rd Engineers and K Company, Sgt. Lloyd Everson.

Conditions were horrible and prison guards were sadistic and mean.

On April 1, 1945, an artillery spy plane flew over the camp and Sam Miller and the other prisoners in the open field removed their shirts and spelled out "American POWs". The next day the U.S. 6th Armored Division liberated the 5000 prisoners held in the camp, 1271 of which were Americans. The Germans guards that had tried to slip away were soon captured and brought back to the camp where the prisoners sought revenge for months of abuse and harsh punishment awaited them.

War correspondent Thorburn Wiant was appalled at what he witnessed and reported the day after the camp was liberated, *Americans Endure Diabolical Treatment At Hands Of Nazis* and told the American public that their boys looked like scarecrows, each having lost 25 to 40 pounds.

More equipment, troops and doctors arrived and the former POWs were kept in the camp turned hospital for twelve days as the troops were chasing the Germans through that area.

After twelve days, the GIs were put on trucks and transported to the airport in Wiesen, Germany where they had C47's waiting to take them to Camp Lucky Strike at Le Havre, France, where they remained for about two weeks before being shipped home.

CHAPTER 10

Unit Recognition

The Battle of the Bulge lasted from December 16, 1944, through January 28, 1945, and has become known as the greatest battle ever fought by the United States Army. It involved more than a million men between the German and Allied forces (600,000 Germans, 500,000 Americans, and 55,000 British).

It is estimated that over 19,000 Americans soldiers died during the Battle of the Bulge and another 23,000 were captured. However, due to the significant destruction of records following the German attacks, exact numbers will never be known. Approximately 100,000 German soldiers were killed, wounded, or captured during the six-week period.

The National Archives WWII POW database (http://aad. archives.gov/aad/) on the 110th Infantry Regiment lists 1,570 men who were reported as MIA/POW during December 20-25, 1944. Twenty-six of these men died while prisoners.

By the end of January 1945, several war correspondents had already published a number of articles recognizing the contributions the 110th Infantry Regiment during the first few days of the Battle of the Bulge–provided in their entirety in *Appendix A*.

Ironically, war correspondent Ivan H. Peterman, with the *The Philadelphia Inquirer*, was already suspicious that the 110th was going to take the fall for their commanders' failure of battle command as he wrote in the final paragraph in his January 25 article, *28th Stood Up Against Big Odds.*

> *"It is because some of our so-called "experts" sometimes place blame before knowing the facts, that outfits like the 28th and the 106th must take blame that is not their fault. I will have more to say of this when discussing what happened to these divisions. For the present I save the foregoing chronology just for itself in the case of the 109th, but almost obliterated 110th, 109th and the equally able 112th Infantry Regiment."*

In February 1945, Col. Hurley E. Fuller sent a letter to Maj. Gen. Norman D. Cota after his POW camp in Poland had been liberated by the advancing Russians, recommending his unit (the 110th) for a War Department Citation for its critical defense of the Ardennes region against the German assault during December 16-18, 1944. General Cota did not act on this recommendation, but it reflects Colonel Fuller's highest regards for the men in his unit:

> *General, I want you to know that Regimental Combat Team 110 fought a magnificent fight in trying to halt the German Advance. We went down and carried out your orders to the letter to "hold at all cost." For that reason, I feel that the following units of Regimental Combat Team 110 are deserving of a War Department Citation, and I so recommend it to you:*
>
> * *110th Infantry, Commanded by Col. Hurley E. Fuller, Inf.*
> * *109th FA Bn, Commanded by Lt. Col. Robert E. Ewing, FA.*
> * *Co B 103rd Engr Bn, Commanded by Captain Jarrett.*
>
> *For your information, in preparing a citation for these units, the following facts are submitted. These units were holding approximately 15 miles of front opposite the Siegfried Line in Luxemburg when the German offensive started on December 16, 1944. Although attacked by two panzer divisions, and one Infantry division these units blocked the advance of this superior hostile force*

for three days along its main axis of advance, thus affording time for the movement of reserves to prevent a disastrous breakthrough by the enemy.

After the first two days of fighting, all elements of the 110th Infantry and Company B, 103d Engr Combat Battalion were completely surrounded. These units continued to fight stubbornly in place, until their ammunition was exhausted, and they were virtually annihilated before they were completely overwhelmed by superior forces of tanks and armored infantry.

There have been several formal applications since the end of WWII to the Secretary of the Army to acknowledge the accomplishments of the 110th Infantry Regiment and award them the Distinguished Unit Citation, now referred to as the Presidential Unit Citation, however, all attempts have been unsuccessful.

Despite that fact, the dedication of the 110th Infantry Regiment to accomplish its "Hold at all costs" order, has caught the attention of many military experts, authors and historians who are passionate about telling their story. The 110th will not remain the unsung heroes of WWII's Battle of the Bulge.

While Peter Elstob's 1971 book, *Hitler's Last Offensive—The Full Story of the Battle of the Ardennes* touches upon many key points in regards to the battle, it is Robert F. Phillips' classic, *To Save Bastogne*, published in 1983, that is the first book to drill down and take an in-depth personal perspective of what happened to and the accomplishments of the 28th Infantry Division those critical first few days of the Battle of the Bulge.

WWII 110th Infantry Regiment veteran, military historian and author, Robert F. Phillips, has dedicated much of his life to researching, interviewing and collecting stories from the men of the 110th Infantry Regiment as well as in-depth research in Luxembourg, Belgium and Germany, interviewing local towns people and WWII experts and historians, and traveling the area in search of the truth. He has unselfishly shared much with fellow authors hoping to continue on where his story left off.

Other well researched books worth reading on the subject include:

- *A Time for Trumpets—The Untold Story of the Battle of the Bulge* by Charles B. MacDonald; 1985
- *Hitler's Last Gamble—The Battle of the Bulge, December 1944-January 1945* by Trevor N. Dupuy, David L Bongard, and Richard C. Anderson, Jr.; 1994
- *The Malmédy Massacre* by John M. Bauserman; 1995
- *Against the Panzers, United States Infantry versus German Tanks, 1944-1945* by Allyn R. Vannoy and Jay Karamales; 2006
- *Alamo in the Ardennes—The Untold Story of the American Soldiers Who Made the Defense of Bastogne Possible* by John C. McManus; 2008
- *Guard Wars: The 28th Infantry Division in World War II* by Michael E. Weaver; 2010
- *Unforgettable: The Biography of Capt. Thomas J. Flynn* by Alice M. Flynn; 2011
- *No Silent Night—The Christmas Battle for Bastogne* by Leo Barron and Don Cygan; 2012

Author John McManus, a University of Missouri history professor, in *Alamo in the Ardennes: The Untold Story of the American Soldiers Who Made the Defense of Bastogne Possible*, agrees that the defense by the 28th Infantry Division, especially the 110th and 112th regiment, were particularly critical to the successful defense of Bastogne.

> *The Germans' failure to occupy this strategic location (Bastogne) was the work of two distinct groups of American soldiers. History has largely focused on the group that endured the siege from the evening of December 20 through December 26. Most of the siege defenders were members of the 101st Airborne Division, and they fought with tenacity and resolve. But I would argue that the contribution of another group—those who fought east of Bastogne and in its outskirts from December 16 through December 20—were every bit as vital and noteworthy. Some of these men were from the*

101ˢᵗ Airborne Division, but the vast majority were not. Most were members of the 28ᵗʰ Division, CCR of the 9ᵗʰ Armored or CCB of the 10ᵗʰ Armored. These soldiers fought a desperate delaying action. They were outnumbered and outgunned. In some cases, the odds were ten-to-one against them. They absorbed the brunt of Hitler's last-ditch gamble in the west.

They fought in what I term the Bastogne corridor, the area roughly along the 25-mile front that the 28ᵗʰ Infantry Division held when the battle began. This front stretched from Lutzkampen in the north all along the Luxembourg side of the Our River, through such towns as Heinerscheid, Marnach, and Hosingen, down the Bettendorf and Reisdorf. The most vital objectives were in the sectors held by the 110ᵗʰ and 112ᵗʰ Infantry Regiments.

Many more stories have been written and tributes paid to the men of the 110ᵗʰ Infantry Regiment for their role in the Battle of the Bulge, but excerpts from several that specifically acknowledge the role of K Company are highlighted below.

"Even the commander of the XLVII Panzer Corps, General von Lüttwitz, paid grudging respect to the Hosingen defenders. After the war, he wrote:

The first resistance of the U.S. 28ᵗʰ Infantry Division was broken in a surprisingly short time, but then, after having overcome the first shock, they fought excellently. Again and again, at points well chosen, they put themselves in front of our advancing columns. A special mention must be made of the defenders of Hosingen. We were able to break the resistance in Hosingen only after the 78ᵗʰ Grenadier Regt of the 26ᵗʰ VGD had arrived on December 17. After Hosingen was taken, the enemy resistance paralyzed considerably. Summing up, I must point out that the resistance of the U.S. 28ᵗʰ Infantry Division was altogether more stubborn than I had expected.[19]

---

19 Vannoy, 214.

In the Epilogue to *Against the Panzers, United States Infantry versus German Tanks, 1944-1945*, authors Allyn R. Vannoy and Jay Karamales also wrote:

> *The defense of Hosingen was a small part of the stand of the 28th Division in front of Bastogne. Other small units clung tenaciously to other small towns at places like Marnach, Heinerscheid, Weiler, Hoscheid, Holzthum, Consthum, Clervaux, and Wiltz. All of these towns fell to the German eventually, but one town the Americans did hold—Bastogne. The failure of the 5th Panzer Army to take this vital crossroads sealed the failure of the Ardennes offensive. And yet, the defense of Bastogne would never have happened had not small garrisons like Company K of the 110th Infantry Regiment and Company B of the 103rd Engineer Combat Battalion held on to towns like Hosingen.*

British Army Training Films

Of particular interest is the fact that the British Army made two military training films in 1980 on the 28th Infantry Division's defensive tactics the first two weeks of the Battle of the Bulge, which are part of the Churchill War Rooms Collection Department at the British Imperial War Museum. Part 2 of 3 films is dedicated to the accomplishments of the 110th Infantry Regiment.

> *The Ardennes Offensive Part 2: Hold At All Costs*
> *The Ardennes Offensive Part 3: Forget Bastogne–Head for the Meuse*
>
> *Made by: Ministry of Defence (Production sponsor) 1980*
>
> *A historical record of the last German Offensive in WWII known as the "Battle of the Bulge". Parts 2 and 3 concentrate on the most dangerous German thrust and show how the heavily outnumbered Americans fought desperately for 2 weeks to delay the advance until a successful counter attack could be mounted. The fog of war, the*

values of leadership and how small but determined groups of men can delay heavy armored attacks are vividly portrayed.

Depicted in a Painting

There is a well-known painting by James Dietz, called "Hold to the Last Round," that depicts the town of Hosingen ablaze while K Company and B Company Engineers fight on. The description of the painting found at http://www.jamesdietz.com, vividly describes the battle in Hosingen:

The 28th Division in the Defense of Hosingen, Luxembourg

On December 16, 1944, began the "Battle of the Bulge," considered by many, including Sir Winston Churchill, as the greatest battle ever fought by the American Army. The 28th Division was positioned in the very center of the German attack, just west of the Our River in a front of about 25 miles. Since this was supposed to be a quiet sector where no enemy action was expected, the three Regimental Combat Teams of the Division could only defend this wide area by establishing isolated strong points to block the main roads leading from East to West. The distances between positions prevented them from being mutually supporting and thus easily surrounded and cut off from reinforcement. In the unlikely event of an attack, the plan was to withdraw and delay.

When the German offensive opened, however, the order was changed to "Hold at All Cost," and thus each of the strong points had to fight its own battle. Rather than giving terrain for time as initially intended, it now became necessary to sacrifice lives for time until reinforcements from reserve units could be brought forward. The strong points of the Division, although surrounded, cut off, and facing increasing enemy forces as the fight went on, held for almost three full days, thus upsetting the German timetable. This gave the Allies time to move major reinforcements forward to Bastogne and St. Vith.

This print was taken from the magnificent painting depicting one of the great strong point actions which occurred in the town of Hosingen, Luxembourg, where "K" Company of the 110th Infantry Regiment and "B" Company of the 103rd Engineer Battalion (Combat) fought for the better part of three days. Although surrounded and greatly outnumbered, the soldiers of these two units held their ground with only a reinforcement of five tanks from the 707th Tank Battalion reaching their position. In this defense, these brave men inflicted an estimated 2,000 casualties upon their attackers and totally upset the German timetable. The 28th Division soldiers fought to the last round and were then authorized to break into small groups and escape as best they could.

The gallant defense of Hosingen, which is depicted in this painting, like the action at the other strong points of the 28th Division, sacrificed men for time. This effort clearly helped save Bastogne, only 18 miles to the west, and bought precious time for the Allies. The painting and the limited edition prints are dedicated to all the brave men of the 28th Division whose courage and sacrifice delayed the German advance and contributed greatly to the final outcome of the "Battle of the Bulge."

Memorial to the American Liberators in Hosingen, Luxembourg

In Luxembourg, many of those that are still alive and remember what WWII was like are still passionate about preserving the memories of those who lost their lives trying to save their's. Monuments and museums are abundant and many soldiers of the 28th Infantry Division soldiers have returned to pay respect to the buddies they lost and to share the experience with their loved ones.

The memorial in Hosingen consists of two plaques on a stone monument on the south end of town. On each side of this monument, there are two flagstones in the grass on which plaques have been mounted.

The text on the red plaque at the monument reads:

> *"WWII American first army Defenders of Hosingen, Luxembourg "K" Company, 110th Infantry Regiment, 28th Division, Captured by German Forces December 18, 1944. Roll on 110."*

and on the second plaque:

> *"Paratus in honor to the valiant men of B Company, 103rd Engineer Combat Battalion, 28th US Infantry Division who gallantly defended Hosingen from December 16 to 18, 1944."*

APPENDIX A

Newspaper Articles published January 1945

Newspaper Articles

The press corps that was stationed in Europe did their best to keep the American population informed of what their boys were doing overseas. Larry Newman, with the International News Service, who covered the Patton's Third Army and was embedded with the American troops in Belgium, wrote *A Saga of Gallant Men; How Heroic 28th Halted Nazis And Saved Our Armies*, on January 6, 1945.

Two Pennsylvania war correspondents, Morley Cassidy with the Philadelphia Sunday Evening Bulletin and Ivan H. (Cy) Peterman from the Philadelphia Inquirer, both followed up with a series of articles in January 1945 that told the heroic stories of the 28th, which usually included references to the 110th and K Company in Hosingen. It was evident to all three of these newspaper reporters and the papers that they wrote for, that the Pennsylvania boys had played an important part at stemming Hitler's advance to Bastogne early in his final offensive. Although not always identified in the articles that follow, the bolded content in the articles provided in this appendix refers to the GIs fighting in Hosingen.

***

A Saga of Gallant Men
How Heroic 28th Halted Nazis And Saved Our Armies
By LARRY NEWMAN
International News Service

WITH AMERICAN TROOPS IN BELGIUM, Jan. 6 –

This is the story of the heroic United State 28th Division. It may well be the story of Marshal Karl Gerd von Rundstedt's failure to reach Sedan and the Meuse – perhaps Antwerp – and to split the Allied armies in his desperate attempt to gain a quick victory.

The famed Twenty-eighth, originally the Pennsylvania National Guard, once was made up almost entirely of Pennsylvania's. It has been replenished and reorganized so many times, however, that other states now predominate among its fighters.

This is the story of men – some hidden in the anonymity of death – who bore the brunt of the initial German assault on the morning of December 16. It is the story of men who kept slugging until they fell in their tracks, of survivors staggering and crawling through encircling enemy lines to regroup and refight again.

The saga of gallantry begins with an American lieutenant speaking over a radiophone. He is weeping and every bitter sob of his rage is communicated back to his commanding officer. He reported to his major:

"We're down to our last grenades. We've blown up everything there is, except the radio. It goes next. I don't mind dying, I don't mind taking a beating – but we'll never give up."

There was a click on the radiophone. The conversation had ended. The major sagged in his chair and glanced at his watch. It was 9:55. He remembered a 4:30 call when this outfit ahead reported its ammunition gone and that there was fighting with grenades from house to house.

They'd held out five hours since that last call and now they were gone.

At Dawn on That Fateful Day!

All this happened two days after Rundstedt began his gamble for victory when he hurled five crack divisions across the Our River into Luxembourg against a thinly-held line covered by the 28th Division known as the "bloody bucket" outfit.

Great as was the defense of besieged Bastogne, many agree that it was these men who made the defense possible. For without that heroic stand we would never have had time to get men and materials through before the Germans would have overrun us.

At dawn on that fateful 16th, under a heavy sky that blotted out air activity, the Germans suddenly burst across the river. They were screaming, shouting, laughing. Some were crying hysterically. Some were more like drunken and doped men than well-disciplined German fighters.

They came wave after wave. They fell into heaps before murderous American machine-gun fire. But still they came.

Near Residorf one Yank unit dug itself in well and held its fire until a solid line of Germans was only 50 yards away. Then they fired.

Nazis Clamber Over Own Dead

From one survivor:

"We racked 'em and we stacked 'em, until the Nazis were clambering over their own dead."

"Their tanks were surrounded and covered with their infantry. The tanks came swiftly toward our doughboys in the foxholes but turn when their infantry lay bleeding and dying, many crushed under the tank tracks."

"But then they came back. More and more and still more died. But the green-clad Hitler lovers still walked into our hail of fire. All that night and into the next day they fought us."

"By Sunday midnight we were surrounded and greatly outnumbered. We radioed battalion headquarters 'Situation

critical.' The answer came back, 'Withdraw if possible.' To that went the reply, 'We can't get out but we'll make them pay.'"

This radio talk went on between the captain commanding the unit and the major at field headquarters. After that the major and the captain did not speak with each other directly. The major related:

"He knew and I knew what the situation was and what can I say to a man at a time like that?"

At nearby Wahlhausen another outfit of the 28th Division was in trouble. Its supporting artillery got the message:

"Heavy German attack coming. Pour it on."

The artillery began sending its shells over and nameless private screamed over the radiophone:

"Closer! Closer! Bring it in. Bring it on top of us. We'll duck." Then the artillery fire came within 50 yards of the doughboys. But the Germans died and doughboys held.

Farther south, at Weiler, a mortar outfit was caught. Pvt. Manuel Wise, of Big Springs, Tex., and his pals from West Virginia and Iowa fought for 48 hours alongside riflemen, cooks and drivers and when their ammunition, food and water were running low a jeep-driver tried to run the enemy gauntlet. He ran into a German ambush. The men heard him scream:

"You'll never get this jeep, you dirty ———."

A machine gun rattled and there was silence. Later four Germans were caught driving the same jeep. They'll never drive another.

Capt. Floyd K. McCutcheon, of Idaville, Ind., together with Pvt. Wise worked their way out of the pocket and up a hill. Four Germans stumbled onto the outpost set up on the height. The doughboys killed two and wounded one. The fourth German bayoneted his own man, then ran. A GI's rifle shot got him.

FOUGHT ALL NIGHT

The outfit fought all night and worked its way into a pine grove, but there found themselves surrounded by Nazi paratroopers. The

Yanks' only escape was to fight their way out. They made a break for it. Wise's trousers were raked from his legs by machine gun fire from a German paratrooper 50 yards away.

Wise kept running, fired once and dropped the paratrooper at his feet. In the gruelling action, Wise became a hero. The private kept the men going and many of them made it safely to fight another day. Here are a few more of the doughboy heroes all Americans should remember:

Pvt. Harold E. Deutschman, of Chicago, a switchboard operator who wandered along in a circle for four days and nights without food and ended up within a few hundred yards of his starting point. For 14 hours he hid in a pile of rubbish and watched the Germans string barbed wire 10 feet away. When a German sentry failed him, Pvt. Deutschman simply walked away.

Then there was Lt. Raymond Fleig, of Ohio, who had just won his silver star. He rushed his tanks to the rest center of Clervaux where the Germans were overrunning everything. He and his boys fought the Germans from alley to alley.

But Fleig, after fighting like a maniac, got cut off from his men. He wandered around for three days – his only food a chocolate bar taken from a dead soldier.

Finally he was found and taken to a hospital, suffering from trench foot and exhaustion. But he pestered the doctors until they released him. Then he hitch-hiked back to his outfit.

Pvt. Harry Stutz, of Detroit, and Sgt. Ben Bertra, of Chicago, message center operators, came close to a German bivouac. They hugged the ground when an enemy flashlight beam swung three feet over their heads. Desperate for food, they walked to the door of a farmhouse and knocked. They stared in amazement when a Jerry opened the door. But they escaped.

One of the greatest of the division's exploits was that of Lt. Glenn Peterson, of Olivia, Tex. He led 50 rear echelon riflemen out of Wiltz on foot. He and his men almost drowned in the icy river. They fought their way through a German guard line over a bridge.

Then Lt. Peterson contacted the Luxembourg underground and got his men safely through the German lines into Bastogne where they fought shoulder to shoulder with the gallant American paratroopers of the 101st Airborne Division in one of the war's epic battles.

***

The following Philadelphia **Sunday Evening Bulletin** articles were written by War Correspondent, Morley Cassidy:

1. *28th Division Battle a Tale of Incredible Heroism,* Jan 17, 1945
2. *Every Man on the 28th Gave All he Had–and more- in Week of a Thousand Battles,* Jan 19, 1945
3. *28th Wipes out Nazi Force After Feigning Retreat,* Jan 20, 1945
4. The PITTSBURGH PRESS, MONDAY, JANUARY 22, 1945– *28th Holds off 9 German Divisions, Upsets Offensive; Keystoners Share Glory of Great Feat of U.S. Military History,* Jan 17, 1945

***

28th Division Battle a Tale of Incredible Heroism

Split, Disorganized and Surrounded by Superior
Forces, Men Fought Furiously and won – Time

By MORLEY CASSIDY
(Bulletin War Correspondent)
(First of a Series of Articles)

With the 28th Division on the Western Front, Jan. 17. – Men with
the red keystone on their helmets had been fighting seven days
and seven nights.

They had been fighting against an enemy who outnumbered
them seven and eight to one, an enemy who had advantage of
supplies and the advantage of machinery, unlimited armor and
artillery.

And now it was the morning of December 22, and the glorious
28th Division was near the end of the road.

At 11 A.M., Major General Norman D. Cota, commanding
general, stood in a battered, dirty field coat on the steps of a
crossroads tavern in the tiny village of Vaux les Rosieres, 12 miles
southwest of Bastogne, on the main road to Neufchateu.

Little Equipment Salvaged

I was a short review. Past him rolled a jumbled column of trucks
and jeeps piled high with disorderly heaps of ration boxes,
ammunition, blankets and gasoline tanks – all that could be
salvaged that morning of a division headquarters pulled out
of the almost encircled village of Sibreh, two miles outside of
Bastogne.

The first job was to count noses. Every man in the column was
ordered into nearby pastures. A few minutes later a colonel from
West Chester, the chief of staff, reported the figures to General
Cota.

The count showed a total of 125 men – clerks, truck drivers, riflemen, cooks, bakers, stenographers, plus 65 men of the signal company.

Threatened on All Sides

And that handful of men, knowing that tanks already headed this way were less than three miles away, knowing every spearhead that was threatening from the north and the south, knowing that German infantry already was infiltrating woods on three sides, dug in for another effort to stop the advance of von Rundstedt's smashing offensive.

That day not only will be remembered as one of the most glorious in the glorious history of the division, but it also will be remembered as the high point in one of the great efforts of American's military history.

Now that the story can be told it is the merest justice to say that the 28th deserves equal credit with the gallant men of the 101st Airborne Division for major fights in the stemming the tide of the German invasion.

Three days before the 101st began its stand at Bastogne the men of the 28th were taking the full brunt of von Rondstedt's mightiest offensive in Luxembourg – fighting desperately in hundreds of scattered battles.

Taking a frightful toll of Germans, many men of the 28th traded their lives for time in which support could be brought up in the breakthrough area. And it takes nothing from the men of the 101st to say that the defense of Bastogne would have been impossible save for the time margin given by the heroism of every man in the 28th division.

But if this heroism paid for the time, then the division paid for its glory – in blood and lives. Its losses make grim reading.

Yet the 28th today stands with head unbowed. Units are reunited into fighting machines.

The story of the 28th is the core of the same story of this breakthrough – and of its failure.

Stretched on 25-Mile Front

On December 15, the "Bloody Bucket Division" and the German main forces were stretched tight as fiddle strings along a 25-mile front on the Our River, from the northeastern tip of Luxembourg to the vicinity of Wallendorf, at the mouth of the Sure River.

It was the widest front held by any division in Europe – five times the normal division front, and bigger than the front of some army corps. But this was a quiet sector whose thin lines seemed justified. It was regarded, in fact, as a rest area. The 28th had fought through the Normandy hedgerows, had helped seal the Falaise pocket, and had been sent here for three weeks of rebuilding after its bloody battle in the Hürtgen Forest, east of Aachen.

A rest center had been organized in the little town of Clervaux. Here the boys came in groups to relax, fish, drink beer, see movies, and visit the Red Cross club set up by Miss Peggy Henry, of Pataskala, Ohio.

They came in trucks from each of three regiments, all serving in the front lines. From the north, in the vicinity of Weiswampach, came the men of the 112th Regiment, covering a six mile front.

Trips Like Picnic Parties

From Heinerscheid and Hosingen came men of the 110th, covering a 16-mile front. From Wallendorf and Bettendorf came the men of the 109th Regiment, holding a three-mile sector on the southern flank. To these battle-weary men the trips to Clervaux were like picnic parties.

Like a clap of thunder came the end of this winter idyll.

At 5:45 A.M. on December 16, the camp at Clervaux was heavily shelled. Soldiers on rest passes were thrown from bed and cut by shell splinters.

Two hours later companies in the line were reporting that patrols of 20 men were pushing across the Our River, in the area of the 110th. At 8 o'clock the 109th, on Reich Lake, reported 30 men trying to cross a little footbridge near Wallendorf. At 8:15 the same regiment reported another patrol of 50 men had crossed the river at Viaden. And then another patrol of 80 men was crossing at Bethendorf.

By 9 o'clock whole companies of green-clad soldiers were fighting their way across the Our River in dozens of scattered spots along the whole front.

Grimly the 28th leaped to attack. Our artillery opened up on the Germans in the vital southern corner, mowing down hundreds as they struggled across a tiny bridge, and holding the flank secure.

In scores of other spots outposts found themselves surrounded, but fought on desperately and turned back ten times their numbers.

Before noon five German divisions of Panzers, infantry, Volksgrenadiers, were hammering at the 28th with rocket guns and artillery. In the afternoon a parachute division joined the onslaught. By nightfall the whole central section of the front was a fluid mass of penetrations and encirclements.

Day of Incredible Heroism

It was a day and night of incredible heroism as the thinly scattered troops fought to hold the paper-thin line.

At Hosingen one company reported 20 tanks coming down two roads from the east. A young captain gathered a weapons platoon, a company of engineers, a raiders' platoon and four tanks, and engaged the enemy.

They battled all that day and the next day. Late Sunday, encircled and outnumbered and with ammunition gone, they radioed battalion headquarters that the situation was critical. The order was given to withdraw if possible.

Two company commanders radioed back: "We can't get out but we will make them pay."

Hours later a young lieutenant from the weapons platoon radioed that he was now the only officer left, and that the men were fighting hand to hand with no weapons except grenades.

For five hours longer this little group held back the foe. Then came another call from the lieutenant. He was weeping now, with pure rage.

Down to Last Grenade

"We are down to the last grenade," he said, "but we've blown up everything there is to blow. I don't mind dying but we'll never give up to these —".

Sob checked his voice. The radio brought the sound of battle noises, and that was the last every heard of that company.

Over and over again the same sort of sacrifice was taking place along the whole division front. On the northern end of the line one company of the 112th regiment for 36 hours stood off every effort to cross a vital bridge.

Over and over German tanks rattled forward with supporting infantry, but ran into a withering hail of fire which stripped away the infantry and drove them back for another try. But finally the tanks succeeded in whittling down the defenders to nothingness.

Calls for Artillery Fire

At Wahlhausen a signal platoon beat off repeated attacks on an observation post, but the Germans came on. Finally a nameless private called for artillery fire.

"German multiple 20 millimeters, on tank and lots of infantry coming down the road," he said. "Pour it on."

As the artillery landed the private pleaded, "Closer, closer," until the blast was heard in earphones. Major Harold F. Milton, of Jasper, Fla., finally demanded to talk to the commanding officer.

A lieutenant came to the phone.

"Bring it in," the lieutenant pleaded. "Bring it on us. We'll duck."

Artillery was laid on their position. No one knows their fate. Perhaps it is just as well.

On Sunday the Germans threw two more divisions – a total of eight at the reeling men of the 28th. Monday they threw in another panzer division.

General Cota's sound judgment already was showing its effect. He was using football strategy. He "kept his tackles strong."

On the two flanks the 109th and 112th moved with the punch, giving ground slowly, but blocking every effort to widen the gap. In the furious day that followed the 110th fought as few men are ever called on to fight.

Split, disorganized, surrounded by immeasurably superior forces, the men fought single, in pairs, in platoons, in companies. In hundreds of furious battles they harassed the enemy, slowed down tank columns, and died storming artillery positions.

They fulfilled their mission to the utmost, but the green hordes pushed westward, threatening division headquarters at Wiltz.

General Stays to Last

Staying to the last hour, General Cota refused to leave until the machine guns already were rattled in the streets. Cooks, clerks, officers at headquarters turned infantrymen to hold off the attack.

The last convoy to leave found a tank blocking the road. It was raked by fire of 88's. Much of the headquarters personnel were forced to take to woods which had been infiltrated or go through surrounding Germans to fall back to new quarters at Secrec, 20 miles away.

They barely reached there when a German column pushing beyond Bastogne besieged the new command post, and forced another withdrawal to Vaux les Rosieres. By this time the 28th had completed one of the greatest feats in the history of American arms against nine divisions which had held so firmly that the German timetable had been thrown completely off.

The capture of Bastogne, which documents showed was scheduled for the first day, never did take place, although the Germans were able to surround the town on the fourth day.

Our command had been given the time to bring in supporting elements, to plant the 101st in Bastogne.

The force of the German drive had been blunted. The flanks had been held. The 28th had made possible the smashing of von Rundstedt's drive.

***

Every Man on the 28th Gave All he Had –
and More – in Week of a Thousand Battles

By MORLEY CASSIDY
(Bulletin War Correspondent)
(Second of three articles)

With the 28th Division on the Western Front, Jan. 19. – A wounded soldier of the 105th Infantry Regiment gave it the right name.

This, he said, was a week of a thousand battles.

As he said it, the 28th (Pennsylvania Keystone) Division was still fighting at the end of the week in which it had met and blunted the full force of von Rundstedt's drive to the west. One of the crucial battles of this war was closing, and the Germans had lost. A great bid for the initiative had failed.

Desperate, Bloody Battles

And the wounded private had spoken truly in saying this was not one battle, but a thousand battles.

For the nine days from December 16-25 were ones in which the men of the 28th had fought singly, by twos and threes, by squads, platoons and companies in endless succession – desperate, bloody battles to gain time for the mobilization of support.

It was a week when lieutenant colonels lay in foxholes next to privates, when majors stood side by side with corporals firing rifles and grenades at tank columns.

It was a week when squads and companies were trapped, escaped, and trapped again. And above all it was a week when every man in the division, down to the newest clerk in the rearmost area, was a fighting man battling against odds few divisions in history ever faced.

The story of this week of a thousand battles never can be told in full. But it can be told that it was a picture of confused, desperate fighting, raging over an area from two to five miles wide by 40 miles long.

Hit on Every Side

Through the center of this area, the 110th Regiment, taking the major force of von Rundstedt's spearhead, was hit on every side, divided, redivided, and driven backwards, platoon by platoon.

Its regimental command post was surrounded. Each time it fought its way out, set up a new position to fight again. And every foot of ground given up is a tale of heroic defense.

There was B Company, for instance, in the village of Marnach. On the first smashing day the captain called battalion headquarters to report: "Hundreds of Jerries outside." He was asked how close. "Close enough to touch," he whispered back.

With a unit of the 707th tank battalion, he was told to hold at all costs. They held all that day and all that night. Once they were attached by six German halftracks and two companies of infantry. The knocked out the halftracks with bazookas and attacked the infantry with rifles.

Moment of Silence

But on the second day, Sunday, the radio man reported German halftracks in front of the company command post, then stopped. For a minute there was silence. Only the clicking of a butterfly switch, then a voice whispered: "Gee, there must be a million Jerries out there."

Then came the sound of furious firing, and the radio went silent.

Not far away, 20 light tanks of D Company of the 707th Tank Battalion tried to clear the highway into Marnach. In one mile 14 were knocked out. The rest were forced to withdraw to aid in stemming the attack on the battalion command post, which already was surrounded.

In the wild melee men fought with whatever weapons came to hand. At Consthum, C Battery of the 687th Field Artillery fired at constantly lowered elevations until the Germans were inside the range, then grabbed rifles and carbines and jumped into foxholes to help the infantry beat off the attack.

Beat Off 5 Attacks

As the Germans retreated, the gunners leaped back to their artillery and sent shells after them. But the Germans came back. Five times the battery beat off attacks. Not a man left his post for 48 hours. They fired until the regular ammunition was gone, then fired anti-tank shells. When those were gone they fired propaganda shells filled with leaflets. Only when those were gone did the battery fall back.

Men tackled jobs they never had been trained for.

First Lieutenant Douglas C. Paul, of Bethlehem, Pa., transportation officer of the 3rd Battalion, set something of a record for variety, even in this mad battle. With Germans attacking the battalion command post, he turned rifleman, organized cooks, clerks, artillerymen and anti-aircraft men for the last ditch fight.

For two days they stood off the enemy. On the third day, with their defences overrun, Paul and Technical Sergeant William B. Schowllenberger, of New York City, tossed an 81 millimeter mortar in a jeep, made a dash through the lies, then set it up and blasted the enemy from the rear.

Drags Out Guns

Forced back to the next town, Paul spied some 105 mm ammunition, and learned of two guns in a nearby ordnance shop. He dragged them out, organized a gun crew from headquarters personnel, and turned artillerymen. Driven out at last, he and his men made a two-day cross country hike through infiltrating Germans, and finally fought as a rifle platoon in defense of the division command post.

Time and again the unit held with the German literally on its doorstep, sometimes escaping, sometimes dying.

At Clervaux, a regimental commander stayed in his hotel headquarters until Tiger tanks stopped in the street outside. The Germans [*content missing*] out the first convoy of vital supplies.

Officers Shift Commands

By this time commanding officers were changing momentarily. Captain Caspar Panicky, of Highland Ave, Chestnut Hill, executive officer of a battery, handled the 109th Field Artillery, took over command in the middle of the German attack, supervised the firing of shells and timed them to burst 200 yards away.

"We were really firing at the whites of their eyes," he said. "We stacked them up in little piles all over the place."

In a crucial moment, Lieutenant Colonel Daniel C. Stickler, of Lancaster, Pa., smiling, leathery-faced executive officer, took over command of the 110th. The defense of Wiltz was his biggest job.

With Tiger tanks already on a hill overlooking the town, he reorganized the regiment, assembled scattered units, localized a force of typists from the adjutant's office, finance office, surgeon's office; division band and military police.

Hold Until Last

The makeshift force held until the most vital material was removed, then piled into the last convoy of 50 trucks. Met by an armored column, the forces which had made the grand stand hit the woods in small groups and made their way west, some to Bastogne to join the air force, some to the division command post at Sibret.

For four days Lieutenant Raymond D. Fleig, of Ohio, led a company of the 707th Tank Battalion in wild dashes, plugging one gap after another. Once it stopped a column of 30 tanks smashing toward Clervaux.

The company fought twice its number of German tanks outside Wiltz, and held until its ammunition was gone. Searching for a new supply, it found an infantry company in the middle of a machine gun attack. Leaving his tank company to consult the infantry captain, Fleig was left standing amid a hail of bullets, his tanks in confusion.

Mission Accomplished

The tankmen fought then as riflemen, only to be driven to the woods, where they wandered for days, with the only food chocolate bars taken from dead soldiers.

Despite the confusion, and with the German spearheads swinging in all directions, the regiment and its units accomplished it mission – delaying the enemy's westward rush. When the division headquarters fell back to Sibert, west of Bastogne, little was left under its immediate command save headquarters personnel, stragglers and scraps attached to units.

With tanks ranging the woods outside the town the division command post pulled out again, but Lieutenant Colonel Thomas E. Briggs, of Wilkensburg, Pa., division operations officer, personally organized a task force as a rear guard.

His adjutant was Lieutenant Stanley Horftman, 2 Sutton place, South New York, public relations officer turned rifleman. Stragglers drifting back from Wiltz were hastily shoved into line. The tiny task force, never more than 50 men, held off repeated attacks by tanks and infantry.

City Officer Escapes

Only when the tanks were coming through a hedge 50 yards away did the force scatter and fall back to repeat the last ditch stand at Vaux les Rosieres. One of the last to leave was Captain Robert A. Hummel, 4918 Baltimore Ave., Philadelphia, who remained firing a rifle until a German tank came around the corner of a building. Then he escaped to the outskirts of the town.

"But then," said one of the enlisted men, "the captain made us stop. He said, 'We've got a job to do here.' Then he took the time to blow up a bridge with tanks coming down the road."

Such deeds, repeated over and over again by the men of the 28th supply the main reason why the German drive failed to crash through to the Meuse. It may have been the crucial moment of the war.

Graduate of Olney High

Captain Hummel, 25, whose wife, Anna, and 20-month old daughter, Jo-Ann, live at 4918 Baltimore Ave., entered the service in July, 1939. At the time he was an accountant for the Pennsylvania

Railroad and was attending night classes at Wharton School of the University of Pennsylvania. He is a graduate of Olney High School.

Lieutenant Paul, 26, is the son of Mr. and Mrs. H. M. Paul, of 522 9th Ave., Bethlehem. A graduate of Bethlehem High School, he went to Mercersburg Academy for two years and was graduated from Lehigh University in 1940. He was a varsity wrestler and played on the hockey and lacrosse teams at Lehigh. In high school and preparatory school, he made the varsity in football and swimming. After leaving college, where was given R.O.T.C. training, he worked at the Bethlehem Steel Co. as a member of the sales department. In July 1942, he was called into the Army as a second Lieutenant. He trained at Indiantown Gap and went overseas in October, 1941. On D-Day, he entered France with the 28th Division, 110th Regiment.

(Concluded tomorrow)

***

28th Wiped Out Nazi Force After Feigning Retreat

Hard-Pressed Troops' Refused Relief . . . That's
the Fighting Spirit of the Keystone Division

By MORLEY CASSIDY
(Bulletin War Correspondent)
(Last of three articles)

With the 28th Division on the Western Front, Jan. 20. – It was
the evening of December 21. For five days the men of the 109th
Regiment, 28th Division, had been holding desperately on the
southern flank of the Germans' smashing breakthrough in
Luxembourg.

Battling two full German divisions – six times their numbers –
the men of the 109th had been rolling with the punch, fighting all
day, giving a little ground each night.

Slowly, the regiment's front had been swung from north-
south to east-west, but the pivot held, blocking the German thrust
southward to Luxembourg City. And, on the evening of December
21, the commanding officer said, came the opportunity for reversal
of tactics.

After the evening clash, he went through the motions of pulling
back his force to a new point on the road leading southwest from
Diekirch, as he had been doing the last four nights. But instead of
pulling back, he withdrew only 200 yards, placed two battalions in
a strong position parallel to the road, and waited.

Morning came, and with it the triumphant Germans started to
sweeps southward again on the road leading to Railon, confident
that they had power enough to smash through a single regiment.

The column moved forward in a long line – artillery, tanks,
trucks, infantry. The triumphal procession lacked nothing except
a blare of trumpets.

While the colonel watched, restraining his men, his two
battalions waited until the two-mile-long column was spread

out directly before them on a road 200 yards away. Then the colonel gave the word, and every gun in the two battalions spoke at once.

Rifles, machine-guns, light artillery, anti-tank guns roared in unison, mowing down infantry, setting the column of vehicles afire. In three minutes the two-mile convoy was a horizontal funeral pyre, black smoke and blazing gasoline filling the length of the little valley.

Trap Works to Perfections
Hardly a German had a chance to fire an answering shot. The trap had worked to perfection.

The colonel later pointed to nearly 2,000 bodies. But that was only a grisly sidelight of more important accomplishments, for the German drive to expand its breakthrough area and push south eastward to Arlon, the surrounded Luxembourg city, had been stopped cold.

Before the Germans could reorganize and replace the annihilated column, support arrived for the 109th, and the southern flank of the breakthrough area had been made impregnable. On the northern side of the bulge, the 112th Regiment, commanded by Colonel Gustin Nelson, formerly of Marlin Road, Overbrook, Pa., was following the same strategy – pivoting slowly, giving ground reluctantly, holding the line like a rock.

Thwarted Nazi Plans
The unshakable stand of these two regiments was vitally important in determining the whole course of the battle. For it thwarted von Rundstedt's plans to widen and exploit the initial breakthrough.

In this stand every man in both regiments forgot all other duties to shoulder a rifle and standoff repeated attacks. And the Germans paid a staggering toll for every foot of ground.

At Reisdorf, L Company of the 109th met the initial breakthrough drive in well dug-in positions.

"We waited until the Krauts were 80 yards away," said one private. "Then we racked 'em and stacked 'em up until the Germans were clambering over their own dead as they came at us,"

Fire at Point-Blank Range
At Bittendorf, the Second Battalion held firm against the first smashing attack at its very doorstep. First Lieutenant Herbert E. Gosling, Jr. of Upper Darby, Pa., regularly a liaison officer, and dozens of others at headquarters, fired at point-blank range from command post windows.

A few miles away, clerks like Joseph D. Cochran, 4828 N. 11th St., Philadelphia, regularly a typist at headquarters, left typewriters and turned riflemen to repel the attach on division headquarters.

Fighting side by side were men of the 107th, 108th and 109th Field Artillery Battalions, and 707th Tank Battalion, the 103rd Engineers, the 28th Signal Company and the 630th Tank Destroyer Battalion.

All turned hands to any shooting that came along. In the fury of battle, Sergeant Hugh F. Coyle, of 822 N. Ringgold St., Philadelphia, a message center chief of the 108th Field Artillery, dropped other work to find the new command post when his battery was forced back, and barely was installed in the new post when that, too, was shelled.

Helps Drive Off Attack
Technical Sergeant John T. (Tim) Lovelace, of 326 Darby Road, Llanerch, Pa., operations sergeant of the same battalion, grabbed a rifle when the Germans stormed his battery and helped drive off the attack.

When the Germans came so close that the guns couldn't be lowered to meet them, in the neighborhood of Diekirch, Captain Leonard Goelz, of Pittsburgh, took a crew and formed a temporary infantry platoon which cleaned out a woods and took 49 prisoners, while three-man gun crews continued to fire.

And the fighting spirit of the 28th never was more apparent than when new divisions came in to relieve the hard pressed 109th Regiment, after a week of fighting which stemmed the German tide.

Refused to Be Relieved

Many men of the 109th refused to be relieved, joined new divisions as casuals, and continued firing. So the regiment was swung south, attached to an armored division, and immediately launched a counter-attack which carried it back to the Sure River, less than 400 yards from the initial position where L Company had mowed down the first Nazi invaders.

The same spirit showed in every regiment of the 28th. Men of the 112th fought first with one division and then another after losing contact with their own headquarters.

***

The PITTSBURGH PRESS, MONDAY, JANUARY 22, 1945 –

28th Holds off 9 German Divisions, Upsets Offensive

Keystoners Share Glory of Great Feat of U.S. Military History

By MORLEY CASSIDY, North American Newspaper Alliance

WITH THE U. S. 28th DIVISION ON THE WESTERN FRONT, Jan. 17 – (Delayed) – 'The men with the red Keystone on their helmets had been fighting for seven days and seven nights.

They had been fighting against an enemy who outnumbered them seven and eight to one, an enemy who had the advantage of supplies and of machinery; of unlimited armour and artillery. [The 28th Division originally was composed of Pennsylvania men.]

And now it was the morning of Dec. 22 and the glorious 28th Division was near the end of the road. German spearheads were now striking savagely west of Bastogne in a desperate effort to reach the Meuse.

At 11 a.m. Maj. Gen. Norman Cota in command, stood in a torn, dirty field coat on the steps of a crossroads tavern in the tiny village of Vaux-lez-Rosières, 12 miles southwest of Bastogne on the main road to Neufchateau. Grimly he reviewed all that was left of his headquarters.

125 Men Left

That morning, division headquarters had pulled out of the almost encircled village of Sibrec, two miles outside Bastogne. Every man in the column was ordered into nearby pastures. A few minutes later a colonel – the chief of staff – reported to Gen. Cota that they count showed a total of 125 men.

Those of us standing there that morning saw Gen. Cota's rough, huge, kindly face tighten a little. A few minutes later the colonel returned to our group to say, "We are standing right here."

That day will be remembered not only as one of the most glorious in the division's glorious history, but it also will be remembered as the high point in one of the great efforts of America's military history.

Deserves Equal Credit

Now that their story can be told, it is merest justice to say that the 28th deserves equal credit with the gallant men of the 101st Airborne Division of Bastogne for the major fights in stemming the tide of the German drive. Three days before the 101st began its stand, the men of the 28th were taking the full brunt of Rundstedt's mightiest offensive in Luxembourg, fighting desperately in hundreds of scattered battles.

On Dec. 15, the "Bloody Bucket" division was stretched tight as fiddle strings along a 25-mile front on the Our River from the northeastern tip of Luxembourg to the vicinity of Wallendorf at the mouth of the Sure River. It was the widest front held by any division in Europe, five times the length of a normal division front and bigger than the front of some army corps.

But this quiet sector with thin lines seemed justified. It was regarded, in fact, as a rest area and the 28th, after it had fought through Normandy hedgerows and helped to seal the Falaise pocket, had been sent here for three weeks of rebuilding after its bloody battle in the Hürtgen Forest, east of Aachen.

The Picnic Ends

The rest center had been organized in a little town of Clervaux. Here boys came in groups to relax, fish, drink beer, see movies, and visit the Red Cross club set up by Peggy Henry, of Pataskala,

O. They came in trucks from each of three regiments all serving in front line. To battle-weary men, the rest trips to Clervaux were like picnic parties.

Like a clap of thunder came an end to this winter idyll.

At 5:45 a.m. on Dec. 16, the camp at Clervaux was shelled heavily. Soldiers on rest passes were thrown from bed, cut by shell splinters. They looked at each other in amazement. This had never happened before.

Three hours later whole companies of green-clad soldiers were fighting their way across the Our River in dozens of scattered spots along the whole front.

Leap to Re-Attack

Grimly the 28th leaped to re-attack. Our artillery trained on Germans in the vital southern corner, mowing down hundreds as they struggled across a tiny bridge, holding their flank secure.

By nightfall the whole central section of the front was a fluid mass of penetrations and encirclements. It was a day and a night of incredible heroism, as thinly-scattered troops fought to hold the paper-thin line. **At Hosingen, one company reported 20 tanks coming down two roads from the east. A young captain gathered a weapons platoon from a company of engineers, a raiders platoon, and four tanks, and engaged the enemy. They battled all day and into the next. Then late Sunday, encircled and outnumbered, their ammunition gone, they radioed their battalion the situation was critical. They were ordered to withdraw if possible. Two company commanders radioed back, "We can't get out, but we'll make them pay."**

One Officer Left

Hours later a young lieutenant from the weapons platoon radioed he now was the only officer left and his men were fighting hand to hand, with no weapons except grenades. Five hours longer this

little group held back the foe. Then came another call from the lieutenant. He was weeping now; weeping with pure rage.

"Down to last grenade," he said. "We've blown everything there is to blow. I don't mind drying, but will never give up to these bastards."

A sob choked off his voice. The radio brought in the sounds of battle noises – the last ever heard of that company.

Face Nine Divisions

On Sunday, the Germans threw two more divisions, making a total of eight at the reeling men of the 28th. Monday, they threw in another panzer division.

On two flanks, the 109th and the 112th Regiments moved with the punch, giving ground slowly, but blocking every effort to widen the gap. In the furious day that followed, the 110th fought as few men are ever called on to fight.

Cooks, clerks and chairborne officers at headquarters turned infantrymen to hold off the attack. Many of the headquarters personnel who had been forced to take to the woods infiltrated through surrounding Germans to fall back to the new quarters at Sibrec, 20 miles away. They barely had reached there when a German column pushing beyond Bastogne besieged the new command post and forced another withdrawal to Vaux-lez-Rosières.

By this time the 28th had completed one of the greatest feats in the history of the American Army. Against nine divisions they had held so firmly that the German timetable had been thrown completely off.

The capture of Bastogne, documents showed, had been scheduled for the first day, but it had taken four to surround it. Our command had been given time to bring in supporting elements, and to plant the 101st Airborne in Bastogne. The forces of the German drive had been blunted; the flanks hand been held. The 28th Division had made possible the smashing of Rundstedt's drive. A wounded soldier of the 105th Infantry Regiment gave it the right name.

Thousand Battles

"This," he said, "was the week of a thousand battles. For the period between Dec. 16 and 25 was one in which the men of the 28ᵗʰ had fought singly, by twos and threes, by squads, platoons, and companies, in an endless succession of desperate bloody battles to gain time for mobilizing of support. It was a period when lieutenant colonels lay in foxholes besides privates; when majors stood side by side with corporals, firing rifles and throwing grenades at oncoming tank columns.

The fighting raged over an area 25 miles wide and 40 miles long. Through the center of this area, the 110ᵗʰ Regiment, taking the major force of von Rundstedt's spearhead, was hit on every side.

Cut off 5 Times

Its regimental command post was surrounded and cut off five times in three days. Each time it fought its way out and set up a new position to fight again. And every foot of ground given up was a tale of heroic defense. There was B Company for instance, in the village of Marnach. On the first smashing day, the captain called battalion headquarters to report "hundreds of Jerries are outside." He was asked how close. "Close enough to touch me."

With a unit of the 707ᵗʰ Tank Battalion he was told to hold at all costs. They held all day and night. Once they were attacked by six German halftracks, and two companies of infantry. They knocked out the halftracks with bazookas and reached the infantry with rifle fire.

But on the second day – Sunday – the radio men reported German halftracks in front of the company command post, then stopped. For a minute, there was silence except for the clicking of a butterfly switch. Then a voice whispered, "Gee, there must be a million Jerries out there."

Then came the sound of furious firing and the radio went silent forever.

14 Knocked Out in Mile

Not far away, 20 light tanks of D Company tried to clear the highway into Marnach. Within one mile 14 were knocked out. The rest were forced to withdraw to aid in stemming the attack on the battalion command post. In the wild melee, men fought with whatever weapons came to hand.

Men tackled jobs they had never been trained for. Lt. Douglas C. Paul of Bethlehem, Pa., set something of a record for variety, even for this mad battle. He turned rifleman, organized cooks, clerks, artillery, and anti-aircraft men for a last-ditch fight.

For two days they stood off the enemy, then the third day, the outer defences were overrun. Lt. Paul and Sgt. William B. Schowllenberger from New York City tossed an 81-mm mortar into a jeep, made a dash through the lines, set up the mortar and blasted the enemy from the rear.

Two-Day Hike

Forced back to the next town Lt. Paul spied some 105-mm ammunition and learned of two guns in a nearby ordnance shop. He dragged them out, organized a gun crew from headquarters personnel turned artillerymen. Driven out at last, he and his men made a two-day cross-country hike through infiltrating Germans, and finally fought as a rifle platoon in defense of the division command post.

Time and again the unit held with Germans literally on the doorstep, some escaping, some dying.

At Clervaux, a regimental commander stayed in his hotel headquarters until Tiger tanks stopped in the street outside, and forced an 88 into the lobby. Headquarters personnel fled through rear windows and escaped to reorganize a few miles back. Capt. Caspar Pennock of Chestnut Hill, Pa., executive officer of a battery, handling the 109th Field Artillery took over command in the middle of a German attack. He timed the shells to burst 200 yards away.

'At Whites of their Eyes'

"We we're really firing at the whites of their eyes," he said. "We stacked them up in little piles all over the place."

For four days, Lt. Raymond D. Fleig of Ohio, led a company of 707th Tank Battalion in wild dashes to plus one gap after another. Once he stopped a column of 30 tanks smashing toward Clervaux. The company fought twice its number of German tanks outside Wiltz and held until its ammunition was gone. Hunting a new supply it found an infantry company in the midst of a machine-gun attack. Leaving his tank company to consult the infantry captain, Lt. Fleig was left standing amid a hail of bullets, his tanks in confusion.

The tank men fought then as riflemen, only to be driven to the woods, where they wandered for days, with the only food chocolate bars taken from dead soldiers.

When the division headquarters fell back to Sibrec, west of Bastogne, little was left under its immediate command save headquarter personnel, stragglers, and scraps attached to units.

Such deeds, repeated over and over again by the men of the 28th supply the main reason why the German drive failed to crash through to the Meuse. It may have been the crucial moment of this war.

***

The following articles were written by Ivan H. (Cy) Peterman, Philadelphia Inquirer War Correspondent:

1. *Full Weight of Foe Hit Jinxed 28th Division,* Jan 22, 1945 (Delayed) (First of a Series)
2. *Pennsylvanians in Ardennes; 110th Followed Orders, But Cost Was Terrible,* Jan 23, 1945 (Delayed) (Second of a Series)
3. *28th Stood Up Against Big Odds,* Jan 25, 1945 (Delayed) (Fourth of a Series)

Used with permission of Philadelphia Inquirer Copyright© 2015. All rights reserved.

***

Pennsylvanians in Ardennes

Full Weight of Foe Hit Jinxed 28th Division

By Ivan H. (Cy) Peterman
Inquirer War Correspondent
By Wireless
Copyright 1945, The Philadelphia Inquirer
(First of a Series)

WITH THE 28TH INFANTRY DIVISION, WESTERN FRONT, Jan 22, 1945 (Delayed)

A SLEEPY non-com in the office of the 110th Regimental Command Post at Clervaux picked up a jangling telephone on the morning of Dec. 16 and said, "What's the matter now?"

"Nothing except there's a helluva lot of artillery coming into our positions and it seems all along the road."

The voice was that of a soldier in battalion headquarters near Marnach and the hour was 5:30 A. M. The non-com made a note, stepped to the door, saw flashes against the low clouds and spoke a word or two to his companions. Presently the telephone rang again.

"The Hunds are coming in against our strongpoints. They are filtering behind the company positions and have overrun our outer liens of resistance. Tell the Old Man it looks serious."

***

THIS time the call was from a battalion leader. The non-com immediately relayed the message to the Divisional Command where Major General Norman (Dutch) Cota was trying to reconstruct the shattered 28th (Keystone) Division.

General Cota's troubles weren't just beginning on the morning of Dec 16 – they were mounting precipitately. He had troubles with the jinxed 28th since the day he took command, reorganizing and restoring a fighting contingent out of the bewildered and somewhat discourage remnants that had but lately emerged from the bloodiest battleground of the Hürtgen Forest.

Ever since its arrival in France the Pennsylvania 28th, the oldest division historically in the U.S. Army, General George C. Marshall's own from the First World War and Lieutenant Omar Bradley's command before he took the Second Corps in Tunisia in this war, had been destined to take the full impact of the Nazi blows.

***

TWAS thus at Mortain where five spearheading Panzer divisions smote them near Gatheme; the same in the Hürtgen Forest where they raced over crests taking Schmidt, only to be chewed up by overwhelming numbers at Rommerscheid, and now…

"German tank – Mark Fours and Tiger Royals – are moving into the Clervaux area."

The telephone jingled incessantly as the General, imperturbable, brave as any man in uniform, aware of the thinly strung lines across almost 30 miles in Luxembourg's "static front," appraised his position.

His division was smack in the path of Field Marshal Gerd von Rundstedt's full counter-offensive. From Ettelbruck it stretched 25 snowy, mountainous and ill-defended miles north of Oudler, curving in and out of hills and ravines and heavily wooded slopes where one could drive 10 miles without encountering a G.I.

Most of the regimental offices were clustered around Ettelbruck, Wiltz and Clervaux. All were busily engaged restoring units, inducting reinforcements and accustoming recruits to the places of those who had been slain, wounded or were missing since the division retired from the Hürtgen nightmare.

***

THIS process had been going on about two weeks, during which the veteran officers and men had leaves in Paris or Britain, and comfortable existence was resumed in old-fashioned houses requisitioned in Wiltz and surrounding towns, first liberated when the 28th made its original penetrations in the Siegfried Line early in September.

Nobody thought much about the attack or about being overrun. The war seemed far away, although the Germans occasionally pitched shells from the opposite ridges.

Up at the 110th Regiment, where the new commander was trying to stop Huns this particular morning, things were not going well. The artillery barrage lasted until 8 o'clock, then the Wehrmacht swirled behind a couple companies, cutting them off. Around Marnach the positions were isolated and presently the 105-mm. Artillerymen were fighting hand-to-hand for possession of our own guns. All but one battery was lost.

***

"WE DISCOVERED the enemy hammering all along the line from Weiswanoach through Lieler trying for the main road toward Clervaux," said Major Glen Roberts, of the 110th. Major Roberts is from Kemmerer, Wyo. He said the attack was a complete surprise to the 28th, which knew the enemy was in opposite pillboxes, but nobody suspected there were tanks.

"All the first day they fought along a straight road toward St. Vith, pushing our infantry back or capturing some, inching toward the Regimental Command Post and moving toward the road net by night," he said.

On the night of Dec. 17 their tanks converged on Clervaux, but not until the bloodiest sort of fight that morning.

(Continued tomorrow)

***

Pennsylvanians in Ardennes

110th Followed Orders, But Cost Was Terrible

(Second of a Series)
By Ivan H. (Cy) Peterman
Inquirer War Correspondent
By Wireless
Copyright 1945, The Philadelphia Inquirer

WITH THE 28TH INFANTRY DIVISION, WESTERN FRONT, Jan 23, 1945 (Delayed)

"OUR fellows murdered them," a major said.

The battle of the bulge was developing; the Yanks were in action, and the comment was in order.

The Second Battalion on the 110th Infantry was ordered to retake Marnach and before the daylight on the morning of the 17th they shoved off. Just as they were moving the enemy struck in an attack to the southwest, their green-clad infantry marching directly into F Company's fire.

The Battalion made good progress after eliminating the Krauts in that local encounter, but nearing Marnach they met several tanks and anti-tank guns. They didn't retake the town but were forced back to a hilltop north of Reuler, from which they could see enemy tanks firing into Clervaux. It was not pleasant sitting there unable to assist, because the Germans were everywhere. The enemy was building up fast.

***

IN Clervaux on the night of the 17th it was hell. The colonel gathered headquarters personnel and formed anti-tank squads, with bazookas and 57 mm guns; he got everyone from a small rest center on the front lines; he manned upper stories of houses with gasoline squads who waited to throw their stuff on tanks to ignite them as they passed. It had been done in other towns.

But Von Rundstedt's overwhelming numbers pushed ahead as if the 28th wasn't there. They came rumbling into Clervaux from the southwest, headed by the Second SS Panzers, a spearhead destined to go with three miles of the Meuse River before it could be stopped, and never to move again.

There, at Celles, under General Harmon's Second American Armored blows, it was utterly destroyed just as now it was destroying the 110th Regiment.

The headquarters boys caught on well. They didn't know much about the bazooka but had learned a lot in an afternoon. They ducked behind buildings when fired upon, but the Germans blasted the buildings. The 110th was overrun.

Someone saw the colonel with a drawn automatic but everything was beclouded by smoke and noise and nobody answered the telephones. About eight o'clock on the night of the 17th, the 110th Regiment, as such, ceased to operate, and the commander was listed as missing in action.

***

"THOSE who got out said civilians cowered in cellars during the brief fight," a major said. "They said their last orders from the General were to hold at all costs. Well, they held – you can't say they didn't try."

It was an eloquent tribute.

On top of Reuler Hill a lieutenant colonel assembled the men who remained from the 110th. It was completely surrounded and was getting heavy artillery fire from three directions. Obviously nobody could remain there long.

The lieutenant colonel ordered everyone to split into small groups to cross the Clerf River and to try and slip through the Nazi lines and recongregate in the vicinity of Donnage, due west along the Bastogne-St. Vith road. By 7 o'clock the next morning a handful of officers and men got through.

"It was a terrible experience, ploughing through snow over hills and through fir trees, getting challenged to be shot." That's what Sergeant Joseph Dail, of Easton, Pa., said. He made the trip. Long afterwards we met men who had hidden among the enemy detoured for days, and finally escaped.

***

"THERE was plenty of opposition, too. Our S2 identified parts of five divisions that were in that area. I thought everything was after us."

Regrouping tattered, tired men, the lieutenant colonel made reconnaissance; G Company had been rushed from the division headquarters to help hold a road and was waiting when the Germans arrived. They hit at about 7:30 o'clock when the lieutenant colonel, in a jeep with two men, was making patrol.

He faced a German half-track, which fired upon the jeep, hitting two enlisted men. Jumping out of the wrecked vehicle, the lieutenant colonel ran toward our unit just as G Company was forced to retire toward Hamville.

"By this time we had met English-speaking Germans in our tanks. Nobody trusted anyone. There were no communications. Orders and everything was haywire. We fell back to Allenbern – there was no order now." I remember the time Lieutenant Jim Flynn, of G Company, said, "By God, we've got Jerry now. He's all around us. We can fire in any direction and kill him."

Private George Nichols, a New York clerk in the rear echelon, escaped ahead of the Panzers with two medics. They trudged all day and night, dodging enemy outposts and eventually found a hayloft in a bar. Climbing a ladder, they fell at once into exhausted slumber.

***

SERGEANT Daily told it: "At daylight one of the medics looked down and there was a swarm of Germans below, eating breakfast.

During the night they had taken the barn for a command post. Well, we couldn't get out and we couldn't eat or get water, for someone was always in the barn."

"Worst of all, Nichols is a notorious snorer – nobody will share quarters because of the noise he makes sleeping. So for the next four days and nights one medic always remained on guard to keep Nichols awake while the other medic slept. Poor Nichols nearly went nuts from fatigue. He said he would watch four times – that's how the fellows kept track of days before the American 26th Infantry brought relief and chased the Germans. Finally they staggered out of the hayloft.

Town by town, a handful of the 110th retreated, through Houffalize to Bastogne, before that place became an unyielding bastion, down to Neufchateau.

***

THE other two regiments fared better because the impetus of two Nazi Panzer armies split them like swinging doors. What they did and how Lancaster's Lieutenant Colonel Dan Strickler helped to defend Wiltz from another chapter of the battered 28th's history. But for the 110th and its handful of survivors the best summary of the feeling of those who got away was provided by Captain Dana Sperr, Of Oakland, Calif., who is regarded as a sort of lay evangelist before battle.

Addressing stragglers after the escape from Reuler Hill and Clervaux that horrible night, he said: "If I ever hear one of you men say we were lucky last night, or credit our escape to anything but the Will of God, I'll personally see that you are court martialled."

Today beside the Meuse the 110th is reassembling as a regiment. They have their old commander, Dan Strickler, back again, and they claim they'll rise from the wreckage. They have a tradition to carry on.

"The Old Man said to hold at any cost. They held until they were overpowered," the major said.

Pennsylvanians in Ardennes

28th Stood Up Against Big Odds

(Fourth of a Series)
By Ivan H. (Cy) Peterman
Inquirer War Correspondent
By Wireless
Copyright 1945, The Philadelphia Inquirer

WITH THE 28TH INFANTRY DIVISION, Western Front, Jan 25.

"THE problems of the 112th Infantry Regiment did not materially improve on Dec. 17, the day after the Germans launched their counter-attack into Belgium and Luxembourg. They were the same old problems of weather and war.

All that day they watched tanks approach, but they held their new lines. Later they fell back to Haldange, but from then on it was a daily move toward ever-receding positions, fighting en route and all the time at different posts.

The routine was always the same, with this exception: From time to time the regiment was attached to different divisions as it swung into line. By Dec. 20 the troops joined the shattered 106th Infantry, which had also been thrust back by the Nazi rush. They held a position at Beiler, Luxembourg. There, K Company fought off tanks and destroyed an ammunition dump and four houses sheltering Heinies.

***

THE Yanks, using mortars, suffered no casualties. Then came orders to march to Rogery, northeast to Bouvigny, some 12 miles through snow. They were no more than there when they were set up for another fight, this time attached to the Seventh American Armored Division. They were also engaged in a fierce delaying action.

This time the battalion fought while the Seventh's tank retired and all vehicles were cleared west of the Salm River. Thereafter the tired Keystone outfit was attached to the 508th Parachute Infantry Regiment, freshly arrive with the 82nd Airborne Regiment.

Between Vielsalm and Salmchateau they defended positions until ordered out when a terrific artillery barrage struck them while going to an assembly area near Hautebodeaux, 10 miles further along.

The battalion then went over to the Ninth Armored, and later, was attached to the Third Armored and the 75th Infantry Divisions before it drifted back to join other 28th elements along the Meuse.

***

A COMBAT team under Colonel Nelson was having similar experiences when the Germans drove upon the regimental headquarters at Ouren with elements of two divisions, including the Second Panzers.

Captain Paul A. Troup, of Reading, Pa., led headquarters company, besides C Company of the 103rd Engineers, under Captain Dick Minton of New Canton, Ill., and restored the positions.

Again on Dec. 17 the Huns struck, and were again repelled with heavy losses, but tanks were in the second attack and the 28th also had losses. In this fight the 630th Tank Destroyer Battalion, under Lieutenant Clarence Bryant, of Atlanta, knocked out a bunch of Nazi tanks.

One Dec, 19 the regiment was ordered back behind a river with few losses, and the 229th Field Artillery, commanded by Lieutenant Colonel John C. Fairchild, of Chesnut Hill, moved with them. Hammering the foe, they held a line in the vicinity of Weiswampach, Luxembourg.

***

A REAR guard action was begun thereafter through Trois Vierges and Huldange, where another shot at the regimental command point was repulsed.

Meanwhile, the whole outfit was attached to the 106th Division, defending positions near Beiler and Leithum, until Dec. 21, when headquarters directed a move to a defensive line at Vielsalm, in Belgium. Under cover of a snowstorm they retired to the new First Army line, which had been established meanwhile.

While fighting here the Nazis cut off the whole First Battalion, plus its regimental headquarters, and elements of other units, in a sudden thrust toward Salmchateau, which prompted one of the outstanding jobs of leadership by the 28th this war has produced.

***

AFTER reconnoitring, Colonel Nelson took personal command of a column of vehicles and footsloggers, leading them first westward then north, slipping through German held territory but always eluding Germans. With loss of few personnel or equipment the outfit escaped back into the American lines. The 112th stands ready to resume against the foe anywhere, its total losses throughout the engagement being slight.

There has been much conjecture at home about the fate of the 28th – as one who passed along its extended Luxembourg line just 48 hours before Marshal Gerd von Rundstedt moved, I admit it seemed impossible how so many escaped.

But aside from the terribly-battered 110th, which was luckiest, perhaps, in the Hürtgen Forest slaughter but certainly hardest hit this time, the 28th Division acquitted itself well and managed to keep its elements together. There was no running, no panic, and no surrender when to stand meant consolidation and preparation.

***

The boys gave a fine fighting account as they dropped back before the onslaught of three or four divisions of the main spearhead that eventually reached within three miles of Dinant.

It is because some of our so-called "experts" sometimes place blame before knowing the facts, that outfits like the 28th and the 106th must take blame that is not their fault. I will have more to say

of this when discussing what happened to these divisions. For the present I save the foregoing chronology just for itself in the case of the 109th, but almost obliterated 110th, 109th and the equally able 112th Infantry Regiment.

(Continued Tomorrow)

APPENDIX B

Partial Roster of the Men Who Fought in Hosingen, Luxembourg: December 16-18, 1944

Name	Unit, Company	Notes	POW Camp(s)
Arbella, Sgt. James S.	110, K*	4th platoon mortar section leader	Stalag 9B Bad Orb
Bryan, S/Sgt. Frank F.	110, K*		Germany
Bulick, Pfc. Frank J.	110, K*		Stalag 9B Bad Orb
Burnett, Pfc. Elbert D. Jr.	110, K		Stalag 9B Bad Orb
Caballero, Pfc. Carlos	110, K*		Stalag 9B Bad Orb
Cornell, Pfc. Edwin H. J.	110, K	Rifleman, K Company	Stalag 9B Bad Orb
Dalgliesh, Sgt. Joseph F.	110, K*		Stalag 4B Mühlberg
Davis, Pfc. Edwin R.	110, K*		Stalag 4B Mühlberg
Dent, Pfc. Earl W.	110, K*		Stalag 2D Stargard Pomerania, Prussia
Epstein, Pvt. Melvin	110, K	1st Platoon gunner	Stalag 9B Bad Orb
Everson, T/5 Lloyd C.	110, K	In water tower when captured	Stalag 9B Bad Orb; Stalag 9A at Ziegenhain
Feiker, Capt. Frederick C.	110, K	K Co. Captain, Died as POW	Stalag 9B Bad Orb; Oflag 13B Hammelburg*
Flynn, 1st Lt., Ex O, Thomas J.	110, K	1st Platoon leader on the North end	Stalag 9B Bad Orb; Oflag 13B Hammelburg*
Forsell, Sgt. John F.	110, K	1st Platoon squad leader	Stalag 3B Furstenberg
Fox, Pvt.	110, K	1st Platoon rifleman	n/a

Name	Unit	Notes	Location
Gallagher, S/Sgt. James H.	110, K*		Stalag 4B Mühlberg
Gasper, Pfc. Edward J.	110, K	1st Platoon rifleman	Stalag 9B Bad Orb
Glick, Pvt. Philip P.	110, K	KIA in Hosingen	—
Gonzalez, Pvt. Andrew G.	110, K*		Stalag 9B Bad Orb
Goursky, Sgt. Edward	110, K		Germany
Gracie, Pvt. William A. Jr.	110, K	4th Platoon, Bazooka on North end of town	Stalag 4B Mühlberg–Escaped
Greene, Pfc. Warren A.	110, K*		Germany
Grove, Pvt. Walter E.	110, K*		Stalag 4B Mühlberg
Grubbs, Pfc. Charles W.	110, K*		Stalag 4B Mühlberg
Guenther, Staff Sgt. Norman R.	110, K	Positioned in churches	Stalag 9B Bad Orb
Hendzel, Pfc. Walter J.	110, K*		Stalag 9B Bad Orb
Howes, Pvt. Oscar M.	110, K		Stalag 4B Mühlberg
Hunnell, T/5 Charles E.	110, K*		Germany
Kappenberger, Pfc. John D.	110, K		Unknown
Kusnir, Pfc. Frank S.	110, K		Stalag 9B Bad Orb
Mc Cauley, Pvt. George R.	110, K		Germany
Mc Crory, Pvt. Charles B.	110, K		Stalag 9B Bad Orb
Mc Glashen, Pfc. Merritt	110, K	KIA in Hosingen	—

Name	Unit, Company	Notes	POW Camp(s)
Mc Grath, Cpl. John E.	110, K		Stalag 9C Bad Sulza
Menefee, Sgt. Scott A.	110, K		Stalag 4B Mühlberg
Miller, Pfc. Thomas J.	110, K		Stalag 4B Mühlberg
Moser, Pfc. Roy D.	110, K		Stalag 9B Bad Orb
Porter, 1st Lt. Bernard U.	110, K	2nd Platoon leader on south end	Stalag 9B Bad Orb; Oflag 13B Hammelburg*
Reynolds, T/5 Councle A.	110, K*		Stalag 4B Mühlberg
Roys, Pfc. Frederick S.	110, K		Stalag 9B Bad Orb
Seidel, Pfc. Harry H.	110, K*	4th Platoon	Stalag 4B Mühlberg
Shanabarger, S/Sgt. Henry D.	110, K*	4th Platoon, In water tower	Stalag 4B Mühlberg
Simpson, T/5 Samuel C.	110, K*		Stalag 4B Mühlberg
Skovbo, Pvt. Alvin P.	110, K	KIA in Hosingen	—
Stanfield, Pfc. Owen E.	110, K*		Stalag 9B Bad Orb
Swartz, Sgt. John E.	110, K*		Germany
Tennessee (nickname)	110, K	1st platoon rifleman; full name unknown	—
Wayman, T/4 Rayburn L.	110, K*		Stalag 9B Bad Orb

Name	Unit	Position	POW Camp
Weaver, 1st Lt. Barrett M.	110, K*	3rd Platoon leader, Hosingen-Barriere outpost	Stalag 3B Furstenberg Brandenburg, Prussia
Webb, Pvt. Thomas E.	110, K*		Stalag 3B Furstenberg Brandenburg, Prussia
West, T/5 Raymond S.	110, K*		Stalag 9B Bad Orb
Whitlatch, T/4 Kenneth L.	110, K*		Stalag 4B Mühlberg
Williams, 1st Sgt. Donald K.	110, K		Stalag 9B Bad Orb
Gallego, Pvt. Ernest P.	110, M	2nd platoon, Hosingen-Barriere outpost; Gustafson's machine gun crew	Stalag 9B Bad Orb
Gustafson, Pvt. Dale L.	110, M	2nd platoon, Hosingen-Barriere outpost; 30-cal MG	Stalag 9B Bad Orb
Kosick, Pvt. Frank J.	110, M	Positioned SW corner of Hosingen–Bazooka	Stalag 9B Bad Orb
Morse, 1st Lt. James D.	110, M	Mortar Section Leader, south half of town	Stalag 9B Bad Orb; Oflag 13B Hammelburg*
Brander, Staff Sgt. Harry A.	103, B		Stalag 9B Bad Orb
Butler, Pvt. Joseph	103, B	Positioned SW corner of Hosingen	Stalag 4B Mühlberg
Devlin, 2nd Lt. Charles F.	103, B	3rd Platoon Leader, Died as POW	Stalag 9B Bad Orb; Oflag 13B Hammelburg*

Name	Unit, Company	Notes	POW Camp(s)
Doyen, Sgt. Darrel J.	103, B	Positioned SW corner of Hosingen	Stalag 4B Mühlberg
Gilmore, Pvt. John J.	103, B		Stalag 4B Mühlberg
Grady, Pfc. Kenneth E.	103, B	Shot during POW lineup after surrender	Transported to Stalag 4B Mühlberg and later died as POW
Gronefeld, Sgt. Lawrence W.	103, B	Died as a result in injuries on 12/18/44	—
Hawn, Pvt. William B.	103, B	Killed in church after he fainted	—
Hutter, 1st Lt. Cary A.	103, B	1st Platoon leader, west side	Stalag 9B Bad Orb; Oflag 13B Hammelburg*
Imhof, Cpl. George H.	103, B		Stalag 9B Bad Orb; Stalag 9A at Ziegenhain
Jarrett, Capt. William H.	103, B	103B Eng. Captain	Stalag 4B Mühlberg
Julien, Pvt. Leland V.	103, B	Positioned SW corner of Hosingen	Stalag 9B Bad Orb
King, Pvt. William	103, B	Positioned SW corner of Hosingen	Stalag 4B Mühlberg
Miller, Cpl. Samuel L.	103, B	Positioned SW corner of Hosingen	Stalag 9B Bad Orb; Stalag 9A at Ziegenhain

Name	Unit	Notes	POW Camp
Pickering, 2nd Lt. John A.	103, B	2nd Platoon leader on south end	Stalag 9B Bad Orb; Oflag 13B Hammelburg*
Slobodzian, 1st Lt. Theodore P.	103, B	Died as a result in injuries on 12/18/44	—
Smith, Pfc. Frank S.	103, B	Captured when he went for medical supplies with John Putz	Stalag 9B Bad Orb
Sterk, Pfc. Jacob J.	103, B	Positioned SW corner of Hosingen	Stalag 13D Nuremberg (Oflag 73)
Stevenson, Cpl. George G.	103, B	Cpl. George G. Stevenson, 103B Eng.	Stalag 4B Mühlberg
Stone, Pfc. Jay E.	103, B	Radio operator	Stalag 9B Bad Orb
Winchester, 1st Sgt. Joseph	103, B	Positioned in churches	Stalag 4B Mühlberg
Wnek, Pvt. John	103, B	Wounded during POW lineup	Stalag 11B Fallingbostel Prussia (Work Camps)
Erickson, T/4 Wayne V.	103, Medical	Medic for K Company	Stalag 4B Mühlberg; Stalag 8A Gorlitz; marched 1500 km; liberated at Horsingen, Germany
Mc Bride, 2nd Lt. Danny R. (nicknamed "Doc")	103, Medical	2nd Lt. male nurse	Stalag 9B Bad Orb; Oflag 13B Hammelburg*
Mc Knight, Sgt. George	103, Medical	Medic for K Company	Stalag 4B Mühlberg; Stalag 8A Gorlitz; marched 1500 km in total

Name	Unit, Company	Notes	POW camp(s)
Putz, T/4 John M.	103, Medical	Medic for 103B Company–Captured when he went for medical supplies with Frank Smith	Stalag 4B Mühlberg (Stalag 9B Bad Orb per son, James Putz, 031514)
Tucker, Pvt. Robert G.	103, Medical	Medic for K Company	Stalag 4B Mühlberg
Dake, Cpl. Leonard G.	630th	2nd Platoon, Tank Destroyer Battalion	Stalag 4B Mühlberg
Freeman, S/Sgt. William O.	630th	2nd Platoon, Tank Destroyer Battalion	Stalag 4B Mühlberg; marched from Gorlitz to Horsingen, Germany where liberated
Payne, 1st Lt. Richard H.	707, A	Tank Company A Co. Platoon leader	Stalag 9B Bad Orb; Oflag 13B Hammmelburg*

* Member of the original K Company that landed on Omaha Beach July 25, '44.
Source: National Archives WWII POW database, Stalag 9B and Oflag 13B POW records
*Captain Feiker was killed by Allied bombing en route from Nuremberg's Oflag Luft III POW camp to Moosburg Stalag VIIA.
*Lt. Charles Devlin, who had been with the 103B Engineers in Hosingen, died while a prisoner of war.
**Flynn and all but seventy-five POWs in Hammmelburg were moved to Nuremberg Stalag Luft III and then Moosburg Stalag VIIA after the Americans temporarily liberated the Hammmelburg Stalag XIIIB camp.
*** After leaving Hammmelburg, he was placed on a forced march to Dachau Prison Camp. Two more escapes led him to American Forces and a return stateside in April, 1945.

APPENDIX C

K Company, 110th Infantry Regiment, 28th Infantry Division Roll Call on July 25, 1944 Omaha Beach Landing

Provided to Sam Oliveto from Robert Peters on September 1988–Commanding Officer, K Company, 110th Infantry Division, 28th Infantry Division on July 25, 1944.

The roster includes two sets of brothers:

- S/Sgt. Frank F. Bryan and Pfc Jack L. Bryan
- T/5 Charles E. Hunnell and Pvt. Wayne E. Hunnell

Status Legend:
MIA – Missing in Action
DOW – Died of Wounds
KIA – Killed in Action
DAW – Died after War
POW – Prisoner of War
W – Wounded
TF – Trench Foot

The classification of casualties as noted after names in this roster are correct is the best of my knowledge and are in no way conclusive nor are the intended to be statement of truth on my part.

Name	Status	Date; Location
Abney, Pvt. Orval W.		
Adams, Pvt. Paul	POW	8/4/1944; N. France – sent to Stalag 7A Moosburg
Andrews, Pvt. Criss W.	MIA	
Arbella, Sgt. James S.	POW	12/20/1944; Hosingen, Lux. – sent to Stalag 9B Bad Orb
Armstrong, Pvt. Herman W.		
Baker, Pvt. Nathan E.		
Balog, Pvt. Frank Jr.	DAW	
Bell, S/ Sgt. John J.	DOW	
Bentz, Pvt. Thomas		
Bianconi, Pfc. Fulvio N.		
Birchfield, Pvt. Charles R.		
Blue, Pvt. Harold M.		
Boling, Pvt. Thomas T.		
Bryan, S/Sgt. Frank F.	POW	12/20/1944; Hosingen, Lux.
Bryan, Pfc. Jack L.		
Buchman, Sgt. Carl R.	KIA	10/5/1944; Rhineland
Bulick, Pfc. Frank J.	POW	12/20/1944; Hosingen, Lux. – sent to Stalag 9B Bad Orb
Burghardt, Sgt. Albert W.	TF	11/8/1944; Hürtgen Forest
Caballero, Pfc. Carlos	POW	12/20/1944; Hosingen, Lux. – sent to Stalag 9B Bad Orb
Campbell, Pvt. John H.		
Chattaway, Sgt. Charles L.	DAW	
Cheskey, Pfc. Carl W.		
Collins, Pvt. Fred, Jr.		
Congrove, Pvt. William W.		

Name	Status	Date; Location
Conklin, Pvt. Herbert C.		
Crivella, Sgt. Carmen J.		
Currey, Pvt. Brennie D.		
Dalgliesh, Sgt. Joseph F.	POW	12/20/1944; Hosingen, Lux. – sent to Stalag 4B Mühlberg
Davis, Pfc. Edwin R.	POW	12/20/1944; Hosingen, Lux. – sent to Stalag 4B Mühlberg
Davis, Pvt. Fleming S.		
Davis, Pvt. Lonnie T.		
Davisson, Pvt. John P.		
Davisson, Pvt. Wade A.		
Debo, Pvt. Joe		
Deems, Pvt. Bert K.		
Dent, Pfc. Earl W.	POW	12/20/1944; Hosingen, Lux. – sent to Stalag 2D Stargard
Depace, Paul J.		
Dickinson, Pvt. Louis A.		
Dill, Pvt. Frank M.		
Dingleberry, Pvt. George H.		
Dinino, Pvt. Leon J.	KIA	8/2/1944; N. France
Doyle, Pvt. Arthur J.		
Drenocky, Pvt. Charles	KIA	8/2/1944; N. France
Dudley, Pvt. Frederick C.		
Dzieszkowicz, Pvt. Eugene M.	KIA	9/22/1944; Rhineland
Eastman, Pvt. Orville M.		
Eckes, Pvt. Elmer P.		
Eckles, Pvt. Earl		
Eldred, Pvt. Arthur T.		
Elerick, Pvt. Willard F.		
Everman, Pvt. Albert J.		
Evix, Pfc. Herman B.	KIA	8/12/1944; N. France

Name	Status	Date; Location
Fisher, Sgt. Edward A.	KIA	9/30/1944; Rhineland
Fleming, Pvt. Ervin T.	POW	MIA as of 8/4/1944
Flint, Pvt. Richard T.		
Fonner, Pvt. James E.		
Francis, Wallace W.		
Friedman, Pvt. Harold H.		
Gagne, Pfc. John L.	KIA	8/4/1944; N. France
Gallagher, S/Sgt. James H.	POW	12/20/1944; Hosingen, Lux. – sent to Stalag 4B Mühlberg
Gandee, Pfc. Oval A.	KIA	10/1/1944; Rhineland
Garvey, Pvt. John L.	DAW	
Gaus, Pvt. Lawrence W.		
Gentry, Pfc. Lawrence J.	KIA	11/5/1944; Hürtgen Forest
Geronimo, Pvt. Anthony J.		
Gibbs, Pvt. Samuel A. Jr.		
Gift, Pvt. Melvin L.		
Glaub, Pvt. John A.		
Gonzalez, Pvt. Andrew G.	POW	12/20/1944; Hosingen, Lux. – sent to Stalag 9B Bad Orb
Godd, John		
Gravitte, Pvt. William M.		
Gray, Pvt. Raymond C.		
Greene, Pfc. Warren A.	POW	12/20/1944; Hosingen, Lux.
Griffith, Harold E.	KIA	
Grilli, Pvt. Valerio		
Grove, Pvt. Walter E.	POW	12/20/1944; Hosingen, Lux. – sent to Stalag 4B Mühlberg
Grubbs, Pfc. Charles W.	POW	12/20/1944; Hosingen, Lux. – sent to Stalag 4B Mühlberg
Hamilton, Robert R.		
Hampton, Pvt. Henry F.	KIA	8/2/1944; N. France

Name	Status	Date; Location
Harris, Pvt. Arley	KIA	8/3/1944; N. France
Harris, Pfc. Eugene	KIA	11/5/1944; Hürtgen Forest
Haun, Pvt. Alva R.	KIA	10/1/1944; Rhineland
Heck, Fred		
Hendzel, Pfc. Walter J.	POW	12/20/1944; Hosingen, Lux.
Hochreiter, Pfc. Richard T.	KIA	8/13/1944; N. France
Hoffman, Pvt. Julian W.		
Huffman, Pvt. Clarence W.		
Hull, Pvt. Melvin C.		
Hunnell, T/5 Charles E.	POW	12/20/1944; Hosingen, Lux.
Hunnell, Pvt. Wayne E.		
Iaquinto, Pvt. Louie	KIA	8/2/1944; N. France
Jauernig, Julius J.		
Johnson, Arthur C.		
Kertesz, S/Sgt. Charles	KIA	10/1/1944; Rhineland
Kittle, Pfc. John	KIA	8/6/1944; N. France
Kladke, Pvt. Clarence A.		
Klein, Pvt. Allan C.		
Kline, Pvt. John F.		
Koslowski, Florian L.		
Krizay, Pvt. Adolph E.		
Kwaisgroch, Pvt. Andrew J.		
Landau, Pfc. Robert E.	KIA	8/2/1944; N. France
Larsen, Pvt. Jack C.		
Leasure, Sgt. Harry B.	KIA	8/2/1944; N. France
Lee, Byron L.		
Lemley, Pfc. Harry L.	KIA	8/4/1944; N. France
Linstedt, Pvt. Alton H.		
Loveless, Pvt. Charles F.		
Malecki, Harry		

Name	Status	Date; Location
Matthews, S/Sgt. Milford E.	KIA	10/1/1944; Rhineland
Matyas, Pvt. John		
McCauley, Pvt. George R.	POW	12/20/1944; Hosingen, Lux.
McCrory, Pvt. Charles B.	POW	12/20/1944; Hosingen, Lux. – sent to Stalag 9B Bad Orb
Mc Elhaney, Pvt. Tim H.		
Mc Vaney, Pvt. Blair S.		
Merrell, Pvt. Eugene A.		
Miller, Quenten		
Minnoe, Pvt. Robert G.		
Monroe, S/Sgt. James E.	KIA	8/13/1944; N. France
Moore, Sgt. Edgar Jr.	KIA	11/5/1944; Hürtgen Forest
Myers, S/Sgt. Harold G.	KIA	7/31/1944; N. France
Newsome, Pvt. William M.		
Oliveto, Pfc. Sam S.	W	11/5/1944: Hürtgen Forest
Orndoff, Pvt. John R. Jr.		
Peevler, Pvt. David L.		
Peterson, Pfc. Thomas J.	DOW	
Pfrogner, Pfc. Eugene H.		
Pierro, Pvt. Michael, A.		
Piper, Pvt. Vernon C.		
Pogue, Charles O.		
Presley, Pvt. Ray		
Przepiora, Pvt. Joseph E.		
Raber, Pvt. Walter J.		
Reed, Pvt. Joe R.	W	11/10/1944: Hürtgen Forest
Reiber, Cpl. Harry J. Jr.		
Renner, Pvt. Homer C.		
Reynolds, T/5 Councle A.	POW	12/20/1944; Hosingen, Lux. – sent to Stalag 4B Mühlberg

Name	Status	Date; Location
Robinson, Pvt. Robert R.		
Ryne, Hayden B.		
Salvador, Pvt. Joseph D.		
Sandidge, S/Sgt. Edgar R.	KIA	8/10/1944; N. France
Sarafian, Pvt. Don		
Schoen, Pvt. Joseph J.		
Schreffler, Pvt. Meredith C.		
Schultz, Pvt. William B.		
Scott, Pvt. Asa H. Jr.	DAW	
Seefeldt, Pvt. Howard E.		
Seidel, Pfc. Harry H.	POW	12/20/1944; Hosingen, Lux. – sent to Stalag 4B Mühlberg
Seifert, Pfc. Eugene F.	KIA	9/19/1944; Rhineland
Shanabarger, S/Sgt. Henry D.	POW	12/20/1944; Hosingen, Lux. – sent to Stalag 4B Mühlberg
Sheets, Pvt. Charles A.		
Shytle, Pvt. Wilburn S.		
Simmonds, Pvt. Robert L.		
Simpson, T/5 Samuel C.	POW	12/20/1944; Hosingen, Lux. – sent to Stalag 4B Mühlberg
Sisty, Norman W.		
Skurla, T/Sgt. Joseph	KIA	8/3/1944; N. France
Smith, Pvt. Howard T.		
Smith, Pfc. Hugh D.		Stalag IXB; 34312889
Smith, Pvt. Lester R.		
Spencer, Pvt. Edward J.		
Spinelli, Pfc. John A.	KIA	10/1/1944; Rhineland
Spivack, Pvt. Hyman		
Staggers, Pvt. Charles J.		
Stanfield, Pfc. Owen E.	POW	12/20/1944; Hosingen, Lux. – sent to Stalag 9B Bad Orb

Name	Status	Date; Location
Steele, Pvt. Henry B.		
Swartz, Sgt. John E.	POW	12/20/1944; Hosingen, Lux.
Szypka, Pvt. William B.		
Terry, Edward E.	KIA	
Thomas, Pvt. Virgil A.		
Tiberio, Pvt. Carlo	KIA	8/4/1944; N. France
Tyran, Pvt. Leon H.	DAW	
Valdez, Eduardo		
Varian, Pvt. Clarence T.		
Veith, Pvt. John A.		
Vincent, Pvt. Howard A.		
Wanner, John A.		
Watson, Waylon R.		
Wayman, T/4 Rayburn L.	POW	12/20/1944; Hosingen, Lux.. – sent to Stalag 9B Bad Orb
Webb, Pvt. Thomas E.	POW	12/20/1944; Hosingen, Lux.. – sent to Stalag 3B Furstenberg
West, T/5 Raymond S.	POW	12/20/1944; Hosingen, Lux.. – sent to Stalag 9B Bad Orb
Wheeler, Pvt. Chester J.		
White, Everett R.		
Whitlatch, T/4 Kenneth L.	POW	12/20/1944; Hosingen, Lux.. – sent to Stalag 4B Mühlberg
Wiedemyer, Francis P.		
Wosilek, Pvt. Charles S.	KIA	8/4/1944; N. France
Zinn, Pvt. Edward D. Jr.		
Zoric, Pvt. William S.		

Officers	Status	Date
Harper, 1st Lt. Malcolm F., (1st Platoon)	KIA	
Jordan, 1st Lt. Archie R., (Executive Officer)		
Peters, Capt. Robert E., (Co. Commanding Officer)		
Templer, 1st Lt. Ernest L., (2nd Platoon)	KIA	11/5/1944; Hürtgen Forest
Tuisl, 2nd Lt. Carl P., (4th Platoon)	KIA	8/13/1944; N. France
Weaver, 1st Lt. Barrett M., (3rd Platoon)	POW	12/20/1944; Hosingen, Lux.. – sent to Stalag 3B Furstenberg

APPENDIX D

K Company, 110th Infantry Regiment, 28th Infantry Division Casualty Report: July 25, 1944–May 1945

Record of all Killed In Action (KIA) from locator cards:
K Company, 110th Infantry Division, 28th Infantry Division–WWII
Listings from Ralph Johnson, Historian 110th Infantry Regiment

Name	Date	Area
Alfke, Pvt. Henry	2/7/1945	Colmar
Bell, S/ Sgt. John J.*	9/9/1944	Rhineland
Bendinelli, Pfc. Ottto A. Jr.	11/5/1944	Hürtgen Forest
Bobzin, Pfc. Stanley J.	11/5/1944	Hürtgen Forest
Bolen, Pvt. William M.	11/9/1944	Hürtgen Forest
Bond, Sgt. Robert L.	9/19/1944	Rhineland
Buchman, Sgt. Carl R.*	10/5/1944	Rhineland
Dimock, Pvt. Erwin C.	2/7/1945	Colmar
Dinino, Pvt. Leon J.*	8/2/1944	N. France
Drenocky, Pvt. Charles*	8/2/1944	N. France
Dress, Pvt. James W.	1/29/1945	Vosges Mts.
Dzieszkowicz, Pvt. Eugene M.*	9/22/1944	Rhineland

Name	Date	Area
Evix, Pfc. Herman B.*	8/12/1944	N. France
Falcone, Pfc. Philip	11/9/1944	Hürtgen Forest
Feiker, Capt. Frederick C.	4/5/1945	Nuremberg, Ger.
Fine, Pfc. Sol	9/2/1944	N. France
Fisher, Sgt. Edward A.*	9/30/1944	Rhineland
Gagne, Pfc. John L.*	8/4/1944	N. France
Gandee, Pfc. Oral A.*	10/1/1944	Rhineland
Gentry, Pfc. Lawrence J.*	11/5/1944	Hürtgen Forest
Gerdes, S/Sgt. Woodrow F.	11/9/1944	Hürtgen Forest
Gipson, 2nd Lt. Woodrow W.	12/30/1944	Ardennes
Glick, Pvt. Philip P.	12/20/1944	Hosingen, Lux.
Hampton, Pvt. Henry F.*	8/2/1944	N. France
Harper, 1st Lt. Malcolm F.*		
Harris, Pvt. Arley*	8/3/1944	N. France
Harris, Pfc. Eugene*	11/5/1944	Hürtgen Forest
Haun, Pvt. Alva R.*	10/1/1944	Rhineland
Hochreiter, Pfc. Richard T. *	8/13/1944	N. France
Huskey, Pfc. Charles G. Jr.	11/5/1944	Hürtgen Forest
Iaquinto, Pvt. Louie*	8/2/1944	N. France
Kertesz, S/Sgt. Charles*	10/1/1944	Rhineland
Kieby, Pfc. John H.	10/27/1944	Rhineland
Kittle, Pfc. John*	8/6/1944	N. France
Landau, Pfc. Robert E.*	8/2/1944	N. France
Leasure, Sgt. Harry B.*	8/2/1944	N. France
Lemley, Pfc. Harry L.*	8/4/1944	N. France
Love, 1st Lt. Lawrence L.	11/9/1944	Hürtgen Forest
Matthews, S/Sgt. Milford E.*	10/1/1944	Rhineland
Mc Glashen, Pfc. Merritt	12/20/1944	Hosingen, Lux.
Milbrandt, Pfc. John F.	11/9/1944	Hürtgen Forest

Name	Date	Area
Monroe, S/Sgt. James E.*	8/13/1944	N. France
Moore, Sgt. Edger Jr.*	11/5/1944	Hürtgen Forest
Myers, S/Sgt. Harold G.*	7/31/1944	N. France
Neu, Pfc. Herbert H.	11/9/1944	Hürtgen Forest
Peterson, Pfc. Thomas J.*	8/24/1944	N. France
Price, Pfc. Robert C.	3/4/1945	Blumenthal, Germany
Rattay, Pvt. Joseph A.	2/7/1945	Colmar
Ricci, Pfc. Edward J.	11/9/1944	Hürtgen Forest
Riddell, Pfc. Jesse J.	11/1/1944	Rhineland
Rogowski, Pfc. William J.	11/9/1944	Hürtgen Forest
Sandidge, S/Sgt. Edgar R.*	8/10/1944	N. France
Scheible, Pvt. Harry C.	11/2/1944	Hürtgen Forest
Scott, Pvt. John W.	11/12/1944	Hürtgen Forest
Seifert, Pfc. Eugene F.*	9/19/1944	Rhineland
Semanik, 2nd Lt. John M. Jr.	11/5/1944	Hürtgen Forest
Skovbo, Pvt. Alvin P.	12/20/1944	Hosingen, Lux.
Skurla, T/Sgt. Joseph*	8/3/1944	N. France
Smith, Pfc. Frederick A.	11/9/1944	Hürtgen Forest
Smoot, Pfc. Walter C.	11/5/1944	Hürtgen Forest
Spinelli, Pfc. John A.*	10/1/1944	Rhineland
Staten, Pfc. James L.	9/19/1944	Rhineland
Stengel, Sgt. Homer J.	8/13/1944	N. France
Stephens, Pvt. Harvey E.	9/17/1944	Rhineland
Templer, 1st Lt. Ernest L.*	11/5/1944	Hürtgen Forest
Thauren, Pfc. John O.	9/14/1944	Rhineland
Tiberio, Pvt. Carlo*	8/4/1944	N. France
Tiernan, Pvt. James A.	1/29/1945	Vosges Mts.
Tuisl, 2nd Lt. Carl P.*	8/13/1944	N. France

Name	Date	Area
Violette, Pvt. Harold M.	1/29/1945	Vosges Mts.
Wosilek, Pvt. Charles S.*	8/4/1944	N. France
Zehr. 1st Sgt. Floyd F.	11/2/1944	Hürtgen Forest

* Member of the original K Company that landed on Omaha Beach July 25, '44.

Bibliography

Books

Astor, Gerald, *The Bloody Forest, Battle for the Huertgen: September 1944–January 1945*. California: Presidio Press, Inc., 2000.

Currey, Cecil B., *Follow Me and Die: The Destruction of an American Division in World War II*. New York: Stein and Day, 1984.

Flynn, Alice M., *Unforgettable: The Biography of Capt. Thomas J. Flynn*. Oregon: Sky Blue Publishing, 2011.

Goolrick, William K., and Ogden Tanner, *The Battle of the Bulge, World War II*. New York:Time-Life Books Inc., 1979.

Huntsberger, Karen B., *Waiting for Peace, The Journals & Correspondence of a World War II Medic*.   Oregon: Luminar Press, 2015.

MacDonald, Charles B., *The Battle of the Huertgen Forest*. Pennsylvania, J.B. Lippencott Company,1963.

McManus, John C. *Alamo in the Ardennes: The Untold Story of the American Soldiers Who Made the Defense of Bastogne Possible*. New York: NAL Caliber, 2008.

Phillips, Robert F., *To Save Bastogne*. Virginia: Borodino Books, 1996.

Vannoy, Robert F. and Jay Karamales, *Against the Panzers, United States Infantry versus German Tanks, 1944-1945*. North Carolina: McFarland & Company, Inc., 1996.

Weaver, Michael E., *Guard Wars: The 28th Infantry Division in World War II*. Indiana University Press, 2010.

Whiting, Robert F., *The Battle of Hürtgen Forest*. New York: Orion Books, 1989.

Articles, Reports, Interviews and Letters

Cpl. Richard J. Berkey, Medic, 14th Armored Division, 68th AIB, C Company, May 1, 1945 journal entry.

Morley Cassidy, Philadelphia Sunday Evening Bulletin, articles by War correspondent attached to the 28th Infantry Division, January, 1945.

Wayne V. Erickson, Medic, 103rd Medical Batallion, *My Part of Time*, May 1990.

Sgt. Lloyd Everson letter to Robert Phillips written in 1994.

1st Lt. Thomas J. Flynn interview, K Company, 110th Infantry Regiment, 28th Infantry Division, National Archives, Record Group 407; May 1-2, 1945.

William O. Freeman, *What Happened In Hosingen, Luxembourg?*. The Bulge Bugle, August 1994.

Col. Hurley E. Fuller *Unit Report No. 5–110th Infantry Regiment, 28th Infantry Division; 01Nov44-30Nov44*, Consthum, Luxembourg.

Pvt. William Gracie letter to Betty Lee and William L. Wilson, April 30, 1945.

Capt. John S. Howe, interview with 3rd Battalion commander, Col. George H. Rumbaugh, 110th Infantry Regiment, 28th Infantry Division, December 15-16, 1944 at 3rd Battalion command post in Consthum, Luxembourg. Part of National Archives and Records Administration, Record Group 407, Records of The Adjutant General, U.S. Army, Combat Interviews (CI-76), 28th Infantry Division, Hürtgen Forest Campaign.

International Red Cross Reports, Bad Orb-Stalag 9B and Hammelburg-Oflag XIIIB, prisoner of war camps, World War II, 1942-1945. Part of National Archives and Records Administration, Record Group 389. Excerpt from Capt. William H. Jarrett's Wartime Log, pgs 27- 67, covering 16 Dec 1944–17 March 1945, p.45.

Cpl. Samuel L. Miller, B Company, 103rd Engineer Battalion, excerpt from interview on WWII given in 2003 for his wife, Dorothy, pages 24-37.

Lt. James D. Morse, Interview given to Al Price, August 16, 1996.

Larry G. Newman, International News Service, *A Saga of Gallant Men, How Heroic 28th Halted Nazis And Saved Our Armies*, article by War correspondent attached to Gen. George S. Patton's press corps, January, 1945.

Ivan (Cy) Peterman, Philadelphia Inquirer, articles by War correspondent attached to the 28th Infantry Division, January, 1945.

Web sites and Online Articles

Ambrose, Stephen E. "Citizen Solders," http://members.aeroinc.net/breners/buckswar/forest.html, (Dec. 29, 2009).

Axis History Forum, Hürtgen Forest, Factory of death, http://forum.axishistory.com/viewtopic.php?f=54&t=66893&start=30, (Dec. 29, 2009).

Battle of Hürtgen Forest, http://en.wikipedia.org/wiki/battle_of_h%C%BCrtgen_Forest, (Dec. 29, 2009).

Bradbeer, Thomas G. *Major General Cota and the Battle of the Hürtgen Forest: A Failure of Battle Command? http://usacac.army.mil/cac2/cgsc/repository/dcl_MGCota.pdf (Dec. 29, 2009).*

Christianson, Lt. Col. Thomas E., *The Destruction of the 28th Inf. Div. in the Huertgen Forest, Nov. 1944,* Scorpio's Web site, The Battle of the Hürtgen Forest, http://www.huertgenforest.be/ScoWeb.php (Dec. 29, 2009).

Department of the Navy, Naval Historical Center, *Online Library of Selected Images: Events, World War II in Europe Normandy Invasion, June 1944, Overview and Special Image Selection,* http://www.history.navy.mil/photos/events/wwii-eur/normandy/normandy.htm (Dec. 29, 2009).

Ethridge, Bill. *Time Out. A Remembrance of World War II,* http://www.moosburg.org/info/stalag/bilder/eth5.jpg (Jan. 12, 2010).

Fact Sheet of the 28th Infantry Division, http://www.battleofthebulge.org/fact/fact_sheet_of_the_28th_infantry.html (Dec. 29, 2009).

Free Republic, LLC, *The FReeper Foxhole Remembers the 110th Infantry at the Bulge (12/16-19/1944) Dec 16, 2003,* http://209.157.64.200/focus/f-vetscor/1041184/posts (Dec. 29, 2009).

Google, *WWII German Panther tank footage,* http://video.google.com/videoplay?docid=3400216787641857936&ei=FPA S4iQC ZWUqAPAtdnmDg&q=WWII+German+Panther+tank&hl=en docid=7186358934547442029 (Jan. 2, 2010).

Hammelburg Raid, The, http://lions44.hubpages.com/hub/The-Hammelburg-Raid# (Sept. 12, 2015).

Holt, Major Jeffrey P., *Abstract of Thesis: The 28th Infantry Division in the 'Green Hell',* Scorpio's Web site, The Battle of the Hürtgen Forest, http://www.huertgenforest.be/ScoWeb.php (Dec. 29, 2009).

LoneSentry.com,http://www.google.com/imgres?imgurl=http://www.lonesentry.com/articles/armoredforces/ (Jan. 2, 2010).

Lone Sentry.com, *Photographs of Stalag IX-B in Bad Orb, Germany,* http://www.lonesentry.com/badorb/index.html (Jan. 8, 2010).

Moosburg On-line, http://www.moosburg.org/info/stalag/bilder/ (Jan. 12, 2010).

Nideggen railroad siding, http://www.restlesswings.com/Documents/missioncals/TRs/December44/TR122444.pdf (Dec. 29, 2009).

Olive-Drab, *SCR-300 Backpack Radio,* http://www.olive-drab.com/od_electronics_scr300.php (Dec. 19, 2009).

Scorpio's Web site, *The Battle of the Hürtgen Forest,* http://www.huertgenforest.be/ScoWeb.php (Dec. 29, 2009).

Strickler, Col. Daniel B. *110th Infantry Action Report of the German Ardennes Breakthrough, as I Saw It from 16 Dec. 1944 to 2 Jan. 1945,* http://history.amedd.army.mil/booksdocs/wwii/bulge/110thInfRegt/Strickler%20AAR%20Bulge.html (Dec. 29, 2009).

U.S. Army Medical Department Office of Medical History, *The Fight for the Hürtgen Forest,* http://history.amedd.army.mil/booksdocs/wwii/HuertgenForest/HF.htm (Dec. 29, 2009).

U.S. Army photo. http://members.aeroinc.net/breners/buckswar/forest.html, (Dec. 29, 2009).

U.S. Army photo; http://members.aeroinc.net/breners/buckswar/kall.html, (Dec. 29, 2009).

Wikipedia, the free encyclopedia, *Post-WWII Sherman tanks*, http://en.wikipedia.org/wiki/Post-WWII_Sherman_tan33s (Jan. 2, 2010).

Wikipedia, the free encyclopedia, *World War II*, http://en.wikipedia.org/wiki/World_War_II (Dec. 29, 2009).

Index

60237605R00162

Made in the USA
Charleston, SC
28 August 2016